Energy-Efficient Houses

Fine Homebuilding®
GREAT HOUSES
Energy-Efficient Houses

The Taunton Press

Cover photo: Bruce Greenlaw
Back-cover photos: top left, Tracey Trumbull;
top right, Tim Synder; bottom left, Joanne Kellar Bouknight

Taunton
BOOKS & VIDEOS
for fellow enthusiasts

First printing: June 1993
Printed in the United States of America

A FINE HOMEBUILDING Book

FINE HOMEBUILDING® is a trademark of The Taunton Press, Inc., registered in the
U.S. Patent and Trademark Office.

The Taunton Press, 63 South Main Street, Box 5506,
Newtown, CT 06470-5506

Library of Congress Cataloging-in-Publication Data

Energy-efficient houses.
       p.   cm.
     At head of title: Fine homebuilding, great houses.
     "A Fine homebuilding book"— T.p. verso.
     Includes index.
     ISBN 1-56158-059-7
       1. Dwellings — Energy conservation   2. House construction.
     I. Fine homebuilding.
     TJ163.5.D86E52275   1992   93-1163
       696 — dc20   CIP

Contents

Introduction 7

Superinsulated Saltbox on the Coast of Maine 8 Owner design and involvement keeps costs low, satisfaction high

Massive Passive 11 Connecticut architect Stephen Lasar combines clean design with solar efficiency

On the Mountainside 16 The south face has sun and a view of the valley; the north face is notched into the wind

Airtight in Massachusetts 23 An energy-efficient house with a Mediterranean flavor

Roll-Top House 28 Plywood and 2x box beams form the structural core of a superinsulated house with a curved roof and a window wall

White Mountain Cape 32 Yankee ingenuity begets an energy-efficient house with an elegant interior

Pool House 38 Antiques, art and a lap pool mix with contemporary details in a passive-solar home

A Photovoltaic Test House 44 Ten years after its completion, this house still sells electricity back to the power company

The Buzzards Bay House 50 Energy efficiency with style

Expressing a Site 56 Materials gathered from the land form a sophisticated, energy-efficient earth shelter

The Double Envelope 62 An architect applies the convection-loop concept with a simple, affordable design

Seaside Solar 68 A traditional shape wraps around an energy-efficient core

Pennsylvania Snowbelt House 72 A passive-solar home on a less than ideal site

Designing for a Temperate Climate 77 How a Maryland architect dealt with seasonal extremes using an arsenal of passive-solar and mechanical systems

An Arc in the Woods 82 A small, sun-tempered house for a retired couple

Shingle Solar 86 Diverse styles shape a Colorado house that incorporates a trombe wall and direct gain

Linear Solar House 90 A patterned concrete floor and stick-built roof trusses accent a simple shape

A Little House with a Big View 94 Though heavily glazed on the north, it remains energy efficient and gets a third of its heat from the sun

Superinsulated in Idaho 98 Lessons learned from an energy-efficient house

Three Sides to the Sun 103 Enough light to cast a shadow can heat this house in the Montana Rockies

Sunspaces 108 A solarium specialist takes a close look at the many factors involved in designing a solar addition

Superinsulating the Non-Box 113 Truss joists and strapping create thick walls in a curved house

An A.O.B. House 116 Meticulously finished, energy-efficient and built to an Alternative Owner Builder code

Solar Adobe 122 A monster greenhouse and labyrinth of ductwork heat and cool a New Mexico house

In the Solar Vanguard **127** In 1946, architect Arthur Brown used industrial components and a simple solar-mass design to temper the desert climate

Cool Details **132** An energy-efficient infill house inspired by Texas vernacular architecture

Southern Comfort **137** Ample ventilation and heat-shedding construction details in a passively cooled south Florida home

Florida Cracker House **142** An indigenous form returns in style

Raised in Style **146** A passively cooled house built on stilts to catch the breeze

Passive Cooling **150** Earth-coupling, shuttered skylights and good venting help keep a North Florida house cool

A Modern Mississippi House **155** Traditional forms find new expression in this design for a hot, humid climate

Introduction

We may like to think that our concern with energy-efficient housing dates from the first oil crisis of the 1970s. But in reality, it goes back to the dawn of human history, when our less-than-upright ancestors first realized that caves were warm in the winter and cool in the summer.

Housing has improved since then, including how we heat and cool our homes. But we've made a century's worth of progress in the last few decades as we've designed and built houses that keep interiors comfortable at reasonable cost and with little impact on the environment. And, as you will see in these pages, the aesthetics of home building have by no means been lost in the process.

Whether cooling houses in the hot climates of Florida, Texas and Arizona or heating them in the chilly winters of New England and Alaska, energy use is an important factor in all home construction and remodeling. In these articles, top-notch designers and architects of energy-efficient houses make available the ideas that have worked for them—and even let you know which ones have failed. They talk about the materials, techniques and styles that they know can help you attain your energy-efficient dream house.

—The Editors

Superinsulated Saltbox on the Coast of Maine

Owner design and involvement keeps costs low, satisfaction high

by Elsa Martz

I spent the summers of my childhood at a camp on the coast of Maine, playing in the fields and woods along the rocky shore, and learning to swim in the frigid waters of Casco Bay. Though I've lived in other nice places through the years, none possessed the magic of the Maine coast. Thirty-five years later, a series of events found me once again prowling the backwoods of Maine, this time in search of a piece of property on which to build.

After just a couple of months of looking, I was fortunate to stumble upon a treasure: a three-acre parcel with a south-facing slope and 265 ft. of frontage on a tidal estuary. Intending to spend the rest of my life in the home I'd build on this land, I took seriously the task of designing it. I dreamed of a house that would be fuel- and water-efficient, and that would require little of my time or energy in upkeep. I spent almost a year researching passive-solar and superinsulation design techniques. When the books started to contradict each other and I felt I could discern which technique or specification was more apt, I knew I was ready to begin.

The time on research was well spent. Not only am I happy with just about every decision I made, but I gained an intimate acquaintance with my home that, I think, is known only by those who've designed and been involved in the building of their own house.

Early design decisions—In siting the house, I struck a compromise between obtaining maximum solar gain (facing true south) and taking full advantage of my view of the water (southeasterly). The house is oriented to magnetic south which, in this part of midcoast Maine, is 17° east of true south. This orientation provides plenty of solar gain.

I wanted a superinsulated, energy-efficient house, but with a relatively traditional look. I drew floor plans and elevations for a 32-ft. by 28-ft. saltbox, with a generously glazed south wall, and set the southerly half of my roof at an angle of 54°, the optimum angle for future roof solar collectors at 44° north latitude (top photo). An architect friend, Sherry Proctor, of-

A house for all seasons. Warm in the winter and cool in the summer, this saltbox features a no-nonsense plan that incorporates energy-efficient and passive-solar design principles, as well as providing ample opportunity for cross-ventilation. The house's R-30 walls, R-40 ceiling and low-e, double-paned windows help to retain heat when the temperature drops and exclude it when the temperature rises.

fered to look at my rough drawings. By repositioning the entrance and airlock entry, he added 80 sq. ft. of living space. I incorporated this and other of his changes to my plan, including the addition of three skylights at the top of the stair. The result is I think, a more elegant design, with more open space and a particularly welcoming entry.

My builder, Bob Randall, also contributed a number of good ideas throughout the project. One of the most significant design changes he suggested was the extension of the second floor by a foot on the south side. Bob's rationale was that this extra bit of floor space would be essentially free and would create an "eave" of sorts to keep the snow, rain and midsummer sun off the downstairs windows.

It also improved the exterior appearance of the south wall by visually splitting its mass.

As built, my house has about 1,800 sq. ft. of living space, plus an attic loft and a basement. On the first floor are kitchen, living room and office in an open, L-shaped layout, as well as a combination utility room/full bath; on the second floor are two bedrooms and full bath (floor plan at right).

Getting started—Bob and I shared the responsibilities of contractor by collaborating on scheduling and the purchase of materials. Once the foundation was poured, the only work we subcontracted was the fiberglass insulation. Bob, his son and another carpenter built the entire house from the sill up, frame to finish, including custom kitchen cabinets, solid-oak stairs, and oak floors throughout. I worked with them—sweeping, stacking lumber, nailing, puttying, moving crushed stone, taking scrap to the dump, staining and painting. My labor saved me money by freeing up Bob and crew, but more important, gave me a sense of real ownership.

Working alone before the carpentry began, I started to apply Thoroseal waterproofing (Thoro System Products, 7800 N. W. 38th St., Miami, Fla. 33166; 305-592-2081) to the foundation. This was one of the worst jobs I tackled. Because I didn't yet have electricity at the site, I had to stir the cementlike mixture by hand for half an hour (to obtain the proper consistency), lug a 50-lb. bucket down to the foundation walls and brush the stuff on while being eaten alive by hordes of mosquitoes. This was a bit more than I cared to suffer alone, so I called on Bob's son, Dave, for help. We finished the waterproofing, then covered it with 2-in. rigid styrofoam insulation to a depth of 6 ft. and 1 in. of insulation below that.

A basement wasn't really necessary, but it provides storage space for firewood and tools, not to mention my fleet: a small sailboat, a kayak and a rowboat. More important, though, the foundation and slab provide a considerable portion of the house's thermal mass.

Because of the foundation insulation and the fact that the basement extends well below

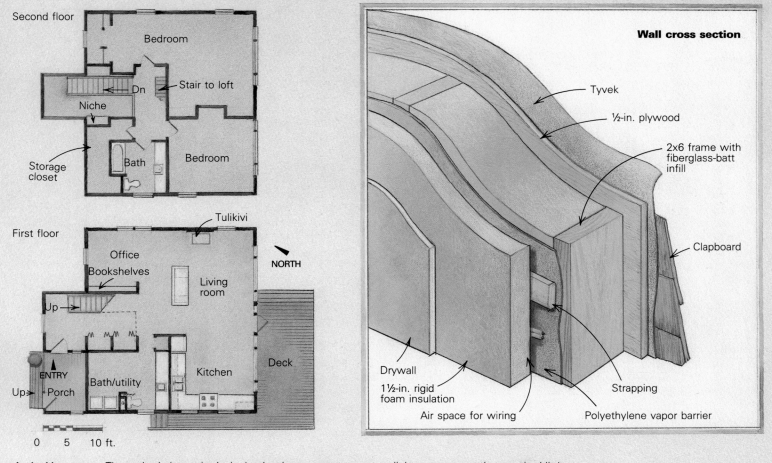

Second floor

Bedroom

Dn — Stair to loft

Niche

Storage closet

Bath

Bedroom

First floor

Tulikivi

Office

Bookshelves

Up →

Living room

Up →

ENTRY

Porch

Bath/utility

Kitchen

Deck

NORTH

0   5   10 ft.

Wall cross section

Tyvek

½-in. plywood

2x6 frame with fiberglass-batt infill

Clapboard

Drywall

1½-in. rigid foam insulation

Air space for wiring

Strapping

Polyethylene vapor barrier

An inviting space. The author's intent in designing her house was to create a light, open space that required little maintenance and was very energy-efficient. The result is a success on all counts. The space is flooded with sunlight, and the glulam beam between the living room and office and entry areas permits an uninterrupted span. The Tulikivi masonry stove provides virtually all the house's heat in winter, with minimal effort and great comfort. The curtain behind the couch can be either opened or closed to adjust the temperature downstairs.

the frostline, the temperature in the basement has never dropped below 37°, even after a week of temperatures hovering around -15°. I wrapped insulation around the water pipes just in case, but also had the water system designed so that if I were to be away for an extended period I could drain the whole system very easily with two faucets.

Tight shell—The walls of my house are 10 in. thick and insulated to R-30. We used 2x6 framing and fiberglass batt insulation, a poly-

ethylene vapor barrier, 1-in. strapping (to provide a channel for wiring runs), 1½-in. rigid foam insulation and drywall to come up with the R-30 rating (drawing above). The ceiling above the second floor is insulated to R-40 with fiberglass, the attic loft being uninsulated.

Windows throughout the house are double-glazed Andersens (Andersen Corporation, 100 4th Ave. N., Bayport, Minn. 55003; 612-439-5150). Because of the depth of the eaves on the living-room side of the house, in midsummer the sun comes in only about 4 inches be-

yond the window sill; in midwinter, sunshine floods the living room and kitchen, reaching in 14 feet.

Keeping the heat in—With so many windows, I knew it would be necessary to prevent all the heat from radiating right back out at night. I discovered a product called "Warm Window," a type of window quilt designed and manufactured by Roc-lon (a division of Rockland Industries, Inc., P. O. Box 17293, Baltimore, Md. 21203; 301-522-2505). It consists of four layers of insulated lining, over which a decorative cover fabric can be sewn. The curtain stacks neatly and unobtrusively above the glass. Magnetic strips inside the edge seams of the quilts line up with magnetic strips attached to the window trim (and painted to match), making a tight seal.

To keep the heat in the living area from rising to the bedrooms, I installed a simple curtain on a ceiling track where the living room meets the front hall. Made of a plain, unlined fabric, it does an amazingly effective job of sealing off the entry and stairs; I've noticed as much as a 10° difference from one side to another. In fact, I use this curtain to regulate room temperature in the winter. When I have company, I can bring the downstairs up to 70° or warmer by keeping the curtain closed. I much prefer a cooler house, however (closer to 60°), so when the temperature in the living room gets above 68°, I open the curtain, allowing the heat to escape upstairs. When not in use, the curtain stacks against a wall at the end of open shelves.

Exterior seal—The entry porch that Sherry added to my design was enclosed on three sides, but open on the fourth. We needed to close off the remaining side to reduce heat loss in winter. The enclosure would need to incorporate a door, yet be simple and light enough that I could set it up and break it down on my own. Sherry designed, and Bob built, a three-section 2x4 frame to hold two sheets of Sunlite, the translucent fiberglass material that we used for the fourth wall (distributed by Solar Components Corp., 121 Valley St., Manchester, N. H. 03103; 603-668-8186). An aluminum storm door completes the setup, creating an effctive airlock entry for the winter. In the spring, I remove the frame, panels and door, and store the pieces until the weather begins to turn cold again.

Heart of the house—With the exception of a small electric bathroom heater, my sole source of heat is a Tulikivi soapstone stove (also called a masonry heater). Because of its density, soapstone has a greater heat-storage capacity than any other masonry material in general use. The stone (two tons of it for my stove) "soaks up" heat from a fast-burning wood fire, then slowly radiates it back for the next 12 hours. The tremendous mass of such a heater requires that it have its own foundation, which is generally built by the foundation contractor when the rest of the house is built. Both stove and foundation were built by Mark McKusick of Hearth Warmers (R.R. 1, P.O. Box 36B, Colrain, Mass. 01340; 413-624-3363).

Building a fire in the Tulikivi takes only about five minutes. I bring in two small log carriers of wood, split into sticks preferably no wider around than my arm, and stack the wood vertically on top of some paper and kindling. One match is all that is necessary. With all the dampers open, the fire roars to life in about a minute, and temperatures in the firebox will reach 1800° in short order. After

about an hour and a quarter, the fire has burned out completely.

My daily fire-building routine, from December through February, is very simple. I light a fire around 7 a. m., and just before leaving for work, after the fire has burned out, I close the dampers. When I return home in the afternoon, the stove is still warm. It's still warm, in fact, when I build the evening fire at 7 p. m. In March and November the sun is high enough on the horizon that I often need fire the stove only once a day, in the evening, and on some sunny days not at all.

We cut quite a few large spruce trees to clear the site, so that's primarily what I burn, along with some poplar, birch, and oak. I save the hardwood for the very cold weather when the extra Btus are really appreciated. Because the Tulikivi burns wood so quickly and completely, there is no creosote buildup and little pollution. For the past two years I've consumed about two cords of wood a winter, mostly softwood. When I check the chimney cleanout in the summer, I find there's no soot buildup and only about one-third cup of fine ash in the cleanout cap.

Air quality—In a superinsulated house, it's necessary to provide a source of fresh air for a wood-burning fire. A floor register near the wall beside the Tulikivi is opened only when the fire is burning. A duct extends from the register, through the basement, and out a 4-in. screened opening in the basement wall.

Everything I read about superinsulated houses indicated the need for an air-to-air heat exchanger (or heat-recovery ventilator), to ensure adequate ventilation while not wasting all the energy (heat) in the exhaust air. I did extensive research on all units then available, and purchased the simplest, quietest unit I could find. I don't use it, though, because it's so annoyingly loud. In my house in the middle of the woods, with no furnace, the loudest noise is the occasional hum of the refrigerator. I'm not about to subject myself to the constant whooshing of the heat exchanger. If I had a house full of people and pets, I'd probably use it some in the winter, but with only one or two people around, it has proved unnecessary. An outside vent for the kitchen stove does an adequate job for cooking odors, and opening windows takes care of the rest.

Saving water, saving energy—I wanted to save wear on both my well and my septic system, as well as be conscientious about conservation, so I had Eljer low-flow toilets installed in both bathrooms. According to Eljer (Eljer Industries, P. O. Box 869037, Plano, Tex. 75086; 214-881-7177), their Ultra One/G model uses only 1 gal. per flush, compared with 3.5 to 7.0 for conventional toilets (for more on low-flow toilets, see *FHB* #61, pp. 62-65).

From April through October, I have a two-stage water-heating system that takes advantage of my south-facing roof. Bob installed a passive-solar batch collector under a skylight on the south roof. It's a 20-gal., glass-lined wa-

ter tank, painted black and placed atop a platform so that it almost touches the skylight. Insulated walls surround the unit because the attic loft is uninsulated. The sun heats the water to anywhere from 70° to 110°, and the heated water is piped directly to a separate faucet at the kitchen sink, as well as to a pair of thermostatically controlled, in-line electric water heaters manufactured by Eemax (Eemax Inc., 472 Pepper St., Monroe, Conn. 06468; 203-261-0684). I have "free" hot water in the kitchen all summer, and elsewhere the preheated water reduces the workload of the in-line units. From November through March, the sun doesn't rise high enough for long enough to heat the water appreciably, so I drain the batch collector. The system seems to work well; my electric bill for the past two years has averaged less than $16 a month at 9¢ per kwh. For one or two persons, this system is excellent. For a family of four, a pair of in-line units in each bathroom would probably be necessary.

Human-energy conservation—House cleaning is not high on my list of priorities; I kept this in mind throughout the design process. I had oak floors installed and covered them with two and three coats of polyurethane, depending on the room. They show dirt less than vinyl or tile floors do, and have proven to be virtually maintenance-free. I don't have forced-air heat, so dust is neither blown into the house nor stirred up. As a result, the house stays amazingly clean and wonderfully quiet.

I also save energy in yard work. Because my home is in a clearing in the woods, a grassy lawn seemed inappropriate. I planted clover and wildflowers in the clearing—no mowing required—and I used the piles of wood chips from the initial clearing to make paths. Wild roses, a lilac and daylilies—all perennials—complete the landscaping.

Cost and value—Exclusive of land, driveway (including some blasting), septic and landscaping, my house cost about $110,000 to build. Though it's hard to compare one region of the country with another, I know I have a very well-built house for the money. Labor is cheaper in Maine, I'm sure, than it is in Boston or San Francisco, but I'm convinced that my approach had something to do with keeping costs down. I worked with (and alongside of) my builder every step of the way and kept an open mind to changes as they seemed to make sense. I used quality materials throughout, but didn't get extravagant.

Although I know what the house cost, I'd have a hard time pinning down the difference in cost attributable to the energy-saving features. Nor could I say how long it will be till they pay for themselves. I do know that it gives me great pleasure to live in a beautiful, comfortable, practical, and very energy-efficient home. □

Elsa Martz is a photographer and adventure-tour leader. She works at Bowdoin College in Brunswick, Me. Photos by the author.

Massive Passive

Connecticut architect Stephen Lasar combines clean design with solar efficiency

The Strasser house in Bethel, Conn. is a 2000 sq. ft. passive solar design in which the structure itself—almost entirely concrete—serves as thermal mass, absorbing the sun's heat, then gradually releasing it back to the living space at night or on an overcast day.

The clients had requested a compact, open plan with built-in furniture, a contemporary appearance and energy efficiency—all within a strict budget. Their house was custom-built for $43 per sq. ft. in the fall and winter of 1979-1980, at a

time when tract houses in the area ranged from $35 to $50 per sq. ft.

Architect Stephen Lasar is increasingly well known for his energy efficient houses. He has built over twenty passive solar dwellings, usually combining suitable fenestration, orientation and overhangs with an integral thermal mass that acts as a heat sink. In the Strasser house, built by Lasar and his builder-partner Larry Neufeld, most of the exterior walls are 10-in. thick poured concrete, externally treated with

Dryvit, a system that incorporates 3 in. of high impact polystyrene insulation and a stucco-like finish. Several interior walls are built of concrete block and they support a second floor made of Flexicore, a prestressed hollow-core concrete plank, precut and put in place by crane. Two inches of concrete poured over the Flexicore and covered with brown tile adds even more mass to the house's main heat sink. The first floor is a 4-in. concrete slab poured over 8-in. block laid on its side to create a plenum, or

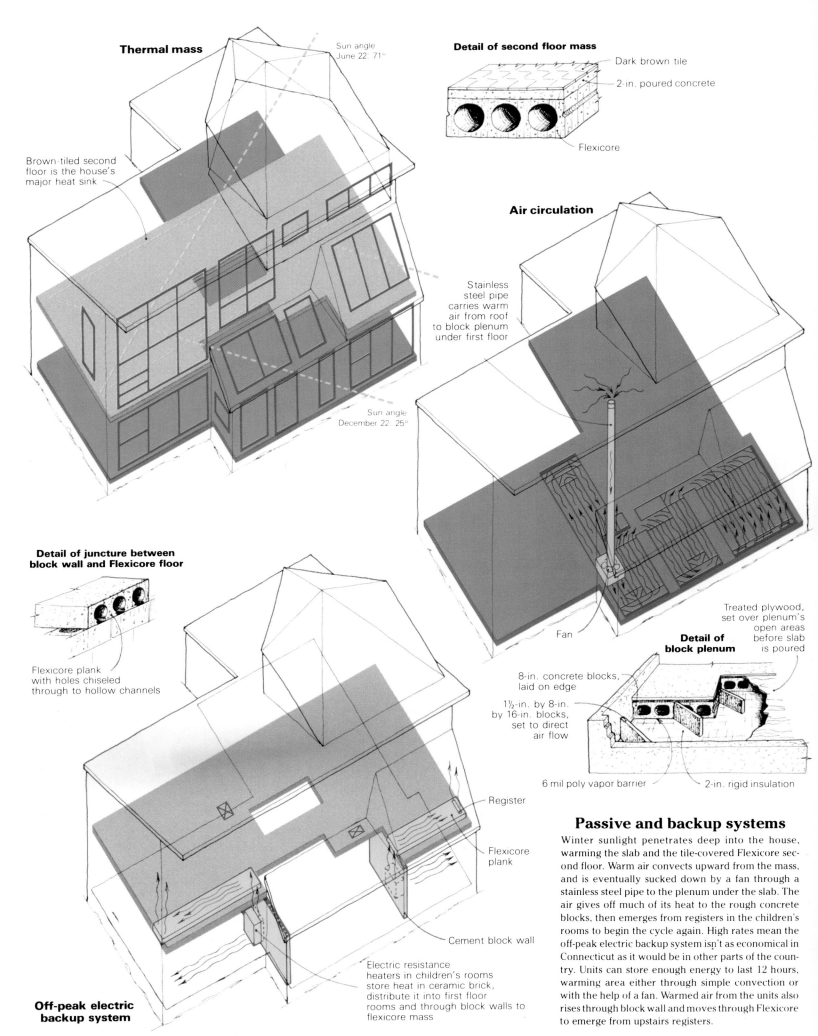

Thermal mass

Sun angle
June 22: 71°

Brown-tiled second
floor is the house's
major heat sink

Sun angle
December 22: 25°

Detail of second floor mass

Dark brown tile

2-in. poured concrete

Flexicore

Air circulation

Stainless
steel pipe
carries warm
air from roof
to block plenum
under first floor

Fan

**Detail of juncture between
block wall and Flexicore floor**

Flexicore plank
with holes chiseled
through to hollow channels

**Detail of
block plenum**

Treated plywood,
set over plenum's
open areas
before slab
is poured

8-in. concrete blocks,
laid on edge

1½-in. by 8-in.
by 16-in. blocks,
set to direct
air flow

6 mil poly vapor barrier

2-in. rigid insulation

Register

Flexicore
plank

Cement block wall

Electric resistance
heaters in children's rooms
store heat in ceramic brick,
distribute it into first floor
rooms and through block walls to
flexicore mass

**Off-peak electric
backup system**

Passive and backup systems

Winter sunlight penetrates deep into the house,
warming the slab and the tile-covered Flexicore second floor. Warm air convects upward from the mass,
and is eventually sucked down by a fan through a
stainless steel pipe to the plenum under the slab. The
air gives off much of its heat to the rough concrete
blocks, then emerges from registers in the children's
rooms to begin the cycle again. High rates mean the
off-peak electric backup system isn't as economical in
Connecticut as it would be in other parts of the country. Units can store enough energy to last 12 hours,
warming area either through simple convection or
with the help of a fan. Warmed air from the units also
rises through block wall and moves through Flexicore
to emerge from upstairs registers.

Owners' perspective

We moved into our house on February 29, 1980. It was an exceptionally cold day, and the off-peak ceramic units in the children's rooms were not hooked up. We spent a chilly night in front of the fireplace. Once the backup systems were connected, winter nights became more comfortable, and we began to learn how the house worked. We soon found that on sunny March days, regardless of the outside temperature, the main level of the house (the second floor) and master bedroom required no supplemental heat to remain at a comfortable 65° F. to 70° F. night and day. The lower bedrooms were fine during the day but required heat at night. Heat loss through unshuttered windows was very rapid.

During the summer, overheating was never a problem. The sunlight never penetrated more than four or five feet into the house, and the windows on the north side assured plenty of cross ventilation.

The only significant negative feature about the house is interior noise. The hard surfaces and open plan combine with two children, a television and a record player to make this a problem we have not been able to solve.

To compensate, though, few noises from the outside penetrate. Even storm winds are barely noticeable. Our house is draft-free, watertight and, from this perspective at least, quiet.

It is important to note that the fine tuning of the house is not yet complete. Each season brings its own adjustments, as we watch the sun change its path and the trees lose and regain their leaves. We feel in tune with the sky and the land, yet protected and safe. It's a very good house.　　　　　　　　　　*—Joe Strasser*

---

air passage. Only the third floor, the roof and utility core areas are constructed of wood. Lasar maintains that this building method is not significantly more expensive than conventional wood framing. "When you figure in the composition of a frame wall—studs, sheathing, siding, drywall—along with joists, subflooring and all that," says Lasar, "the costs are very close." He estimates that the small difference would be made up in well under a year through the superior performance of the concrete mass. Masonry construction also cuts air infiltration, a factor even in carefully built frame structures, to near zero.

Heating Systems—450 sq. ft. of south-facing double glazing admits the sunlight that in Lasar's estimation will provide 60% of the heat for the Strasser house. When the sun shines, air within the house is warmed, and it rises in a normal convection pattern toward the roof, where it is sucked by a small $\frac{1}{40}$th horsepower fan down through a stainless steel pipe and into the block plenum under the slab. There it gives up much of its heat to the concrete before emerging, much cooler, to begin the cycle again. Simultaneously, solar energy is being absorbed and stored by the tiled second floor and the other concrete areas being struck by the sun's rays.

When direct gain from the sun stops, this stored energy is gradually surrendered, and it helps to keep the house warm long after the sun

ceases to shine. When the air at the top of the house is no longer warm enough to spare heat for storage in the plenum and slab, a thermostat turns off the fan, and the system begins to operate by convection alone.

The combination of direct solar gain and the release of energy stored by the thermal mass sees the Strasser house through much of the heating season. For especially cold weather and periods of little sunshine there are several backup systems. The primary one is a Lange wood-stove on the second floor. Also on this level is a Preway fireplace, which draws oxygen from outdoors so as not to use heated house air for combustion. There are electric baseboard units on the north wall of the dining and living areas, as well as in each bathroom. Most interesting, however, are two Control Electric Corporation off-peak electric storage units on the first level. These units include a resistance coil, ceramic brick and a fan, and are controlled by thermostats inside and out. Depending on the outside temperature, they heat up at night to a maximum of 1,200° F., storing in the brick enough heat to last 12 hours. The amount of heat actually stored can vary from a fraction of the full capacity up to 100%, depending on outside temperatures. The fan in the unit is turned on by the inside thermostat when the interior air temperature falls below its setting. This is rare, and heat is usually distributed through the room by simple convection. Some warm air also makes its way up through the block wall and then through the hollow Flexicore, warming the mass before emerging from registers on each end of the second floor. The system is sophisticated, using off-peak power, allowing for fine-tuning, and providing for storage as well as heat production. Lasar, however, is not altogether happy with the way it has worked out in the Strasser house. "Off-peak power in Connecticut isn't that much cheaper than full rate. The political reality of the rate structure has to be taken into account with systems like this. It would work great in New Hampshire, but here we just about break even."

Reality is something Lasar stresses when talking about the efficiency of the system in the Strasser house. "There's too much emphasis on calculations of solar gain," he says. "It's more important to understand how the house is going to work." He feels that calculations are most useful in comparing designs, but that the working efficiency of the house is largely determined by the habits of the owners, most of whom have been accustomed to setting a thermostat and forgetting about it. Lasar emphasizes that moving into a passive solar house requires a change in living patterns. "It takes a while to get things working properly and to learn how to deal with the subtle systems in a house like this." Some people take a long time to adjust. "It can be quite a challenge," says Lasar, who went through the process himself after moving into one of his own houses.

Approached from the north and well back from the road, the Strasser house is set in a gentle hollow between low knolls on a two-acre lot. Its appearance was largely dictated by solar requirements, and the sharp differentiation between the south facade, with its large area of glass, and the other three sides, with their mostly windowless walls and bermed-earth covering, is marked. This is an aesthetic problem that all builders and architects will have to learn to deal with as they come to grips with the design imperatives of passive solar gain. Lasar feels that a single facade is seldom seen in isolation, and that by carrying similar colors, textures and modular elements through all four sides he has unified disparate elements and pulled the forms together into a satisfactory whole. He's had a lot of practice. Over the past six years, Lasar has designed more than 20 passive-solar houses, many of them built by the Neufeld-Lasar Design Build Co. Partner Larry Neufeld does much of the masonry work and wood framing himself. "He's a real artist," says Lasar.　→

The interior spaces of the Strasser house, particularly the second and third floors, provide pleasing and varied living space. Dark brown ceramic tile covers the entire second floor (above), and gives a forceful visual counterpoint to the changing heights and textures of the varied second-story space. This dark tile also provides a solar-energy-absorptive surface over the poured concrete and Flexicore beneath it. The white-walled living room (below left), two floors high, has 450 sq. ft. of floor to ceiling glass on its south wall. On winter days sunlight passes through the double glazing, heating the massive floors and walls of the house. At night insulated shutters and shades will keep the precious stored heat from escaping the same way. The roof overhang combines with the shade of tall oaks (left undisturbed during construction) to screen the high summer sun during warm weather. On the eastern end of the second floor, the ceiling drops down to a single level, creating an intimate, enclosed space with heavy, natural-finish oak beams and tongue-and-groove planking overhead (below center). The oak stairs leading to the third floor could have cut this area off from the rest of the house, but they have been left without risers (below right) allowing the spaces to flow into one another. The first floor, which includes the ochre-tiled entry, the two children's bedrooms, and a bath and storage area, works to keep the children's living quarters well separated from the master bedroom.

Lasar feels that solar building has been dominated by engineers who have done valuable work in assessing various systems and calculating their effectiveness, but who have often neglected other aspects of design. While Lasar will design only energy-efficient structures, he sees a house as an aesthetic object as well as one that must operate as efficiently as possible.

A

F

B

E

Clockwise from upper right: A small segment of wall in the second level den areas (A,B), is angled at 60° from the horizontal to provide for spring and autumn heat gain, and also to allow light to penetrate the dining area. The Danish woodstove provides backup heat. The pipe that passes warm air from ceiling to plenum hadn't yet been installed when this picture was taken looking down into the first floor entry (C). The stairway between the second and third stories is of oak, and exhibits some nice joinery (D). Overlooking the main living space of the second floor is a small study (E,F). Also on the third floor is the master bedroom and bath complex, and a closet housing the hot water heater which is part of the thermosyphon system. The collector for this system (G), is built into the 45° angle over the entrance, and so fashioned that warm house air may circulate around it during cold weather to keep the water from freezing. It supplies preheated water to the electric heater, which acts as a booster.

C

On the Mountainside

The south face has sun and a view of the valley;
the north face is notched into the wind

by A. J. Davis

The south face. **On this sunny fall day, operable skylights exhaust excess solar heat from the greenhouse and the sunroom. A yellow awning helps to control solar gain in the two-story sunspace behind the wall of windows. The large main deck is flanked by small triangular decks framed between the wing walls and the rectangular floor plan. The screened deck on the left is off the master bedroom. A second-floor bedroom deck faces due south. On the far right, the breakfast deck is directly below another bedroom deck.**

A s an architect, I've experienced a love/ hate relationship with many of the places I've lived. I love the potential for design, but I hate living in a construction project. This dilemma affected my wife Linda and me acutely soon after we purchased a run-down 1847 Victorian two-family house in Newton, Mass. We proceeded to renovate with all the naive enthusiasm of children aspiring to run one week after learning to walk. Through the trials of re-plumbing, endless plastering, adding a new porch, refinishing both kitchen and bath, sanding floors, carpeting and painting, we learned a great deal. We came to appreciate the benefits of having a quality-conscious contractor do most of the work for us. We also learned that quality construction is time-consuming. We finished the renovation two weeks before we sold the house, and swore that next time we were going to live in the design, not the construction.

Beginning anew—The opportunity to design and build a new house arose when we relocated to the mountains of southwestern Virginia. By this time, we had a two-year-old daughter, and Linda was expecting our second child. Our standards were admittedly high, but we set out to define our dwelling in terms that would transcend the floor-plan orientation of most housing solutions. We wanted the living space, its enclosure and the site to interact like three friends in constant dialogue.

The lot we selected is five acres of mixed hardwoods on the south-facing slope of a small mountain. The elevation is 2,650 ft. above sea level. Here the wind blows with predictable regularity 250 days of the year, ranging in intensity from soft breezes to harsh, piercing winter gales. The average annual snowfall is between 25 in. and 30 in., and the temperatures can range from $-15°F$ in winter to $90°F$ in summer.

As a place to hike and cross-country ski, this location was ideal for us. The southerly view down the mountain was also a major attraction. But we wanted shelter from the wind too, and there was only one place on our five acres where we could enjoy the view and also benefit from wind-deflecting topography.

The hollow where we chose to build slopes $15°$ to the south. Even with the necessary trees removed, the landscape offered excellent wind protection. There was also some historical precedent for building here. A wagon road dating back to the 18th century cut diagonally across the site, and was in just the right place to become part of our driveway.

The design program for this house was tightly interwoven around three conceptual dichoto-

mies. First, the house design and site should be not so much "of" the site as "with" the site. It could be spatially complex but not complicated. And finally, the design should encompass personal qualities of place without being a collection of rooms. There had to be unity.

I began designing in October 1984, and finished up by the end of December. Models were the primary means of design because to get the house to work spatially, I had to work in three dimensions. After several prototypes, each with its own follow-up drawings, we developed the one that was built. As it turned out, the final model was not only a design asset but also assisted the carpenters in understanding the larger context of what otherwise might have appeared to be isolated tasks.

On the third weekend in February during an early winter thaw, a friend and I cut down and cleared away 45 trees to make room for the house. Splitting up this dividend, along with subsequent construction debris, we had enough fuel for two woodburning households the following winter.

As we cleared the land, I grew concerned with water movement down the slope. As far as I could tell, during snow melts and after heavy rainstorms, water traveled southward down our lot on top of a clay layer that went about 30 in. deep into the ground. Both the foundation and the septic field would need protection from such substantial runoff. In fact, we decided that the best location for the septic field, based on percolation tests, would be above the house site. Waste would have to be pumped 35 ft. up to the fields from holding tanks below the house. Forty more trees had to come down over the septic fields.

Clearing these two areas of trees and brush was a tiresome, weight-loss regimen. Our only solace was in the thought of early settlers traveling our road. They must have struggled months to accomplish what we did in a couple of weekends with chainsaws.

In spite of the demands of the septic contractor, we saved a 40-ft. long bank of rhododendrons at one edge of the site. Beyond this boundary, which we can see from the house, the landscape is as wild and unaltered as before our arrival. As if to emphasize this, massive glacial outcroppings on a ridge above the rhododendrons form another natural barrier.

Between two hands—In addition to providing natural protection, the hollow also encouraged design responses that helped to determine the approach to the house, its entry, and ultimately its overall organization. From the parking area, an entry walk leads you through a circular opening an extension of the northeast wall of the house (top photo, p. 19). This 9-ft dia. circle frames a view of the rock outcropping. The walk then turns $90°$ and proceeds to the main entry.

The entry door is in one of two walls that have no windows. These walls, which extend 3 ft. beyond their right-angle intersection, symbolically and physically shelter the house, embracing it like two open hands touching at their wrists. The primary floor plan sits juxtaposed to these walls at $45°$, using them for support and

From *Fine Homebuilding* (Spring 1987) 38:24-30

protection against cold winds from the north and west. Each of the two main walls is penetrated by a corner of the main floor. The two cantilevered triangular punctures, painted a contrasting white, emphasize the rectangular plan as well as the importance of the main walls (drawings and photos, facing page).

A walk through—The front door, sheltered by a small roof, is located just to one side of the intersection of the main walls. Directly inside, there is an implied vestibule under an upper-level walkway. One step more and the space opens up, flooded with natural light from an 80-sq. ft. triangular skylight in the roof 18 ft. above. Horizontally, the primary view is of the fireplace core (photo, p. 20), seen across the half-wall that encloses the sofa in a sunken living room. Symmetrically and symbolically, the fireplace is the heart of the house, while the entry is its circulation hub. As shown in the floor plans, stairs from the entry lead down to the studio and up to the children's bedrooms and playroom.

The rectangular floor plan is in fact composed of three smaller rectangles, or bays. These divisions are visible in the axonometric drawing at right. The sunken living room is in the center bay, and is focused on the hearth—a fireplace at the center of the chimney mass flanked by built-in shelves. On both sides of the chimney, steps lead up to the sunroom. This is a two-story space with a tiled floor that can be heated by the sun or by a large woodstove, depending on the weather.

The right bay (viewed from the entry) is a private space, containing the master bedroom and a bathroom. Part of this bathroom's cubic form penetrates the northwest wall of the house. Its counterpart in the northeast wall is a kitchen corner that cantilevers through the wall with its own triangular skylight that illuminates the entire kitchen area. The kitchen, dining room and greenhouse make up the third bay.

Though small, the kitchen is efficiently organized around a central cooking island. From this work station, it's possible to look through a shuttered wall opening into the living room, or into the dining room and greenhouse beyond it.

The accessibility of the dining room is important. The "eat-in kitchen" is a concept that has no place in our family. When we gather for a meal, we want it to be in an environment where we can talk, relax and enjoy being together. As much as possible, we want to avoid the hit-or-miss, fast-food, commando action that dining can easily become, especially with two small children. When the weather is nice, there's a small "breakfast deck" accessible from the kitchen through a predominantly glass door.

Just to the south of the dining area is a two-story greenhouse. This enclosed space heats up far more rapidly than the sunroom (temperatures in the greenhouse have climbed to 80°F when it's below freezing outdoors). During the day, we usually keep this sunspace closed off from the main part of the house. Then at night, the accumulated heat can be released into the house through a dining-room door and through a pair of operable windows in an upstairs bedroom. If the greenhouse heat isn't needed to

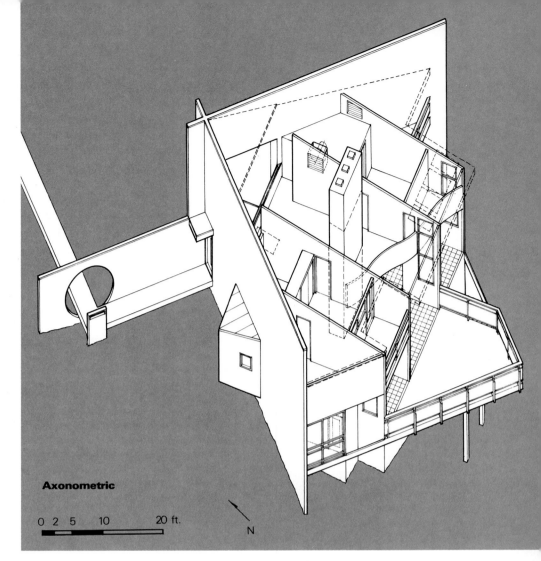

Axonometric

0 2 5 10 20 ft.

N

help heat the house, it can be vented outside through three operable skylights.

Though the greenhouse is a reliable source of solar gain, the two-story sunroom is the primary passive-solar heat source for most of the living space. Its dark tile floor is set on a 4-in. concrete slab. This mass combines with that of the chimney to provide ample thermal storage. Once warmed by the sun or woodstove, sunroom heat rises naturally into the upstairs rooms. A variable-speed paddle fan in the ceiling above the sunroom augments this convection. The entry overlook provides a path for cooler air to move back downstairs.

The curved wall that overlooks the sunspace has an important softening effect on the otherwise angular floor plan. The curve extends across the width of the upstairs playroom and continues through the greenhouse (photo p. 21). The curved wall receives light in varying amounts during the day, creating pleasing changes in color and tone inside the house.

Windows and decks—The greenhouse, sunroom and master bedroom all share a south-facing window wall 35 ft. long and 14 ft. high (photo p. 16). This wall has thirty-four windows and three glass doors. With this much glass area, night-time heat loss during the winter was an important concern. Rather than design a massive system of movable insulation just inside the glass, we decided to use "Low-E" windows by

Weathershield (Weathershield Mfg., Medford, Wis. 54451). These windows are manufactured with a low-emissivity coating that reflects radiant heat back into the living space. With a U-value of .30, these windows are about 60% more efficient than conventional insulated-glass units.

The window wall is protected from undesirable summer sunlight by a 2-ft. roof overhang and an adjustable yellow awning. The yellow fabric casts a warm glow on the interior, while substantially reducing heat gain. With tree cover and a fairly high summer sun, very little unwanted sunlight actually strikes the wall. If we do use the awning, it's usually in spring or fall, when the sun is still low in the sky.

The south deck extends outside the sunroom and the master bedroom, its polygonal shape completing the square plan implied by the walls. This is the largest of the house's five decks and is a favorite place for entertaining guests or for family gatherings.

Going from the deck into the master bedroom, one passes through a small sunspace. There's room here for a whirlpool bath, and this is where we intend to soak after running, hiking or cross-country skiing. The room can be open to views and winter temperatures independent of the rest of the house. Also off the master bedroom is a small screened deck, just large enough for two people and a candle.

Upstairs, each bedroom has its own small, private deck. The east deck is covered by the main

Drawings: Bill Galloway

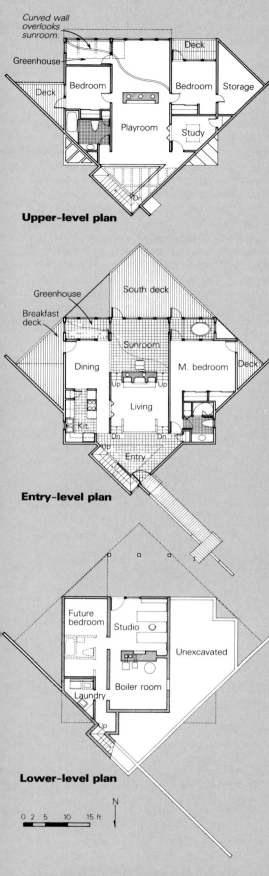

Curved wall overlooks sunroom.

Greenhouse

Deck

Bedroom

Deck

Bedroom | Storage

Playroom

Study

Dn

Upper-level plan

Greenhouse

Breakfast deck

South deck

Sunroom

Dining

M. bedroom

Deck

Living

Krt.

Up

Dn | Dn

Up

Entry

Entry-level plan

Future bedroom

Studio

Unexcavated

Boiler room

Laundry

Up

Lower-level plan

0 2 5 10 15 ft

N

High wing walls intersect at 90°, forming a north-facing wedge that deflects winter winds around this mountainside residence, right. The rectangular floor plan intersects the wing walls at 45°, creating twin triangular penetrations that are painted white to contrast with the roughsawn cedar siding. A view from the west, above right, looking toward the driveway, shows the circular opening in the low entry wall as well as the highly glazed south face of the house. The central chimney is surrounded by standing-seam metal roofing.

Photos: Daniel Terrell

Facing page: The curved wall of the upstairs playroom stretches across the sunroom and extends into the greenhouse, which is visible through the windows at right. Dark quarry tile set on the sunroom's 4-in. thick concrete slab provide thermal mass for heat storage.

The hearth and a sunken living room are at the center of the house. Shelves built into the chimney mass flank the fireplace. The kitchen is visible through a shuttered wall opening. Steps on both sides of the chimney lead up to the sunroom.

roof. It overlooks the dining deck and also commands the best view of the valley. The south-facing bedroom deck extends above the roof of the tub room, and is designed to be easily removed should the soldered tin roof need repair or repainting.

The playroom is the hub of the upstairs living area. Like the house core on the main floor, it's pierced by the chimney, which has a shelving niche for books and toys built into it. As shown in the floor plans, the playroom is flanked on the east and west by bedrooms and a bathroom. The curved wall on the south side overlooks the sunroom (photo facing page), and on the entry side, the roof's skylight triangle is repeated in a triangular opening above the entry. On two sides of this opening, 3-ft. high walls form a planter balcony. The planter is lined with heavy plastic sheets and filled with soil over loose gravel. With plenty of sunlight from the skylight above, the various forms of ivy we've planted are now cascading down the walls above the entry.

Downstairs—The lower level is the business portion of the house. Here we have the laundry room, boiler room, a workshop and an office. The primary heating system is hot water, fired by two boilers—one burns wood; the other, oil. Each is capable of heating the house, and they are linked in series so that the oil boiler acts as a backup. The house is divided into three zones, roughly one for each level. The Swiss-made Runtal radiators on the entry level are thin, flat-painted steel units built much like a car radiator. They are distributed in the U. S. by Fittings, Inc. (380 Boylston St., Boston, Mass. 02116). The rest of the radiators in the house are conventional white fin-tube design.

During periods of clear winter weather, approximately 30% of the total heating can be met with the direct solar gain through the south window wall. On mild winter days, the upstairs woodstove is adequate. In severe weather, either of the boilers may be used.

Construction—Though the design concept was spatially complex, the construction concept was fairly simple. This was important because we wanted a special house, but we didn't want the risks or high costs associated with tricky construction details. Early in January, I contacted three contractors to give bids. One declined, and we were left with just two bids. We selected local builders Peter and Mike Adamo of Adamo Building Corporation. We were impressed with their skill, honesty and eagerness to begin.

The foundation went in with little difficulty, save for the extra care that was taken in waterproofing and drainage. The steepness of the site as well as several severe rainy spells during construction led me to specify extra gravel and ample runs of drainage tile.

We got a little depressed after the block work was done. Walking between the foundation walls, I wondered how we could ever live in such a small place. The dark grey concrete block and the dirt floor seemed hopelessly confining. I searched for early drawings, fearing I had used one scale for the floor plan and another for the furniture. The skeptical client and the professional were at war inside the same head. Fortunately, my dimensions were right, and as framing began, the spaces started to open up.

The exterior walls were framed with 2x6 studs spaced on 2-ft. centers. Horizontal 1x4s were let into the studs every 2 ft. on both sides of the wall. Though it was time-consuming to gang-notch the 2x6s, the horizontal 1x4s were necessary to stiffen the wing walls, which rise 40 ft. above grade in some places. The 1x4s also provided nailing for the vertical shiplap cedar siding. The walls hold R-19 batt insulation, and directly beneath the roughsawn siding there's a layer of Tyvek (a wind barrier) over ½-in. thick Celotex insulation board.

The house is tight, but not superinsulated. After the builders installed the windows, I sealed and insulated the shim spaces using cans of urethane spray foam. On this particular site,

controlling wind infiltration is probably just as crucial as insulation. Except for the two triangular penetrations, the wing walls present a windowless face to northerly winds. The south-facing parts of the house are meant to catch the sun. We've spent two winters in the house now, and this strategy seems to have been more than adequate in terms of energy conservation.

The framing took about six weeks, but we had to wait three months for the open-web steel joists that support the tiled concrete floor of the sunroom and greenhouse.

Framing the curved wall that overlooks the sunroom could have been a major construction snag, but the builders took this part of the job in stride. First, the pattern of the curve was drawn and cut in the ¾-in. plywood that would be used as upper-level subflooring. Then a double 2x10 header was installed across the sunspace and greenhouse, running diagonally and roughly tangent to the planned curves. The upper-level subfloor was installed so that its curved portions cantilevered beyond the header. To pick up these minor cantilevers structurally, a curved box beam was built and nailed to the diagonal header. The box beam's 2x frame is skinned on top and bottom with ¾-in. plywood. The bottom and top plates for the curved balcony wall were cut from ¾-in. plywood, and 2x4 studs for this wall were set on 8-in. centers. The entire assembly was then covered with ¼-in. plywood.

Because the wing walls extend above the top of the roof, we couldn't vent the roof in the usual way. To vent the top of the roof, button vents were installed in the wing walls about 10 in. above the roof line. Several vent holes had to be drilled through the roof joists so that air can move into the exterior walls and escape out the button vents. Conventional soffit vents were installed along the eaves. The roofing is standing-seam galvanized metal, and the gutters are notched into the ends of the rafters.

Looking back, my only regret is that I chose painted gypboard for the interior wall finish. On expansive, uncovered areas of the wall, you can see the drywall joints as soft undulations on the surface, especially when evening light rakes through the windows. Thin-coat plaster over rock lath would have been a better, though more expensive, choice, and it would have yielded a more pleasing texture.

All in all, we're very pleased with the house for the comfort, privacy and togetherness it affords. After two years here, nature is reclaiming much of what it lost, and the dialogue that we hoped to achieve between structure and site is indeed occurring. Outside the house, we planted grass and wildflowers over the septic field and scattered pine bark on steep slopes to help control erosion. Eventually these areas will be covered by flowers, shrubs and white pines. The cedar siding is slowly aging, its color blending more into the landscape. □

Built atop a platform of battered masonry walls, the house extends long and low, commanding great vistas to the south and west. In the winter view above, two pointed patios extend beyond the shelter of a cantilevered flat roof. The small one is off the master bedroom; the larger serves the living room. On the facing page, skylights, copper flashing and a pointed chimney refine the hip roof form at the center of the house. An earth berm against the northeast side of the house, top, offers privacy from a neighboring house as well as protection from noise and temperature extremes.

Airtight in Massachusetts

An energy-efficient house with a Mediterranean flavor

by Paul Fisette

"That's a bunch of bunk." This is how builder Paul Bourke views the common notion that energy-efficient houses are inherently ugly. According to Bourke, energy-savers don't have to resemble clunky, 1970's-style solar homes any longer; nowadays, almost any style home can be energy efficient.

Bourke's environmental conscience, like that of many of his peers, was forged during the energy crunch of the 1970s. That's when energy-conscious builders first divided into two camps: those who installed solar panels and lots of south-facing glass to trap the maximum amount of solar heat, and those who superinsulated building envelopes to limit the amount of energy consumed in the first place. The controversy inspired Bourke, of Leverett, Massachusetts, to develop a unique building system that combines solar orientation, airtight-envelope tightening and a tidy heating, cooling and ventilation system. And, as demonstrated by one of Bourke's latest projects, the Terrazza house, energy-efficient detailing doesn't have to compromise sound aesthetic design.

Hugging the hillside—The red tile roof, white stucco walls and Mediterranean style of the Terrazza house defies traditional New England architecture. Yet, notched into the south-facing slope of a hillside lot, the house fits perfectly into the wooded landscape of western Massachusetts. On approach from the north, even the most observant visitor can be fooled into thinking that the house is split-level and earth-bermed (top photo). But out back, the south wall of the house reveals two full floors tucked neatly into the hillside below the entry level (bottom photo). Bourke used terraces surrounded by stone walls to create three levels in the yard on the west side of the house (thus the name Terrazza). The terrace elevations match those of the three floors.

The lot faces south, so Bourke laid the long axis of the house east to west, maximizing its southern exposure. Inside the house, a tiled stair decends 6 ft. from the entry platform to the main floor—a synthesis of crisply faceted ceilings, arch-top doorways and skillfully crafted mahogany details (photo, p. 27). Another stairway drops to the children's floor in the basement, where three bedrooms surround a central indoor "courtyard" that serves as a family room.

Though the design of the Terrazza house is noteworthy, the promise that the house's 3,200

The Terrazza house looks like a split-level, earth-bermed house from the front (photo above). But a walk around back reveals two full floors of living space (photo below), each embraced by a stone-walled terrace hugging the hillside. A stuccoed concrete retaining wall capped with stone forms a seamless connection between the house and the garage. The house's sleepy Mediterranean façade belies its airtight, superinsulated envelope and sophisticated HVAC system.

sq. ft. of living space can be heated for $450 per year is even more compelling.

Building theory—To work right, an energy-efficient building must have systems for controlling moisture movement and for minimizing energy loss through the building envelope. Vapor diffusion, the movement of moisture through building materials, is typically controlled by installing a polyethylene vapor retarder. The effectiveness of the vapor retarder is a function of surface area; for example, a vapor retarder with holes punched into 2% of its surface is still 98% effective.

Controlling *air-transported* moisture, however, is far more important than controlling vapor diffusion. That's because air can transport 100 times more water vapor than can move through materials by diffusion. The truth is, most problems associated with moisture condensation can be avoided by controlling air leakage and the temperature of framing components.

Air barriers can be placed anywhere in a building envelope, but they must be continuous to work and they must be rigid to remain continuous. That rules out the use of Tyvek and other housewraps as air barriers because, even if their seams are caulked or taped, the seams can (and do) rupture with time under the stress of fluctuating air pressure. Any holes in an air barrier will funnel air-transported moisture into a building's envelope. Thus, few houses built today have an effective air barrier.

In the Terrazza house, Bourke installed an effective vapor retarder and air barrier, plus a layer of insulation, in one step: by virtually encapsulating the house in a 1-in. to 2-in. thick bubble of foamed-in-place polyurethane insulation. In addition, Bourke beefed up the R-value of the envelope by adding fiberglass batts and expanded polystyrene (EPS) foam board. Bourke's attention to energy-efficiency, though, began with the basement slab.

Concrete solutions—Conventional reinforced concrete footings and stepped foundation walls support the basement slab and the house itself. Before pouring the slab, Bourke established a level grade 8 in. below the top of the footings, using sand where needed to fill in the low spots. Next, he installed a double layer of 2-ft. by 8-ft. by 2-in. thick extruded polystyrene (XEPS) board over the level grade. The XEPS board in the top layer is oriented perpendicular to the board below, and the joints are staggered to limit heat loss. At the footings, both layers of XEPS abut a 1-in. thick layer of XEPS that wraps over the footings and continues about 2 in. up the interior face of the basement walls. This layer of insulation serves as an expansion joint and a thermal break between the slab and foundation.

Bourke stretched a 6-mil polyethylene vapor retarder over the insulation board, then spread a 2-in. deep layer of clean sand over it, bringing the subslab surface to within 2 in. of the top of the footings. Bourke was now ready to pour a 4-in. thick slab, which finished out 2 in. above the top of the footing. The use of

sand directly below the slab is critical. It provides a firm, level base for the concrete, protects the vapor retarder during the pour and allows the water in the concrete to dissipate for proper curing.

Instead of using wire mesh to reinforce the slab, Bourke specified the addition of an additive called Fibermesh (Fibermesh Co., 4019 Industry Dr., Chattanooga, Tenn. 37416; 615-892-7243) to the concrete mix. Fibermesh consists of fiberglass fibers that are distributed uniformly throughout the concrete during mixing. At a cost of about $7 per cu. yd. of concrete, Fibermesh is comparable in price to wire mesh (including installation) and it's a lot easier to work with.

Once the concrete cured, the 1-in. XEPS around the slab's perimeter was trimmed flush with the top of the slab. Later, the foamed-in-place polyurethane bubble surrounding the house would terminate at the top edge of the XEPS and literally fuse to it, forming a continuous insulating seal.

The exterior of the basement walls below grade is sealed with two coats of Thoroseal (Thoro System Products, 7800 NW 38th St., Miami, Fla. 33166; 305-592-2081) and finished above grade with a synthetic plaster that's part of a system called Outsulation (an exterior insulation and finish system). Outsulation was also used as the exterior finish of the house itself (more on that later).

At the time Bourke poured the slab, he was unaware of any radon problems in the Leverett area. But soon after he finished the house, he discovered that several houses in the area *did* have radon problems, though fortunately the Terrazza house wasn't one of them. Nevertheless, Bourke says next time he'll add a 4-in. thick layer of ½-in. to 1-in. clean, crushed stone (the size of the stone must be uniform) beneath the double layer of XEPS insulation. That way, if high levels of radon are detected later, a 4-in. dia. hole can be drilled through the slab down to the stone to accommodate a 4-in. PVC pipe linking the slab to daylight. An inline, continuously-operating centrifugal fan will then depressurize the subslab, sucking the radon out. Bourke seals all penetrations through concrete slabs with polyurethane sealant.

A warm frame—For the most part, Bourke follows the tenets of conventional wood-frame construction, with one exception: wherever possible, he eliminates thermal bridges (materials that extend from the interior to the exterior of a house and conduct heat through the envelope), gaining in the process the maximum amount of space for sprayed polyurethane foam insulation (drawing facing page).

For the Terrazza house, Bourke framed 2x4 perimeter walls on the interior side of the foundation walls. The stud walls and foundation walls are spaced 1 in. apart to provide a convenient chase for wiring and a cavity for containing sprayed polyurethane foam insulation. Next, Bourke bolted a 2x6 pressure-treated mudsill to the tops of the 8-in. thick foundation walls, holding the outside edge of the mudsill 1½ in. back from the building line. The mudsill sup-

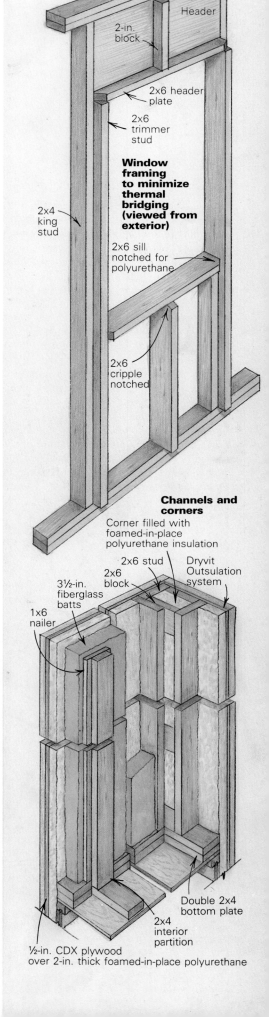

Header

2-in. block

2x6 header plate

2x6 trimmer stud

Window framing to minimize thermal bridging (viewed from exterior)

2x4 king stud

2x6 sill notched for polyurethane

2x6 cripple notched

Channels and corners

Corner filled with foamed-in-place polyurethane insulation

2x6 stud

2x6 block

Dryvit Outsulation system

3½-in. fiberglass batts

1x6 nailer

Double 2x4 bottom plate

2x4 interior partition

½-in. CDX plywood over 2-in. thick foamed-in-place polyurethane

Drawings: Michael Mandarano

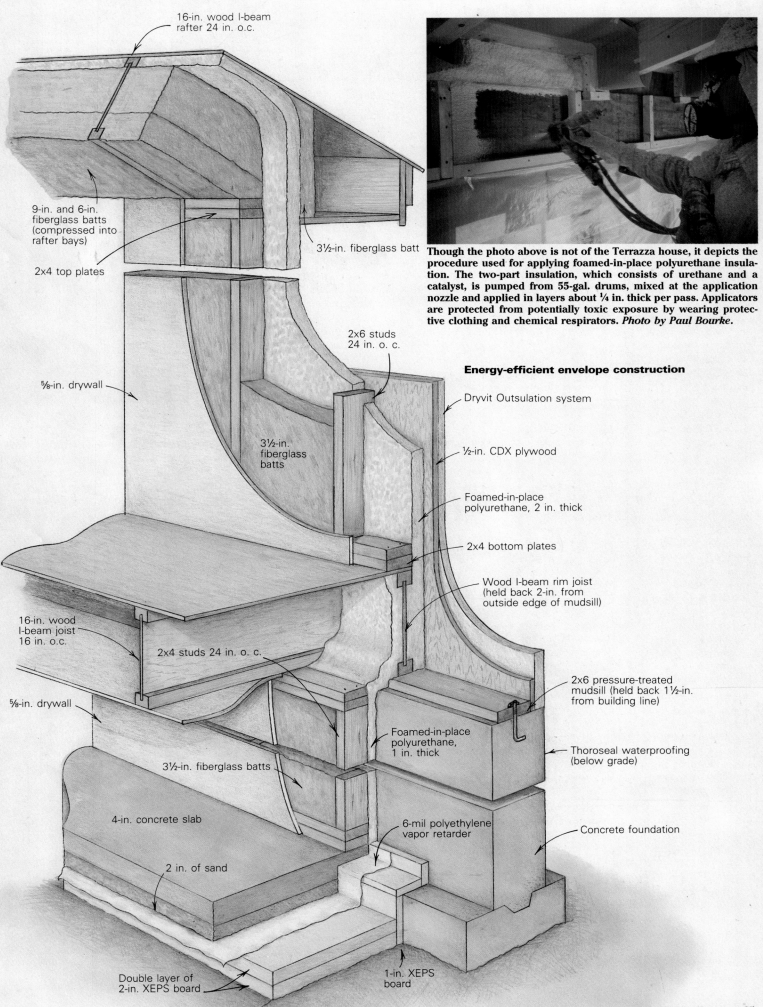

16-in. wood I-beam
rafter 24 in. o.c.

9-in. and 6-in.
fiberglass batts
(compressed into
rafter bays)

2x4 top plates

3½-in. fiberglass batt

2x6 studs
24 in. o. c.

⅝-in. drywall

3½-in.
fiberglass
batts

16-in. wood
I-beam joist
16 in. o.c.

2x4 studs 24 in. o. c.

⅝-in. drywall

3½-in. fiberglass batts

4-in. concrete slab

2 in. of sand

Double layer of
2-in. XEPS board

Foamed-in-place
polyurethane,
1 in. thick

6-mil polyethylene
vapor retarder

1-in. XEPS
board

Though the photo above is not of the Terrazza house, it depicts the procedure used for applying foamed-in-place polyurethane insulation. The two-part insulation, which consists of urethane and a catalyst, is pumped from 55-gal. drums, mixed at the application nozzle and applied in layers about ¼ in. thick per pass. Applicators are protected from potentially toxic exposure by wearing protective clothing and chemical respirators. *Photo by Paul Bourke.*

Energy-efficient envelope construction

Dryvit Outsulation system

½-in. CDX plywood

Foamed-in-place
polyurethane, 2 in. thick

2x4 bottom plates

Wood I-beam rim joist
(held back 2-in. from
outside edge of mudsill)

2x6 pressure-treated
mudsill (held back 1½-in.
from building line)

Thoroseal waterproofing
(below grade)

Concrete foundation

ports 16-in. wood I-beam floor joists, installed so the exterior face of the rim joist is held back another 2 in. from the outside edge of the sill.

Bourke framed the perimeter walls above the basement walls with double 2x4 bottom and top plates and 2x6 studs spaced 24 in. o. c. (double bottom plates were used throughout the house to provide solid backing for the baseboards). The plates and studs are aligned flush on the interior side of the walls, and the walls are positioned so that the studs are in the same vertical plane as the mudsills below. That allows the walls to be tied to the mudsills with ½-in. CDX plywood sheathing.

The point of all this is to forestall air infiltration and to prevent the foundation walls, rim joists and wall plates from wicking heat out of the house. But Bourke took the concept a step further. Rough window and door framing consists of 2x6 trimmer studs nailed to 2x4 king studs (drawing, p. 24). Headers are double 2x's sandwiched around a ½-in. plywood core, and sills and header plates are 2x6s. These framing members are also aligned flush with the interior face of the wall so that, around doors and windows, only the trimmer studs, header plates and sills extend all the way through. Wherever possible, Bourke uses a corner framing detail that allows polyurethane foam insulation to be injected into it and substitutes single 1x6s for three-stud channels where interior walls butt into exterior walls (drawing, p. 24). Roof framing consists of 16-in. deep wood I-beam rafters spaced 24 in. o. c.

Flash and batt—The primary insulation system used for the Terrazza house, called "flash and batt," combines foamed-in-place polyurethane with fiberglass batts.

Foamed-in-place polyurethane insulation is a two-part liquid system consisting of polyurethane and a catalyst. The ingredients typically arrive on the job site in a pair of heated 55-gal. drums nestled in the back of a panel truck. The liquids are pumped to the house via separate hoses that converge at the application nozzle, where they're mixed to the proper proportion.

During application, the nozzle is held anywhere from a few inches to 18 in. from the surface to which the foam is being applied (photo preceding page). The foam is typically applied in a layer about ¼ in. thick per pass. When necessary, the nozzle is adjusted to create a narrow spray that can penetrate those tight spots around the windows and doors.

The polyurethane liquid expands into foam immediately when it hits the surface, as the catalyst reacts with the polyurethane. The foam hardens within two to three minutes. Applicators protect themselves from potentially toxic exposure by wearing protective coveralls and chemical respirators (once cured, the insulation is non-toxic). The Terrazza house was insulated during the summer because polyurethane foam doesn't expand as much when it's applied during cold weather, decreasing the yield and driving up costs. Application at temperatures under 32° F is possible, but should be avoided whenever scheduling permits.

To prepare for the application of the foam, Bourke braced all rough window and door openings more than 4 ft. in width by tacking a 2x4 to the trimmers horizontally, using duplex nails for easy removal. That prevented the openings from distorting under the pressure of expanding foam. That done, Bourke gave way to the insulation subs. Before spraying foam, though, they covered the openings with plastic sheeting and masked off electrical outlets, pipes, plumbing vents, ventilation ducts and other wall penetrations (all wall penetrations were made prior to the spraying operation).

The application of foamed-in-place polyurethane foam can be tricky, and it's best controlled by an expert. Beginning at the basement slab, polyurethane foam was applied in a 1-in. thick layer between the foundation walls and the adjacent 2x4 walls. This layer continues up over the mudsill and up the back side of the rim joists, dying into the underside of the floor deck. Next, foam was sprayed into the 2-in. space between the plywood sheathing and the exterior side of the rim joists and bottom plates. This layer of foam continues up the inside surface of the plywood sheathing between the 2x6 studs, and fills the gap between the sheathing and top plates. Cavities behind headers and king studs and at the corners were also filled with foam. Where necessary, framing members were notched to gain access to hard-to-reach places. Up top, fiberglass insulation was stuffed into the soffits, and polyurethane was sprayed over it, continuing in a 2-in. thick layer along the underside of the roof deck all the way up to the ridge.

Once the foam cured, stud cavities were insulated with 3½-in. fiberglass batts, and 9-in. and 6-in. batts were compressed into each of the rafter bays. With this system, Bourke gets the best of both worlds—an insulating air barrier and the low cost of fiberglass batt insulation. The final touch in Bourke's insulation system is a layer of rigid 1-in. EPS foam insulation installed over the sheathing. This brings the exterior surface of the walls flush with that of the foundation walls and adds an extra buffer against the weather (the thermal rating of the EPS is R-5).

Not including the 1-in. EPS insulation, which is a part of the Outsulation system, the wall's insulation/vapor retarder/air barrier system is rated at an airtight R-25 for a total installed cost of about $1.15 per sq. ft. of wall area. A more conventional wall system incorporating Tyvek, a polyethyene vapor retarder and 6-in. fiberglass batts costs between $.58 and $.88 per sq. ft. of wall area, depending on the quality of the job. True, Bourke's wall is more expensive, but its R-value is higher (R-25 versus R-19) and it's significantly tighter.

It took five days to insulate the Terrazza house from prep to clean-up, including three days to apply the polyurethane foam. This time schedule is comparable to other systems.

Hot roof—The Terrazza house is capped by an unvented roof. There is no attic space and the rafter bays are completely filled with insulation,

so there is no airspace to ventilate. This hot-roof construction is controversial and should be used cautiously, but is permitted by most building codes. It's crucial that hot roofs be absolutely airtight and incorporate high levels of insulation, the amount of which depends on the location of the house. The hot-roof design used for the Terrazza house was approved by an architect who specializes in energy-efficient design.

According to some people, the biggest problem with hot roofs is that they can cause the premature degradation of asphalt shingles. Most asphalt-shingle manufacturers will void the warranty if their shingles are installed on an unvented roof. Bourke installed high-density concrete roof tiles (Vande Hey Roofing & Tile Co., Inc., 1665 Bohm Dr., Little Chute, Wisc. 54140; 414-766-0156) on the Terrazza house, so shingle degradation was not an issue. And because the tiles are raised above the deck on 1x sleepers, the roof *is* vented to a degree (this also keeps the tiles at the ambient temperature, helping to prevent ice dams).

Bourke's roof-insulation system scores a thermal rating of R-60 and costs $1.87 per sq. ft. of roof area. That is comparable to a more conventional system that includes a polyethylene vapor retarder, 15-in. fiberglass batts and a roof ventilation system.

Insulating the outside—The transition between wood siding and a stepped foundation has always bothered Bourke. For the Terrazza house he wanted to use a siding material that would blend with the foundation. The solution was provided by a product called Outsulation (Dryvit Systems, Inc., One Energy Way, West Warwick, R. I. 02893; 401-822-4100).

Outsulation is sold to listed applicators only, who act as subcontractors. It consists of a 1-in. to 4-in. thick layer of EPS insulation board that's glued to the exterior sheathing; a reinforced fiberglass mesh stretched over the EPS; a cementatious base coat within which the mesh is fully embedded; and an acrylic finish coat.

While the Dryvit system seems expensive ($5 per sq. ft. of wall area in western Massachusetts or $20,000 total for the Terrazza house), its lifetime cost compares favorably with vertical-grain Western red cedar clapboards. Installed clapboards with cedar trim (including two coats of stain or paint) cost $4.25 per sq. ft. of wall area according to Bourke's best estimate, or almost 20% less than Dryvit. But add the installed cost of 1-in. EPS board and future maintenance costs of clapboard siding and you have a different story. Dryvit comes in a variety of textures and colors and never needs painting.

The finish coat only of the Dryvit system was applied over the exposed foundation walls, and a horizontal control joint was placed where the foundation and stick-framed walls meet. Next time, Bourke says he'll frame the perimeter walls so that the exterior face of the plywood sheathing is flush with that of the foundation walls (instead of offset by 1 in.). Then he'll apply the entire Dryvit system, EPS included, over both the foundation walls and the stick-framed walls, smoothing the intersection between them.

Though built on speculation, the Terrazza house was designed according to concepts presented in the book, *A Pattern Language*. On the main floor (photo above), multi-faceted surfaces are accentuated with polished mahogany trim, tiled stair treads and oak floors.

HVAC havoc—Building a house as tight as a thermos bottle is only half of the equation; making the house a safe place in which to live is the other half. That means installing a mechanical ventilation system that exhausts stale air and replaces it with fresh air.

In the Terrazza house, Bourke initially installed what *seemed* to be a nifty HVAC system that integrated the heating, cooling and domestic hot-water (DHW) system with a heat-recovery ventilator (HRV). The HVAC system consisted of a Vent-Aire model ECS4038 HRV, a 2½-ton air-conditioner and a propane-fired, stainless-steel, condensing domestic hot-water heater (designed to supply both heat and domestic hot water) with an AFUE rating of 94%. The HRV was equipped with built-in heating and cooling coils to which the water heater and the air-conditioner were hooked up directly. A blower in the HRV was supposed to force fresh air across the coils and, depending on the season, distribute either cooled or heated fresh air through the supply ducts to the various rooms in the house. Stale air would be sucked out of the house in the usual manner—through strategically placed exhaust registers. On paper, the system sounded great. Unfortunately, it didn't work.

With the system up and running, Bourke quickly discovered that, though the heating system worked fine, the 3-speed blower in the Vent-Aire HRV wasn't powerful enough to propel air-conditioned air through all the supply ducts in the house. After an on-site demonstration, a representative from Vent-Aire came away convinced that the unit was underpowered for a

3,200-sq. ft. house (though they say it works fine for houses of 2,500 sq. ft. or less). They recommended that Bourke either add a booster fan or a second model ECS4038 HRV to the system. Unconvinced that either solution would work, Bourke decided to revamp the system.

The new HVAC system isn't quite as lean as the original, but it's efficient. Bourke replaced the original HRV with a less ambitious Vent-Aire model ECS22 HRV (Engineering Development, Inc., 4850 Northpark Dr., Colorado Springs, Colo. 80918; 719-599-9080), which contains no heating or cooling coils (Vent-Aire, to their credit, sold him the unit at cost). He also added to the system a new MOR-FLO model VH30HAC3 vertical fan-over-coil air handler (MOR-FLO Industries, Comfort Systems Dept., 18450 S. Miles Rd., Cleveland, Ohio 44128; 216-663-7300) that combines a powerful blower with a heating core and cooling coil. The heating and cooling systems are now routed to this blower unit, and from here warm or cool air is distributed to all rooms in the house via supply ducts. Return air is drawn through three return-air registers: two on the second floor and one on the first floor.

The 100,000 Btu Polaris model DVPB-35 hot-water heater (also made by MOR-FLO Industries) is the heart of the heating and DHW system. The sealed-combustion water heater draws combustion air directly from the outdoors through a 2-in. dia. ABS pipe. Because indoor air isn't used for combustion, the indoor air pressure remains balanced with the outdoor air pressure, which ensures maximum air quality in the house and helps protect

against radon infiltration. Exhaust air is cool enough to be vented through an ABS pipe at the base of the water heater—no chimney is required.

The HRV is linked to the outdoors at the basement level with a pair of 6-in. double-walled, insulated, flexible ducts—one for fresh-air intake and the other for stale-air exhaust. The exhaust port is located 25 ft. away from the intake port so that exhaust air isn't recirculated through the intake port.

Fresh air from the HRV is dumped directly into the MOR-FLO blower unit, where it's mixed with heated or cooled air and distributed throughout the house. Stale air is drawn from the house through exhaust registers located in the kitchen and bathrooms, where indoor air pollution is greatest. Each register is equipped with a timer that boosts a fan housed in the HRV from low to high speed during peak hours.

The result of all this trouble is an HVAC system that's similar in principle to the original, except that there's now an extra piece of equipment in the utility room. The costs of the two systems are comparable, too, except that Bourke spent both time and money in upgrading the system. In the end, the cost of the entire mechanical system including ductwork was $11,000 (not factoring in the expense of revamping the original HVAC system)—still not bad considering the average yearly heating bill (figured at $1/ gal. for propane) is only $450 per year. □

Paul Fisette is director of the Building Materials Technology and Management Program at the University of Massachusetts at Amherst.

Roll-Top House

Plywood and 2x box beams form the structural core of a superinsulated house with a curved roof and a window wall

by Tim Snyder

William Maclay's first acquaintance with box beams came with the building (with Jim Sanford and Richard Travers) of Dimetrodon in Warren, Vt., an experimental collection of living and working spaces constructed around and within a giant framework of 2x members sheathed with plywood. Box beams are made by fastening a rigid skin (plywood) to a framework of dimensioned lumber. Structurally, neither the frame nor the skin can stand alone, but by combining them, exceptionally strong beams can be made in various shapes and sizes. (For more on box-beam construction, see *FHB* #2, pp. 56-59 and *FHB* #14, pp. 27-29.)

By using a number of box beams, both curved and straight, Maclay designed the unusual curved-roof house shown here. Tucked into a beech forest on the north, the house has a solar south face that overlooks a meadow in Vermont's Champlain Valley. While the roll-top roof is the most obvious evidence of unconventional framing, the window wall was also built using box beams, and it extends from bottom plate to attic level with no structural tie to the second-floor joists. Since it's mostly glass, the window wall gets its racking resistance from an inner wall just 2 ft. away that separates the second-floor bedrooms from the sunspace.

House anatomy—It's easy to mistake this house for a double-envelope design (see pp. 62-67) because of its curved roofline and its

From *Fine Homebuilding* (February 1985) 25:38-41

Facing page: Below its curved roof, top photo, the south face of the house holds two levels of fixed glass between upper and lower bands of awning windows. A small balcony off the master bedroom is tucked beneath one section of the curved roof. Bottom, the house is shaped to welcome the sun but deflect north winds over its superinsulated roof.

The window wall, right, extends a full two stories with no direct structural tie to second-floor framing. Racking resistance is provided by the sheathed 2x4 wall that separates the second-floor bedrooms from the sunspace.

independent window wall. But rather than relying on natural convection to move heated air around the house, Maclay chose an active system for distributing and storing solar heat. Warm air near the window wall rises naturally, reaching the second-floor bedrooms through openings in the inner wall. The warmest air eventually collects in the attic, where a large fan pushes it down through a duct to a rock-storage bin located beneath the first floor. The bin extends from the north wall to within 12 ft. of the south window wall. The fan can be controlled automatically with an adjustable thermostat, or manually, depending on when and how it's best to store or retrieve heat from the 14-ton rock mass. A woodstove in the dining room and a small quartz heater provide auxiliary heat.

As shown in the drawing on p. 31, the rock bin separates the first floor into two levels. The kitchen, bath and study on the first floor are 2 ft. 8 in. above the living room and dining area, shown in the photo at right. The second floor contains three bedrooms and a bath. The attic, because it's insulated and open, can be used as a play area, an office or a guest bedroom.

East and west walls—The unconventional design of the roof and south wall led Maclay and head carpenter Peter Laffin to frame these areas last. Once the foundation walls and 4-in. thick floor slab had been poured, the crew framed out the rock bin and the east and west walls. Maclay designed these walls to be superinsulated, with separate outer and inner 2x4 framing yielding 12 in. of insulation space. But at this stage of construction only the inner structural wall was framed so that the roof could go on as quickly as possible. The 2x8 joists for the two upper floors run from east to west. They're supported by these end walls and by an inner post-and-beam frame that picks up the joist breaks between rooms.

Box-beam joinery—At the south face of the house, the curved roof dies into a lintel that's held 20 ft. above the slab by the west-wall framing and by four box-beam posts. The lintel is actually a series of four horizontal box beams that butt together in a single line above the three central posts. The posts define the window bays along the south wall. Toenailed into the lintel over each post is a curved box beam that forms the arching roof. The curved beams support 2x8 purlins on 16-in. centers that run east and west, completing the roof's framing. A look at the unsheathed skeleton (photo next page) reveals the

Box-beam construction. Structural beams with 2x inner frames and plywood skins can be fashioned in just about any size and shape. The framing skeleton (photo left) includes three box-beam posts 20 ft. high, a four-piece box-beam lintel, and five curved box-beam rafters. Dissecting part of the south wall and roof (drawing, facing page, right) reveals the gridwork of inner framing crucial to beam strength. The small drawing shows the floor plans and energy performance.

relative positions of the box beams. For a closer look at the joinery, see the drawing, facing page.

Peter Laffin built all the box beams in his workshop and then trucked them to the site, where they were installed with the help of a crane. The workshop proved to be a dry haven during an extremely rainy fall. It also provided ready access to a bandsaw and plenty of flat space for layout and construction.

The construction sequence for all the box beams was the same: cut the ½-in. CDX plywood faces of the beam to their blueprint dimensions; use panel adhesive and 6d nails to fasten the 2x inner frame to one face; then enclose the frame by attaching the other face.

The box beam's inner frame is designed to maximize the strength of the completed structural member without adding unnecessary weight. Each 20-ft. post, for example, has two 2x4 edges and a doubled 2x4 center support. Edge and center 2x4 stock runs the full height of the post. Unable to locate 20-ft. long 2x4s, Laffin butt-joined shorter 2x4s, making sure to stagger the joints by at least 2 ft. Blocking is glued and nailed between vertical 2x4 runs every 4 ft. and wherever solid backing is required for nailing into the box beam. Offsetting the joints in the plywood skin between the two beam faces is also critical.

To trace the curves for the roof box beams onto the plywood and 2x stock, Laffin used a compass made from a furring strip with a nail protruding at one end and a pencil at the other. In these beams, three layers of 2x stock were bandsawn to the beam's curve and then laminated face-to-face to make the inner frame. Again, all butt joints were offset by 2 ft., and blocking was glued and nailed across the width of the beam at the edges and every 4 ft.

The south roof has five curved box beams— one at each end of the house and three located directly above the window wall's three center posts. The two centermost box beams each have an outside radius of 8 ft. 2¼ in. The radius for the other box beams is 7½ in. smaller. This allows the 2x8 purlins that bear on the smaller outer beams to butt against one of the two inner

box beams, where they're attached with joist hangers (photo above and drawing, facing page).

The window wall's posts were erected first, and then the four horizontal box beams went up to form the lintel. Finally the curved roof beams were set down on the lintel and secured with temporary braces that came off as the purlins were nailed up.

While they are strong in compression, the four 20-ft. box-beam posts that support the south face of the house were precariously shaky when they were first installed. Laffin toenailed the base of each post into a 2x12 sill, and he toenailed the top of each post into the lintel beams that butt together above it, and added a ½-in. plywood gusset over the lintel-beam joints. Then the tripled 2x4 and 2x6 cross members were nailed between columns to act as rough sills and headers for the glazing.

Even with all the box beams and rough sills installed, the array of temporary braces holding the columns plumb had to stay put. This is because racking resistance for the window wall is provided by the conventionally framed second-floor wall just behind it. This inner wall encloses the bedrooms and is connected to the window wall through west-wall and attic-floor framing. Beneath its drywall finish there's ½-in. plywood sheathing (shear panel) nailed to the 2x4 framing for racking resistance.

The high end walls on the east and west of the house were also shear paneled to provide greater stiffness from the other direction. Sheathing the roof's 2x8 purlins with ½-in. plywood bent to the roof curve further stabilized the window wall. Just beneath the roof sheathing, Laffin nailed 1x furring strips to the purlins 16 in. o. c. to create a vent space for the insulation under the sheathing.

The curved eave along the north side of the house and the curved roof dormer above the second-floor bathroom were built using the same box-beam and purlin detail that Maclay designed for the south face. Insulating the 2-ft. thickness of the roof framing with fiberglass batts gave it a rating of R-76. Building the outer walls on the east and west sides of the house

completed the framing and enabled Laffin to insulate them with 12 in. of fiberglass (R-38).

Maclay installed most of the 6-mil poly vapor barrier himself. On the east and west walls, it's stapled directly over the ½-in. shear panel that covers the inner wall. On the ceiling it's just under the drywall, with the ceiling-to-wall junctures caulked and stapled to reduce air leakage.

With the rest of the house superinsulated, Maclay needed to minimize heat loss through the south wall to maintain energy efficiency. This had to be done economically, and triple-glazed windows or double-glazing with insulated curtains proved to be too expensive. Maclay's solution was to use two layers of standard 46x76 sliding-glass door replacement units for all fixed glazing. By installing two double-pane units in the same opening you get less conductivity than triple glazing (three airspaces instead of two) for about $8 per sq. ft. There's also less solar transmittance, but this is a safe tradeoff given Vermont's long, cold winters.

Before the fixed glass was installed, all the box-beam posts, sills and headers were trimmed out with redwood. Then each glass panel was sandwiched between redwood stops, its bottom edge resting on two neoprene setting blocks. Exterior stops were silicone-caulked where they meet glass. At the base and top of the south wall, insulated awning windows were installed to provide fresh air when the owners want it.

Except for bending the drywall to fit against the curve of the attic ceiling, finish work inside the house was fairly straightforward. Decoratively routed and painted white, the posts and beams that help support the upper floors lend a formal air to the living and dining rooms, which still await finish flooring (photo previous page).

Passersby who view the roll-top house from the road often comment on how out-of-place it is amid the neighboring farmhouses that were built a century earlier. But Maclay's view is different. Ingenuity and craftsmanship, he says, are traditional New England values very much embodied in the roll-top design. Maclay's aesthetic goal was to express, simply and honestly, the functional goal of integrating passive-solar gain with superinsulation. Such basic energy-efficient features, he feels, shouldn't have to be forced into the confines of conventional construction or appearances. Thus the curve of the roof back to the berm on the north side of the house.

The energy performance of the house has been good. It takes about two cords of wood to heat the 2,000-sq. ft. living space during the year, and heat loss through walls and glass is slow. Even in midwinter, the owners can leave for the weekend without stoking the woodstove or worrying about the need for backup heat. □

Illustration: Christopher Clapp; Photo this page: William Maclay

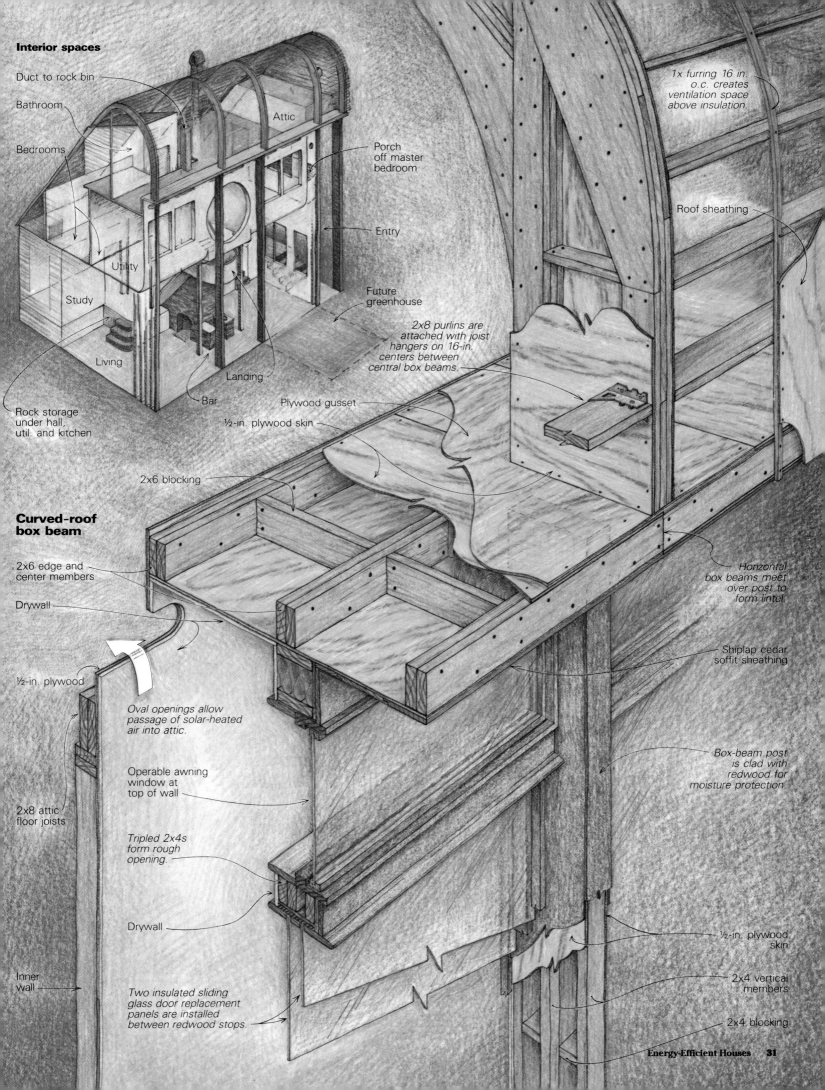

Interior spaces

Duct to rock bin

Bathroom

Bedrooms

Attic

Porch off master bedroom

Entry

Utility

Study

Future greenhouse

Living

Landing

Bar

Rock storage under hall, util. and kitchen

2x8 purlins are attached with joist hangers on 16-in. centers between central box beams.

1x furring 16 in. o.c. creates ventilation space above insulation.

Roof sheathing

Plywood gusset

½-in. plywood skin

2x6 blocking

Curved-roof box beam

2x6 edge and center members

Drywall

Horizontal box beams meet over post to form lintel.

Shiplap cedar soffit sheathing

½-in. plywood

Oval openings allow passage of solar-heated air into attic.

Operable awning window at top of wall

2x8 attic floor joists

Tripled 2x4s form rough opening.

Box-beam post is clad with redwood for moisture protection.

Drywall

½-in. plywood skin

2x4 vertical members

Inner wall

Two insulated sliding glass door replacement panels are installed between redwood stops.

2x4 blocking

White Mountain Cape

Yankee ingenuity begets an energy-efficient house with an elegant interior

by John Starr

I first became interested in energy-efficient construction for two reasons: the energy crunch of 1973-1974, and seven years of living in Fairbanks, Alaska. When my wife and I relocated to the White Mountains of New Hampshire, I designed and built a superinsulated house with double-wall construction, R-60 walls and ceiling, direct-gain passive-solar heating and lots of thermal mass. We've been living in the house now for five years and have had no cold feet, cold drafts or overheating of the second story. Primary heat is furnished by a single woodstove that uses only two cords of wood per winter to heat 3,000 sq. ft. — not bad for a 9,000 degree-day climate.

But most of my work as a small custom designer/builder is quality conventional construction. Clients just haven't had a burning urge to build and pay for a superinsulated house (superinsulation adds almost 7% to the cost). One client was an exception. The comfort of our home convinced her that superinsulation was a good idea for her new house.

Aesthetics and efficiency — My client had strong ideas about what she wanted. The house had to capture the graciousness of her former 19th-century Boston townhouse. New technology was acceptable, but it couldn't interfere with the impression of stately Boston living created by the interior design. Interior form and function were more important than exterior shape. Lighting, both natural and artificial, was important. My client also wanted the option of leaving the house untended, confident that it could survive on its own for long periods of time.

Apart from these general considerations, there were specific requirements. The ceiling in the parlor had to be 10-ft. high to accommodate a tall grandfather clock. Three bedrooms, each with its own bath, were mandatory, as was a view of the mountains from the master bedroom. My client also wanted a bowed exterior wall in the parlor and a gracious curved stairway to serve as the centerpiece of the house (floor plan, facing page). We settled on a basic Cape for the exterior shape, with the roof sitting on top of the first-floor walls and the upstairs rooms nestled under the rafters (photo facing page). My client chose roof windows instead of dormers because she doesn't like the look of dormers. Besides, the extra floor space provided by dormers wasn't needed.

I was given complete freedom to design for energy efficiency and low maintenance. In addition to superinsulation, the house would have wood primary heat, a heat-recovery ventilator (HRV), direct-gain passive solar and backup heat to allow extended absences. To me a low-maintenance exterior means no paint or stain. I chose Western red cedar shingles, with cypress trim and T&G cedar soffits, all untreated (photo below). Low maintenance also means no shoveling of roofs and no ice dams. I decided to build a steep-pitched roof (10-in-12) with metal roofing and large overhangs (32 in. at the eaves and 24 in. at the rakes) to protect the siding.

I couldn't come up with an intelligent way to give just the parlor a 10-ft. high ceiling, so I raised all the ceilings on the first floor to 10 ft. I felt that this would add to the 19th-century feel of the house.

The building site offered southern exposure and a south-southeastern view. I oriented the long dimension of the house so that it faced 15° east of south in order to strike a compromise between the view and the sun. I then oriented the ridge so that it ran across the short

The exterior is designed to be maintenance free, with red cedar shingles, T&G cedar soffits and cypress trim, all untreated. The continuous soffit vents draw cool air into an airspace above the roof insulation, and warm air is exhausted through standard gable-end vents.

dimension of the house (north/south). This positioned the gable ends so that the second-floor windows would capture the maximum amount of solar energy. As an added benefit, this also provided headroom over the maximum area upstairs.

The north/south orientation gave the roof a total span of 44 ft., calling for rafters about 32 ft. 3 in. long. That's a long 2x12. I knew that I could use finger-jointed 2x12s for the rafters, having used 26-footers before, but the local lumberyards said they didn't have a source. I was also familiar with laminated-veneer lumber. The lumberyards could get Trus Joist wood I-beams, or TJIs (Trus Joist Corporation, 9777 W. Chinden Blvd., P. O. Box 60, Boise, Idaho 83707), for me, but they wanted me to take them 60-ft. long or pay a stiff cutting charge. I solved that problem by using wood I-beams for the floor joists as well as for the rafters and ordering the same size (14 in. wide) for both. That way, I was able to place a big enough order to reduce the price, and the variety of lengths required for the floor joists minimized waste.

The wood I-beams allowed me to span 20 ft. in the floors. To cantilever a greenhouse 6½ ft. off the first floor I added web stiffeners to the wood I-beams directly over the rim joist (web stiffeners are 2x4 blocks nailed vertically to opposite sides of the plywood web between the flanges). The cantilever exceeded that recommended by the product literature, but by figuring the actual loads associated with the greenhouse instead of the assumed roof loads, I calculated that it would be safe (for more on laminated-veneer lumber, see *FHB* #50, pp. 40-45).

Please note that for anyone who lives and works in areas covered by building codes, calculations like this should be figured by a licensed engineer or architect. If you live in a rural area, you have more freedom to exercise your own judgment. But I strongly recommend the services of a professional if you are using materials in unique ways — one structural failure is one too many.

Backup heat — My next design priority was backup heat. I wanted to avoid using electric heat because electricity is expensive in New Hampshire (9¢ to 10¢ cents per kwh). Fortunately, the conventional propane water heater I planned to use for the domestic hot water provided a solution. Scouring the product lit-

Drawings: Gary Williamson

The exterior of the house is a basic Cape with red cedar shingles and simple detailing. The roof is clad with commercial-grade, galvanized-steel roofing and features roof windows instead of the traditional dormers. The greenhouse in the left of the photo is supported by Trus Joists cantilevered out from the first floor, and the basement windows below it are fixed sliding-glass door replacement glass. The dry-laid wall in the foreground is built of granite dynamited from the basement area.

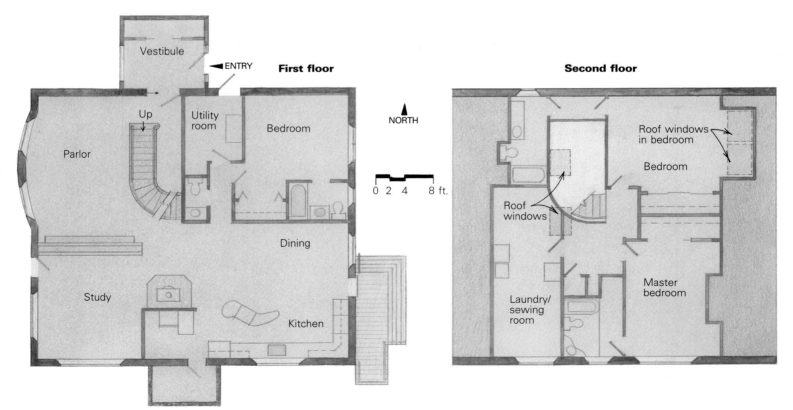

First floor

Vestibule

◀ ENTRY

Up

Utility room

Bedroom

Parlor

Study

Dining

Kitchen

▲ NORTH

0 2 4 8 ft.

Second floor

Roof windows in bedroom

Bedroom

Roof windows

Master bedroom

Laundry/ sewing room

From *Fine Homebuilding* (October 1989) 56:58-63

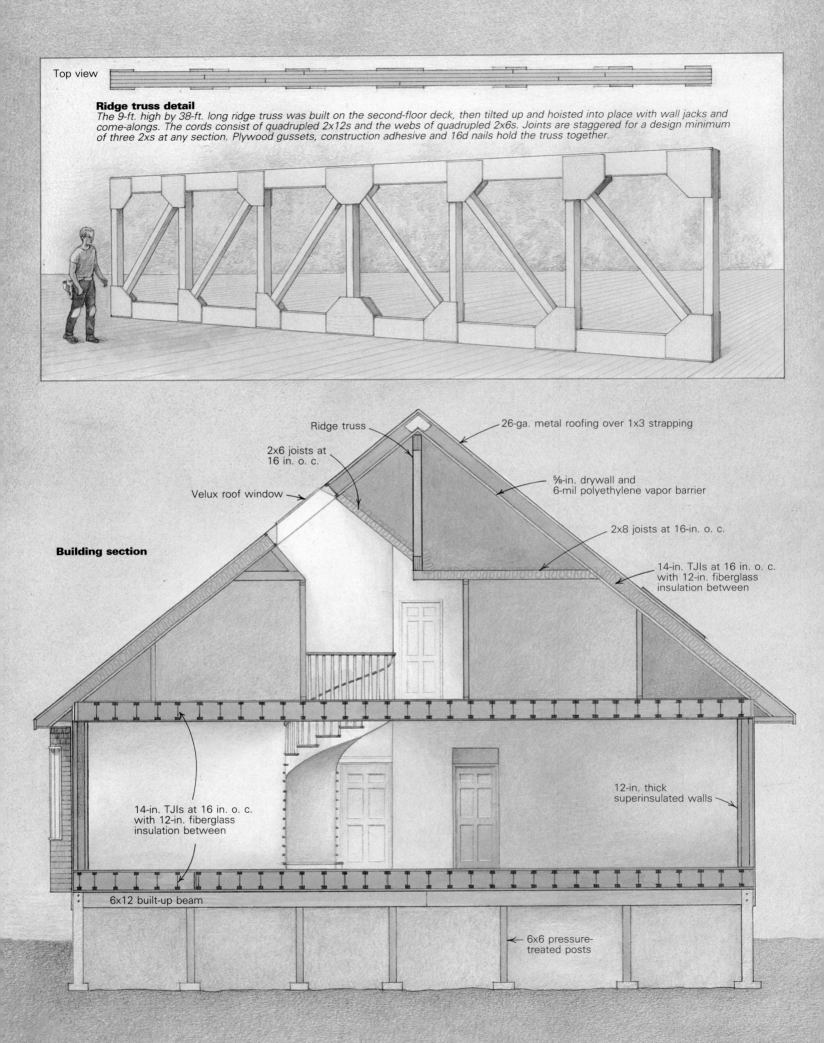

Top view

Ridge truss detail

The 9-ft. high by 38-ft. long ridge truss was built on the second-floor deck, then tilted up and hoisted into place with wall jacks and come-alongs. The cords consist of quadrupled 2x12s and the webs of quadrupled 2x6s. Joints are staggered for a design minimum of three 2xs at any section. Plywood gussets, construction adhesive and 16d nails hold the truss together.

Ridge truss

2x6 joists at
16 in. o. c.

Velux roof window

Building section

26-ga. metal roofing over 1x3 strapping

⅝-in. drywall and
6-mil polyethylene vapor barrier

2x8 joists at 16-in. o. c.

14-in. TJIs at 16 in. o. c.
with 12-in. fiberglass
insulation between

12-in. thick
superinsulated walls

14-in. TJIs at 16 in. o. c.
with 12-in. fiberglass
insulation between

6x12 built-up beam

6x6 pressure-
treated posts

erature, I discovered that I could use the water heater for backup heat by installing a separate fan/coil unit made by the same company that manufactures the water heater (Mor-Flo Industries, Inc., 18450 South Miles Rd., Cleveland, Ohio 44128), and a circulating pump. The system works by pumping hot water from the water heater through a coil in the fan/coil unit, where fan-forced air picks up heat from the water en route to the interior of the house.

Now the question was how to distribute the backup heat in the house. I had already worked out an HRV system with its supply and return ducts. Because backup heat was needed only to prevent freeze-ups during prolonged absences in the winter, why not use the HRV ducting to distribute the backup heat? After all, when the house was empty and needed backup heat, it wouldn't need ventilation.

I was reluctant to go ahead with this plan unless I could find a competent mechanical sub who was comfortable with it. Fortunately, there is an excellent commercial mechanical sub in town, and he didn't see any problems with the plan as long as we had a mechanical and electrical lockout system to prevent both systems from functioning at once. Essentially, the cost of backup heat turned out to be the cost for the fan/coil unit and circulating pump (about $700 in all).

A sculptural stair—The staircase I designed consisted of nine straight steps, six radiused steps to turn 90° and two more straight steps up top. I drew the stair as completely freestanding, but I wasn't sure whether it would be stiff enough. I did some rough deflection calculations and decided that stringers could be laminated out of plywood and ash in such a way that they wouldn't be too springy when a 250-lb., slightly inebriated guest jumped on them. I included red oak treads, painted birch risers and a laminated cherry rail. The outboard stringers would be capped with painted birch skirtboards, and the underside of the stair would be finished off with 3-coat plaster. I hired out the stair to a local architectural millwork shop (Littleton Millwork, Corp. Lafayette St., Littleton, N. H.), which fabricated the parts and did most of the installation work. The stairs turned out to be strong and elegant (photos next page).

Daylighting—When I was beginning to think about detail drawings, the owner asked me, "How are you going to light the upstairs hall and stairwell?" I realized that I had ignored direct natural lighting altogether in the stairwell. The only way to supply it here was with roof windows, but the problem was how to install them so they'd look good.

After a lot of head-scratching, I hit upon the idea of building a vaulted ceiling over the stairwell, with a pair of roof windows installed in one side of the ceiling (photo left). With a little bit of fine-tuning, I was able to extend the side of the ceiling opposite the roof windows in an unbroken line into the top of the roof-window wells, and to extend the wall directly below the roof windows up into the bottoms of the window wells (bottom drawing, facing page).

Though I was pleased with this solution, I realized once I began to draw the sections for the whole house that the vaulted ceiling would cut through most of the ceiling joists that were to act as collar ties. The only way around the problem that I could see was to eliminate collar ties altogether by using a load-bearing ridge. The ridge would have to span 38 feet, so I considered using glulams, steel, or Micro=Lams for it. I ended up ruling out glulams and steel because they were too heavy and expensive, and Micro=Lams because the 38-ft. span and load-bearing requirements were too much to ask of them.

A site-built truss—Once I exhausted the high-tech possibilities, I looked into site-building a truss for the ridge out of conventional lumber. Because of the steep-pitched roof, the distance between the second-floor ceiling joists and the ridge measured over 9 ft., which gave me a lot of room to work with. After running a series of calculations, I discovered that a 9-ft. 1-in. deep truss would span 38 ft. with no problem.

The truss would consist of quadrupled 2x12s for the cords and quadrupled 2x6s for the webs (all of #2 spruce), with the joints staggered to assure a design minimum of three 2xs at any section (top drawing, facing page). Fourteen pairs of ¾-in. plywood gus-

The vaulted ceiling was created over the stairwell by adding a false ceiling between the top of the roof windows and the bottom of the site-built ridge truss (concealed behind the soffit in upper right of photo). A catwalk links the bedroom to the right with a full bath. The main entry is directly below the catwalk. Dark mahogany rails contrast with the white walls, which serve to reflect natural light into the stairwell.

sets, construction adhesive and 16d nails (driven with a pneumatic nailer) would hold the truss together. Rafters would bear on top of the truss, and the bedroom ceiling joists would terminate beneath it. We planned to build the truss on the second-floor deck and raise it into place. It would be inexpensive to build and light enough (about 1,950 lb.) so that it could be lifted into place without a crane (more on that later).

Hands on—The site was sloped, and ledge (the local name for bedrock, which in this case was solid granite) was only about 12 in. down. My crew and I cleared the trees, yanked the stumps from the site and scraped off the topsoil to expose the ledge. I carefully figured out exactly where the foundation was to go and how much rock had to be dynamited out of the way. The plans didn't call for a basement—just a minimal crawl space. The blasters decided to load the charge a little heavy so we wouldn't end up with chunks of granite too big too move. After a truly impressive blast, we had a three-quarter basement instead of a crawl space, with some chunks of rock in it that it took a D-6 to move. We piled up the rock on site, knowing we would eventually use a good bit of it for driveway fill and stone walls.

Foundation work was straightforward except for the weather. We poured in December during a cold snap, but by draping poly over the walls and heating the air underneath it with propane space heaters, we avoided any problems (for more on pouring concrete in cold weather, see *FHB* #51, pp. 41-42).

Double walls—The double-wall construction for the exterior walls was no problem because I had done it before and had worked out a system. The 1-ft. thick frame consists of two standard 2x4 walls with single top and bottom plates and a 5-in. space between them. The outer wall is clad with Western red cedar shingles over ½-in. plywood sheathing and Tyvek. The inner wall is sheathed on its exterior side with ½-in. plywood over a 6-mil poly vapor barrier and is finished with ⅝-in. drywall on its interior side. Both the inner and outer walls are filled with R-11 fiberglass insulation, and the space between them is filled with R-19 fiberglass insulation installed horizontally.

The walls are tied together top and bottom with 12-in. wide, ½-in. plywood plates, and the window openings are splayed to allow the maximum amount of light into the interior.

The bow wall in the parlor is a double wall, too. We bandsawed the plates, sills and headers, assembled the wall on the deck like any normal wall, and then tilted it up. I was pleasantly surprised when it tilted up as easily as a straight wall. The wall bears on wood I-beams that extend from a Micro = Lam header and cantilever out beyond the building line.

The most exciting part of the framing was the ridge truss. My Proctor wall jacks (Proctor Products Co., Inc., Box 697, 210 8th St., South, Kirkland, Wash. 98083-0697) are rated

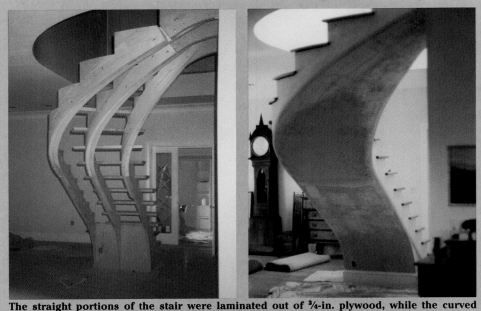

The straight portions of the stair were laminated out of ¾-in. plywood, while the curved portions were glue-laminated out of a combination of plywood and ¼-in. thick plies of ash (photo above left). The underside was finished off with 3-coat plaster over metal lath, and the outboard stringers were capped with painted birch skirtboards (photo above right). The stair was then topped off with red-oak treads to match the strip flooring. A glue-laminated cherry rail was added later.

for 1,000 lb. each, so theoretically they could handle the weight of the truss. We built the truss flat on the second floor, kitty-corner to its final location so it would fit on the deck. Then we stood the truss up. We now had to raise it 8 feet. We set up the two wall jacks on opposite ends of the truss, blocked them up about a foot off the deck so they would have enough lift and guyed them off to the deck.

Things went well for the first 7 ft., but then the first wall jack failed. All the cable had wound up on one end of the drum, and the uneven pressure broke the drum and ratchet (the instructions say to make sure the cable winds up evenly on the drum, but that's not easy to do when there's close to 1,000 lb. of tension on the cable). To its credit, the wall jack failed safely, meaning nothing fell down, but the jack wouldn't go up either.

We blocked up the bottom of the truss with 2x6s, braced the top and jury-rigged a come-along to finish the lift. The same thing happened to the other wall jack a few minutes later, and we solved the problem in the same way. (The Proctor Wall Jack Company sent out replacement parts at no cost, which endeared them to me.) The last foot of the lift went smoothly. We were able to position the truss at the top of the wall by hoisting it up an extra inch or so and easing off on the guy lines.

I had subcontractors for the plumbing and for the mechanical and electrical work whom I had worked with before, and who knew their business. The mechanical sub and I figured out how to run the ducting for the HRV, and he installed the ducts before I allowed the plumber to run his drain and supply lines. Finally, I let the electrician rough in.

This avoided the usual problems of two trades competing for the same space and set the priority for who got first pick on the available space.

I used ⅝-in. drywall throughout because it isn't much more expensive than ½-in. drywall, yet it provides some fire rating, is stronger and feels more solid than ½-in. drywall. For the bowed wall and for curved sections above the stairwell, we used double ⅜-in. drywall because it bends easily. To deaden sound transmission between the first and second floors, we substituted resilient channel in the ceiling for the strapping that is traditionally installed around here between the floor joists and the drywall.

I went with commercial grade 26-ga. galvanized-steel roofing. It was heavier than the usual 29-ga. roofing available in the lumberyards. Better yet, the supplier would cut it to length, supply all the flashing and even bend valley flashing in matching colors to meet my requirements. Also, the supplier had no problem handling long lengths. My previous experience with 29-ga. residential roofing was that it was available in 2-ft. increments only, just a few stock flashings were available, and no matter what the manufacturer's literature said, if you wanted long lengths you couldn't get them because the local yard couldn't handle them without damaging them. While this last problem is no doubt a local one, it was still real to me. By going with a commercial roofing, I paid more, but I got more in terms of product and service.

Vapor and moisture control—We installed Tyvek on the exterior of the house between the siding and sheathing, but I wonder if it's worth the cost. Plywood sheathing makes a

Though the kitchen and dining area are an open plan, they're separated visually by a free-form island and a curved soffit, and by the transition from vinyl flooring in the kitchen to oak strip flooring in the dining area. The framing for the window openings in the superinsulated walls is splayed to capture the maximum amount of light and the optimum view. The coved ceiling in the kitchen is illuminated with indirect fluorescent lighting, and the cornice molding is Focal Point resilient urethane foam molding.

good air barrier except at the seams and openings, but I think I can effectively caulk seams (provided there's at least a ⅛-in. gap between adjacent sheets of plywood) more cheaply than I can install Tyvek.

Installing the vapor barrier 3½ in. into the wall allowed the plumbing and electrical work to be done without puncturing the poly. The only penetrations in the ceiling were for the plumbing stack and the chimney for the woodstove. I don't like to use vapor barriers in floors, because the idea of trapping moisture in finish flooring makes me nervous.

The main floor is insulated with R-38 fiberglass insulation, and the second-floor rim joist is insulated with 3-in. Thermax fitted between each joist and then caulked. In the roof, the 14-in. rafters allow for 12-in. fiberglass insulation with a 2-in. airspace above it. To prevent the insulation from encroaching on the airspace, I stapled Rafter-Vent (Foam Plastics of New England, Inc., P. O. Box 7075, Prospect, Conn. 06712) to the underside of the sheathing between the rafters. Rafter-Vent consists of corrugated foam cut into 1-ft. by 4-ft. sheets. Air enters the airspace through a continuous soffit vent. I have yet to find a ridge vent that I like for use on a steep-pitched metal roof, so I used big gable-end vents to allow warm air to escape from the attic.

Interior finish — The baseboard, casings and four-panel doors were all made by the same company that built the staircase. Poplar was used throughout, except for the exterior doors, which were built out of maple. The baseboard and casings are similar to those found in my client's old house. We went with 7-ft. doors and larger baseboards and casings on the first floor to complement the 10-ft. high ceilings, and installed 6-ft. 8-in. doors with scaled-down casings and baseboards on the second floor, which has standard 8-ft. ceilings.

The free-form island countertop in the kitchen (photo above) was designed to mirror the curvature of the soffit directly above it. The soffit and island are important design features because they separate the kitchen from the dining area. During the day, the kitchen/dining area is an open plan, and the island and built-in range function as part of the kitchen. But at night, with the task lighting in the kitchen turned off and the chandelier in the dining area turned on, the soffit effectively separates the dining area from the kitchen, and the island becomes part of the dining area. The cornice molding on the first floor and the rosette for the chandelier are stock patterns from Focal Point (P. O. Box 93327, Atlanta, Ga. 30377-0327). The molding is of flexible urethane foam, which was easily persuaded to follow the curvature of the soffit and the bow wall.

I chose Forbo-Smarag vinyl flooring (Forbo North America, Inc., P. O. Box 32155, Richmond, Va. 23294) because it comes with a cushion, it's tough, and though the wear surface is thick, it can be coved up the wall to ensure a watertight installation. For hardwood flooring we installed traditional 2¼-in. red-oak strip flooring. After the first heating season, shrinkage of the flooring was noticeable, but not excessive. I don't have a good solution for this. The wood had plenty of time to acclimatize in the house before installation, but the change in relative humidity from July in an unheated house to February in a heated house is substantial.

Down the road — One potential problem lurks out in front of the main entry. The valley formed by the intersection of the garage roof and the entry roof could unexpectedly launch an avalanche of ice or snow right on top of an unwary pedestrian. To avoid this, a small eyebrow roof will be built that will extend 3 ft. out from the edge of the entry roof and will deflect ice and snow to either side of the line of travel.   □

_____

John Starr is a custom builder in Littleton, New Hampshire.

Pool House

Antiques, art and a lap pool mix with
contemporary details in a passive-solar home

by Stephen Lasar

From *Fine Homebuilding* (Spring 1988) 45:76-81

Although my client Chris Smith had always lived in old houses and enjoyed their warmth and craftsmanship, he had planned for years to build a new house. The new house would have to be a blend of the contemporary and the traditional—a setting where his antiques wouldn't seem out of place, but where space would be open and flowing from room to room and from floor to floor.

Smith came to my office after seeing some passive-solar, energy-efficient houses I had designed. He was also intrigued by the design/build business I own with Larry Neufeld, a sculptor turned builder who has worked with me for 12 years on over 40 projects. Neufeld and I think alike and complement each other's trades. Unlike the traditional and sometimes adversary relationship between architect and contractor, our relationship is a partnership.

We've spent some time building a network of good independent craftspeople to hire as subcontractors, and we like to bring their expertise and preferences into a project early. I have more control over the construction when Neufeld is the contractor. He knows what sorts of details I'm looking for, and I know what he and his team are capable of producing. Finally, because we write contracts that allow decisions to be made in the field, owners are able to wait until they actually see the built space to choose details, colors and finishes. I tell clients about their options for hiring a contractor—competitive bidding, negotiated bidding and contracting for design/build services—and tell them which I prefer. As Chris Smith did, many choose a design/build contract and work with us on a cost-plus-a-fixed-fee basis. I think the best houses come from this kind of collaboration.

On this job, our teamwork began even before Smith had selected the site for his house. A friend and subcontractor of ours told me of a south-sloping site at the top of a hill, where you could see miles of the Connecticut countryside. I showed it to Smith, and he decided that day to buy the land.

Harmonic concurrence—I like to design houses that are in harmony with their sites and regions. The individual parts of a structure can be in tension with the form of a site, but overall the house should fit the site. For this reason, I prefer to use some vernacular materials and forms when I design contemporary houses. For

Smith's house, I intended to use forms indigenous to New England houses and barns, such as a central stone chimney, steeply sloping roofs, shingles on both walls and roof, and berming on the north side of the building. We should be building houses for our time that will also stand the test of time. Like a New England farmhouse or a Shaker barn, a house designed today ought to inspire us for as long as it remains functional.

My appreciation of the way that ancient non-Western civilizations dealt with the siting of buildings influenced the placement and design of the Smith house. A Chinese *feng shui* practitioner could detect the energy of a site, which is found in its terrain, orientation, weather and view, as well as in the stars and seasons, and would use the resulting energy map to determine the most auspicious location for a house.

While Westerners may be skeptical of this kind of unseen energy, there's a practical basis to energy mapping that we can all understand. Roughly, the best siting for a house is on a south slope with its entrance to the south. It should be protected from weather by high hills or thick woods to the north and by gentle hills to the east and west. A winding stream downhill is a boon to health, as the house won't be flooded and the water can be appreciated from the house. Spiraling lines and gentle angles are thought to conduct good energy, perhaps because they control speed better than straight lines and sharp angles.

Smith's property seemed the perfect site for a house that could harness energy, both solar and terrestrial. It is a south-sloping piece of land with hills on three sides and a meandering stream to the south. The site is bounded on all sides by old stone walls and covered with wildflowers in the summer (photo facing page). There's hardly a house or barn to be seen in the distance, and the view stretches 20 miles on clear days.

Setting the course—Chris Smith wanted a house big enough for his wife and their children, who range in age from eight to mid-twenties. He also wanted to be able to watch the moon rise from the window of the master bedroom and to have space for his art collection and antiques. It was a given that we would include passive-solar design techniques and overall energy efficiency. The challenge that loomed largest was to incorporate an indoor lap pool into the design. An-

The sloped southeast facade of this house in northwest Connecticut turns its four stories to the sun (above). Most of the windows on this wall are skylights, including the large windows at the lower pool level, and are unshaded to allow for solar gain. Skylights on the upper levels can be covered by integral exterior shades. An abundance of local fieldstone was put to use in retaining walls, interior fireplaces and the chimney. Many interior rooms open to the outside at decks or terraces, like the large trellised patio off the dining room. The entry facade faces downhill toward a long drive. A view from the northwest (right) shows the half-below-grade garage. From this vantage point, the narrow silhouette of the house, with its steep roofs, dormer and few windows, looks somewhat medieval.

other specific request from Smith—in fact, one of his reasons for working with us—was that Larry Neufeld build at least one of his signature stone fireplaces.

From plan to house—I find it easiest to clarify the program by beginning the design process with floor plans. As I work out the plan with my client, the arrangement of rooms suggests volume and flow. Next, I design the massing and elevations, working from the inside out. Designing this way creates interesting facades that pique a viewer's curiosity about what is inside.

Smith and I agreed that the house should have four levels, each more private than the one below, from the pool on the lowest level to the study on the top floor (drawings, below and facing page). The slope allowed me to bury the house in the hill. I aimed the major elevations of the house to the south to get full benefit of the sun. One elevation faces southeast and the other is angled 45° to face southwest. This turning forms the angles that appear inside the house, and it makes the house seem as if it is following the sun.

The southwest entry facade is massive and nearly symmetrical, presenting an almost traditional face to the south and the long, curved drive (photo p. 38). But a steeply sloping roof takes over the southeast facade, making most of its windows into skylights. As the hill rises around the house, terraces and retaining walls step up with it, allowing access to the outside from almost every interior level. On the north

As shown in the photo at left, a fieldstone fireplace dominates the living room and defines the edge of the dining room, to the left, and the library, behind it on the right. Flagstone finishes off the cabinet top along the wall at the right. Custom registers, which allow heat to flow from convection units behind the cabinets, fit into the kickspace of the cabinets and between the flagstone tops and window sills along the living-room walls (level-two plan, below). A small library is several feet below the level of the living room (photo facing page). Warm red paneling contrasts with the light, smooth walls of the rest of the house. Belgian block cobblestone edges the brick fireplace.

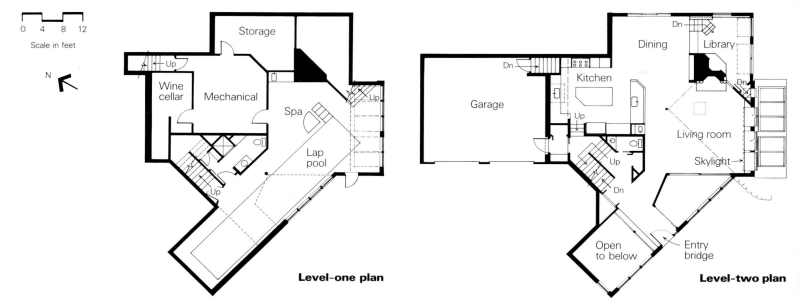

0   4   8   12
Scale in feet

N

Level-one plan

Storage

Wine cellar

Mechanical

Spa

Lap pool

Up

Up

Up

Level-two plan

Dn

Dining

Library

Kitchen

Garage

Up

Dn

Up

Living room

Dn

Skylight

Open to below

Entry bridge

and west sides of the house, the one and two-story walls have few windows and look hunched against the northwest winds (photo p. 39).

Though the massing of the Smith house isn't traditional, its shingled roof and sidewalls are. Formal granite steps along a curved, off-center stone retaining wall lead to the front door. Just inside, the traditional foyer is replaced by a glass walkway that spans the lap pool below.

Like the exterior, the interior is a mix of contemporary and traditional detail, and spaces are at once flowing and well defined. Sun angles influenced several of the rooms. A central switchback stair connects the four levels of the house, and a few steps link the library with the living room and the pool below. Near the front door, visitors are funneled from the glassed bridge through a slightly angled hall into the living room, where a fieldstone fireplace anchors the soaring space (photo facing page).

The circulation flows from space to space in overlapping spirals. Most rooms are entered from a corner, or at least at a diagonal, so that you can't get a head-on look into a room or take in the view until you get there (although a piece of the view may intrigue you from a distance). You find your bearings in this house from the many views, both controlled and panoramic, of the surrounding hills and fields.

There's an unexpected contrast of color, mood and size between the bright contemporary living room and the tiny library around the corner, with its rich, red paneling (photo right). Then, if you open the little door in the corner of the library and go down a few steps, first narrow, then broadening, you come to the lap pool, a dark blue-green rectangle in a tall, white room with lots of glass (photo p. 43). Even the air is different there.

The pool room—The lap pool is the thermal and formal focus of the house. I cut away part of the second level so that you can see it from the entrance bridge before you actually get to it from the library or the central stair, and also to allow more surface area for the transfer of heat from the pool to the rest of the house. The sides and floor of the

Level-three plan

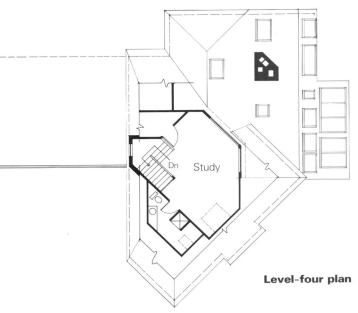

Level-four plan

Bluestone surrounds the pool and the half-moon whirlpool at one end (above). The pool room takes up space from the floor above to bring in light. A glassed-in bridge upstairs overlooks the bright space and its dark pool (facing page).

A light-colored, round maple inlay accents the curve of the walnut railing in the library.

pool were sprayed with gunite and then coated with dark grey marlite. The dark color absorbs heat well and makes the pool look blue-green during the day. The sun helps to heat the pool water to around 78°F, and the surrounding air is kept one or two degrees higher to prevent mist and condensation from forming. Moisture is drawn from the air by a Dry-o-tron system (Dectron, Inc., P.O. Box 2076, South Burlington, Vt. 05401). This state-of-the-art dehumidifier cools the air below its dew point to condense it, then returns the water to the pool; it also warms the room air with heat generated by the compressor.

Heat from the pool space conducts slowly through insulated interior walls and windows to the rest of the house. This system works so well that the baseboard heating system we installed as a backup has hardly been used over the two winters that the family has lived in the house.

As an additional humidity control, we installed vapor barriers on the pool side of the wood stud walls. All drywall surfaces in the pool room are finished with a thin layer of Keenes Cement (United States Gypsum, 101 S. Wacker Drive, Chicago, Ill. 60606), a plaster, lime and water mixture that creates a tough, crack-and-water resistant surface. Most other surfaces near the pool are water resistant. The siding is cedar, the pool deck and window sills are bluestone, and the windows trim is painted wood. Glass between the first and second floors, at the bridge and in the living room is insulated and fixed, but the windows between pool and outside can be opened to the breeze (photo top left).

Collaborating on the details—Many details were purposely left to be developed during construction. Designing and building the library, with its cobblestone fireplace, detailed paneling and fine stair rail, involved us all, from owner to subcontractors. Smith wanted the library to be cozy, comfortable and more traditional in detail than the rest of the house. He suggested surrounding the fireplace with red-painted wood paneling, I sketched the paneling, and Neufeld and Dan Dommenel, of Picton Construction Co., detailed the design and made the paneling. Neufeld chose the Belgian block cobblestones of the fireplace, and Al Lord designed and crafted the walnut handrail with its light-colored maple inlay (photo bottom left). In the kitchen, I designed the layout while Smith worked with Neufeld and Lord as they detailed and built the cherry cabinets. For the master bedroom, Lord and Smith collaborated on a beautiful, curved-end curly maple bed unit.

Some years back Neufeld had acquired a long, nicely shaped stone and had since been thinking about how to use it. He decided that it would make a perfect lintel for the living-room fireplace, so he fit fieldstone around it like puzzle pieces. Upstairs, he set smoothly cut Indiana limestone for the fireplace surround and for a dresser counter. Outside, there's more Neufeld-inspired stonework—he and Smith chose stone from a local supplier, and Neufeld supervised the construction of granite slab steps to the front door and the installation of the two pillars that mark the driveway cut through an existing fieldstone wall. □

A Photovoltaic Test House

Ten years after its completion, this house still sells electricity back to the power company

by Charles Wardell

"The truth of the matter," says Steve Strong, "is that innovation in the housing industry is very, very slow." He should know. As president of Solar Design Associates, a group of architects and engineers who design and build "environmentally responsive" homes, Strong has been testing new housing technologies since the mid-1970s. So it was no surprise when, in 1982, Boston Edison asked his firm to design an energy-efficient demonstration house in Brookline, Massachusetts. The "Impact 2000" house combined passive-solar design, superinsulation and highly efficient mechanical systems. But the project's centerpiece was a 4kw photovoltaic array designed to supply half of the home's power needs (top photo, facing page). When the home's electric demand exceeds that supplied by the roof, the grid-interactive system draws power from the utility; when roof output exceeds demand, the home sells power *back* to the utility.

Great ideas, but does the house still work after 10 years, and what have we learned from it? I recently visited Strong to find out, and in doing so I discovered that there's more to a successful photovoltaic house than a bunch of solar cells on the roof.

Creating demand—Even today, most people don't know much about photovoltaics. But one reason for building the "Impact 2000" house was to highlight energy-saving technologies that would become commonplace *after* the turn of the century. Some of these have already entered the mainstream, while others are well on their way.

One message that emerged from the project was that the early market for such technologies can be created by someone other than the designer, the builder or the client. In this case, it was the electric company, and utilities across the country have since jumped on the energy-efficiency bandwagon. A combination of rising demand, escalating construction costs and public opposition to new power plants has made it more cost-effective for utilities to reduce their loads than to add capacity. "Utilities have undergone nothing less than a full-scale revolution in the way that they do business," says Strong. "Until a few years ago, only a handful of farsighted utilities understood that they could profit from conservation. Now, nearly all of them realize that it's far cheaper and better to lower demand." Impact

2000 showed how energy-saving measures could dramatically lower electric demand without sacrificing comfort.

A different approach—Strong likes to say that flexibility and unconventional thinking are required when designing energy-efficient homes. A passive-solar home is a good example of this. Although solar houses can be of any architectural style, they tend to be contemporary for good reason. "You need a lot of design flexibility," he says, "and contemporary designs allow that freedom." Flexibility proved crucial in developing what was, at best, a difficult site: a south-facing hill that had once been a private landfill. A house had stood at the top until the 30s or 40s, and remnants of its foundation remained. But current setback limits left no room for a conventional house, so the site had been passed over as unusable.

Strong took full advantage of the site by designing an earth-bermed solar contemporary that turns its back on the street. The austere (bottom photo, facing page), low-profile street façade helps shield the house from harsh winter winds; well-placed shrubs and trees serve as an additional buffer (dense rows of evergreens planted 50 ft. or so from a structure can actually direct winds up and over it). The design allowed Strong to open the living spaces to the sun without sacrificing privacy or quiet.

But to call Impact 2000 a solar house is only half the story. Strong's forte is "building integration," a design approach in which "the architecture is conceived in concert with the mechanical and energy-systems design." Impact 2000 was the first photovoltaic house in the United States that was built in a fully integrated manner. Strong's architects and engineers worked as a team on all aspects of the design, including the interior spaces and the mechanical systems. This is a major departure from standard practice, where the architect fixes the design and then the subcontractors fit the systems.

Walls and spaces—According to Robert Erb, a designer at Strong's firm, the Impact 2000 house was conceived as "a high-quality, casual living environment." The quality is evident in the house's architecture, as well as in its performance. The interior is bright and airy. The 2,800-sq.-ft. floor plan stretches out along

the east/west axis. Living areas face south (top photo, p. 46), while bathrooms, stairs, closets, mechanical spaces and the garage back up to the north. The upper level includes a master bedroom, a dining room and an eat-in kitchen that serves as a casual family area; the formal areas, a study and two extra bedrooms occupy the lower floor (bottom photo, p. 46). The master bedroom is acoustically isolated from the rest of the house and is accessed via a bridge from the entry. The lower-level bedrooms are located as far away from the master suite as possible, near their own stairway to the kitchen.

One of the reasons that the interior seems so comfortable is the integration that Strong speaks of. Spaces were designed with an eye to thermal comfort, as well as to aesthetics. The south side is lined with 440 sq. ft. of heat-mirror glass. A coating in the glass acts as a one-way mirror, letting short-wave solar radiation into the living spaces but keeping long-wave heat radiation from escaping. In winter, warm air rising from a sunspace at the home's midpoint helps warm the upper floor.

The house is superinsulated with R-68 ceilings, R-30 walls and R-25 floors. A continuous 6-mil vapor barrier prevents air leakage. Good air quality is maintained by a mechanical ventilation system with heat recovery. The system replenishes indoor air at a variable rate of up to one air change per hour.

To maintain even indoor temperatures, a passive-solar home needs a lot of thermal mass. The mass serves as a storage battery, soaking up warmth during the day and giving it off slowly at night. Impact 2000 has some thermal mass in every room. In keeping with the integrated approach, Strong designed the mass into the home's structure. All exterior walls and four interior walls consist of concrete block (bottom photo, p. 48). The inside was finished with a coat of plaster. A block fireplace core rising through the home's northwest corner contributes additional mass. A lot of this mass lies beyond the reach of the sun's rays, making it three to five times less effective than directly illuminated mass. But this deficiency is more than overcome by the sheer volume of the mass.

Heating and cooling—The design program specified that the house burn no fossil fuel. Auxiliary heating and cooling are provided by

From *Fine Homebuilding* (February 1992) 72:70-75

Energy craftsmanship. This photovoltaically powered home in Brookline, Mass., is now 10 years old. It helped to popularize energy-efficient building techniques.

Low profile. Performance of the house was enhanced by an earth-bermed design. The louvers at the peak of the roof serve as the roof's ridge vents and also cool the photovoltaic cells.

a geothermal heat pump connected to a 750-ft. deep well. A heat pump works like a refrigerator in that it transfers heat energy from one mass to another—in this case from the ground to the house in the winter and from the house to the ground in the summer.

Geothermal units take advantage of relatively stable, below-ground temperatures, making them suitable even for northern climates. Instrumentation on the heat pump shows that it delivers four times as much energy as it consumes. The people at Boston Edison, however, were initially skeptical about the heat pump's efficiency. When the utility sold the house to a private owner, they installed what Strong calls a "massive" backup electric heating system. It's never been used.

The house gets 80% of its hot water from a solar drainback system with 150 sq. ft. of high-efficiency, integrated collectors and two stone-lined storage tanks (for more on solar hot water, see *FHB #68*, pp. 50-55). The collectors separate the roof's two photovoltaic arrays. Laying the collectors directly over the roof sheathing helped reduce back-losses and raise efficiency. The home gets the remaining 20% of its hot water from a desuperheater on the heat pump. The desuperheater extracts any residual energy (energy that's not used for space heating) from the heat pump's refrigerant loop. Use of this strategy means that the house gets its hot water practically free.

The home also includes two closed-combustion fireplaces. A series of vents in each unit let house air circulate around the back of the firebox, enhancing heat transfer to the living spaces. Because the fireplaces don't use house air for combustion, any heat sent to the living space is a net gain.

Solar electricity—Heat pumps, high-quality insulation and the like are now standard fare in many energy-efficient homes. The most striking aspect of the Impact 2000 house is the 4½kw photovoltaic array lining its south roof—a marriage of one of our most advanced and one of our most traditional technologies. The 24 solar modules generate an average of 450kwh of electricity per month (a typical family uses about 750kwh). Each module consists of hundreds of wafer-thin crystalline silicon cells. In principle, solar cells work like any semiconductor (sidebar, p. 49). The difference is that solar cells go a step further, using sunshine to generate direct-current (DC) electricity.

But in an electric power system driven by alternating current (AC), DC is awkward to work with. Impact 2000's ambition was to enter the mainstream. Before the home could plug into the grid—and before the occupants could plug in their household appliances—the DC flowing from the roof would have to be converted to AC. This transformation or conversion takes place inside a solid-state device that's called an inverter.

The inverter does more than change DC to AC—it's the heart and the brain of the system. To drive most household appliances safely and to ensure that its output meshes easily with that of the grid, the inverter's electronic circuits must maintain a stable voltage, frequency and waveform—the pulse and the blood pressure of an electric service. It must also disconnect from the grid the moment it senses a power outage; otherwise, electricity flowing from the inverter to the grid might electrocute line workers. In other words, the success of a utility-interactive system depends on the quality of the inverter.

Unfortunately, early inverters were known mostly for being unreliable. Inverter performance had improved dramatically by the time the Impact 2000 house was built (and it's even better today, thanks to ongoing research in the electronics industry), but Boston Edison still wanted to see how an inverter would hold up in the real world over a long period—which was one reason that the house was loaded with instruments. "They had images of unacceptable harmonics, a poor power factor and the possibility of all sorts of fireworks," says Strong. But after several years of study, what may have been most abnormal from a utility point of view was the lack of problems. "The researchers reluctantly shrugged their shoulders and concluded that everything was just fine." In fact, the power quality coming from

Let the sun in. All living areas face south. The two-story sunspace at the far end of the dining room helps warm the upper floor.

Livable spaces. The ground floor includes the formal areas and a study. The emphasis of the interior design was on comfort.

PV past, present and future

Photovoltaic systems have no moving parts, require little or no maintenance and — in theory at least — never wear out. They make no noise, cause no pollution and generate no waste. Their modular design makes them versatile enough to power a single lightbulb or a small town. So why aren't photovoltaic systems more widely used?

The answer is that they're not yet cost competetive with conventionally generated power. Cell manufacture is highly capital intensive, so prices remain high. "The name of the game from my point of view is cost reduction," says Stephen Shea, a senior engineer with Solarex Corporation, a leading cell manufacturer. Prices have fallen dramatically since the technology was first introduced as a means of powering communications satellites. The initial cost per watt of peak generating capacity (the power a cell will put out at noon on a sunny day) has dropped from more than $2,000 in the mid-1950s to about $5 today, or around 30¢ per kwh. At that price, it's now less expensive to install photovoltaics on a home that's one-half mile or more from the electric grid than it is to extend power lines. But photovoltaics still can't compete with 10¢ per kwh power from the nearby utility pole.

A choice of futures — Substantial savings have already come from streamlining the process of making traditional crystalline cells. But a potentially more promising effort involves the development of thin-film photovoltaics: semitransparent sheets of the type used to power hand-held calculators.

Thin-film sheets are less efficient but far less costly than crystalline cells. And if current research efforts are successful, thin-film silicon could be included as a power-generating component of tinted window glass. "We've been trying to use photovoltaics only to generate electricity," says Roger Taylor of the Solar Energy Research Institute in Golden, Colorado. "But if we're smart, we'll get them to provide a variety of functions, especially if we can underwrite the cost of the modules with things like glass that have to be made anyway." The most advanced thin-film research is going on in Europe. Germany's Flaschglaff Solar, which has 70% of the European market for architectural glass, has teamed up with two German cell manufacturers to develop a 30% transparent solar module. They're also working on a technology for depositing a semitransparent amorphous silicon film on glass.

The problem with thin films is that they degrade when exposed to direct sunlight. Most people in the industry believe that degradation can be minimized and that thin film will eventually dominate the market. But not just yet. "I measure that on the order of decades," says Shea. "First, there's a lot of physics we have to go through."

Meanwhile, Texas Instruments and Southern California Edison are testing a new product that is neither a thin film nor a crystalline cell. The new cells, which are slated to hit the market in the the mid-1990s, consist of tiny silicon "microspheres" embedded in a thin aluminum foil at a density of 17,000 spheres per 4-in. square. The product uses metallurgical-grade silicon, considered too unstable for photovoltaics until now. Material costs are $1 per lb., as opposed to $35 per lb. for semiconductor-grade silicon. The companies claim that the new product will generate electricity for 14¢ per kwh, "the greatest single cost reduction in the history of PV technology," according to a leading industry newsletter.

Signs of hope — No one can say for sure where such efforts will lead. Crystalline silicon, on the other hand, is a seasoned performer with a proven track record. As such, it remains a technology to watch. Paul Maycock, a leading industry consultant and head of the Department of Energy's (DOE) photovoltaic effort during the Carter administration, cautiously predicts crystalline cell prices of $3.50 per peak watt by 1995. "At that point," he says, "some roof-integrated systems will begin to break even," mostly in areas with high peak-power charges.

Maycock's scenario depends on what he calls "a favorable government environment." He believes that federal and state policies favoring solar technologies "would cause venture and risk capital to put their money where their mouth is." This is already happening in Europe, where a powerful environmental movement has popularized all forms of renewable energy. Germany, for instance, has banned the construction of nuclear power plants, and the German government offers tax credits of $3 per kw for renewable energy systems. The situation is similar in Japan. The Japanese government now spends at least as much on photovoltaics as does the United States. Just about every large Japanese company is involved in the effort, with each one tackling the problem from a different angle. The upshot is that Germany and Japan now seem positioned to take the lead in photovoltaics. Indeed, the U. S. share of the international market has fallen from 60% to 35% in the past 10 years.

There are some signs of hope. The DOE's 1991 photovoltaics budget grew to $45 million, a substantial increase from a mid-80s' low of $28 million, but still far from the $150 million budget of 11 years ago. More important, the DOE has shifted much of its funding from basic research to getting that research out to manufacturers.

But while such efforts are important, some observers are less than sanguine about the government's ability to create a market. "It's very hard to create a large-scale market based on the American political system," notes Christopher Flavin, vice-president for research at The Worldwatch Institute in Washington, D. C., "because it's so fickle." Manufacturers, says Flavin, are understandably reluctant to invest in markets created by legislation that may be repealed after the next election.

This doesn't mean that the photovoltaic industry isn't healthy. World shipments of photovoltaic modules doubled from 1986 to 1990. But most of that growth was in markets independent of the American political system: remote applications in Third-World countries that Flavin calls "the thatched-roof market." Flavin doesn't see a widespread market for grid-connected homes developing until after the turn of the century.

Before that happens, electric rates will have to rise. "Energy is neither particularly expensive nor particularly scarce at this point," says Flavin. Gas, for instance, is now priced at the oil equivalent of $8 per barrel, and electricity can be generated for 5¢ to 6¢ per kwh. That could change if environmental costs somehow get factored into the price of electricity. "The environmental side of things is really going to be a driving force," he adds, "and it could have a very, very substantial impact."

Building issues — But whether it develops in five years or in 15 years, the grid-connected market is potentially huge. The Electric Power Research Institute in Palo Alto, California, estimates that 60% to 70% of all roofs could accept productive photovoltaics. First, however, a host of related issues must be resolved. Zoning laws must be revised to ensure solar access; building codes will have to address the proper design and installation of modules and other components; installation methods will have to be streamlined; installers will have to be trained; and regulators will have to establish fair buy-back rates. In short, the industry needs to be standardized. "There are still fewer than 100 projects a year that see an inspector," notes Paul Maycock. "We're just not pervasive enough. Because they're so few," he adds, "photovoltaic projects require you to educate several people every time you do one."
— C. W.

Integral mounts. The photovoltaic system includes two arrays of 12 modules. Mounted directly on the rafters, they double as the roof's weather shed.

Block and more block. To even out temperature extremes, every room includes some thermal mass. The architect designed much of that mass into the home's structure, in keeping with an integrated approach to design.

the inverter has proven consistently better than that flowing from the grid.

Integral mounts—Photovoltaic modules can be mounted in three ways. They can rest on metal rails that lift them several inches above the finished roof surface; they can be attached directly to the roof sheathing; or they can be laid over the open rafters, doubling as the roof's weather shed. Strong prefers the third approach. Impact 2000's roof consists of two integrally mounted arrays of 12 modules each. Making the modules part of the roof structure meant that they could be cooled by the roof vents—unlike solar hot-water collectors, photovoltaic cells work best when they're cool. The soffit on the south side is fully vented, while north-facing louvers protrude above the peak of the roof along its entire length (bottom photo, p. 45). This configuration both cools the modules and removes heat from the attic.

Besides heat, the next biggest threat to a photovoltaic array is moisture. The modules are mounted on wide wooden caps that are fastened to the top chord of the roof trusses (photo above). The modules themselves sit on rubber baseplates and are made watertight in much the same way as a sloped-glazing unit (for more on sloped glazing, see *FHB* #72, pp. 76-80). The modules are factory-sealed. Temperatures in New England's damp climate range from below zero in winter to +90° in summer. Daily extremes can be quite pronounced, too. But despite the stress that such temperature swings place on the photovoltaic system, the owner describes it as trouble-free. "I had some concerns when we moved in," he says about the the roof, "but it's the tightest roof we've ever had."

Counting costs—As desirable as such a system may be, it's far from inexpensive. In fact the first problem most people bring up at the mention of photovoltaics is cost. When Impact 2000 was built, photovoltaic systems cost about $10 per watt—hardly affordable electricity. Today an equivalent array costs half the price and delivers more power. But will photovoltaics remain so expensive? Strong, of course, thinks not. Prices are dropping steadily, though not as dramatically as they did during the last decade (sidebar, p. 47). "This house is typical of what you'll see in 2005, 2010 or 2015," says Strong. He also believes that improvements in systems and appliances mean that "you'll see houses with arrays this size that put out more power while at the same time using far less."

Taking lessons—Impact 2000 was a demonstration house. The reams of computer data it generated proved that a photovoltaic residence could operate for several years without problems. But Strong points out that the project had some things to teach that the computer couldn't quantify.

One of these concerned the thinking required to build such a house. Because building integration blurs the traditional boundaries of several disciplines, it demands an unusual attention to detail. Roofs, for instance, must be framed to ⅛-in. tolerances (you can't trim a photovoltaic module to fit inaccurate framing). And the energy features must be thought of as the gears of a single machine rather than as discrete systems. Finding people to work together at this level of detail can be a challenge. "Though there are a lot of PV businesses out there," says Strong, "many don't know a hoot about architecture and building." But his experience has shown that there are also a lot of talented builders who are willing to tackle an unfamiliar building type. "The talent is there," he says, "but someone who's knowledgeable about integration needs to be involved in the building process to direct it."

The other lesson learned from Impact 2000 is that people can live comfortably in such a house. "We've never been in a house that works as nicely as this," say the current owners, who are enthusiastic about the place. When they speak about their home, they use words like "quiet," "clean," "healthy," "dust-free" and "reliable." Says Strong, "All the data I need is for the clients to say, 'We love the house, and it works very well.'" □

Charles Wardell, a former assistant editor of Fine Homebuilding, *is now a builder in Boston, Mass. Photos from Boston Edison except where noted.*

Making a solar cell

Driving north on I-270 in Frederick, Maryland, the unprepared observer is apt to do a double-take. Off to the left, near where the highway intersects Route 70, an array of 3,100 2-ft. by 5-ft. photovoltaic modules rises from the ground at a 45° angle. This is the south face of the Solarex Corporation Technology Center, a facility the company calls its "solar breeder" (photo below). The 200kw array combines an interactive grid connection with 2.1Mwh of battery storage. Its purpose is to help power a manufacturing line that transforms chunks of silicon—refined from high-purity sand—into small DC generators: wafer-thin cells that make electricity from sunshine.

Inside the plant, chunks of silicon are placed in disposable ceramic molds (manufactured in-house in a decidedly low-tech operation called "the flowerpot shop"), then melted in 1,400° casting ovens. The heat refines the silicon's crystal structure, making it a better carrier of electrons, and causes any conduction-retarding impurities to rise to the top where they're sliced off and discarded. The silicon emerges from the casting ovens as 10-in. square ingots about a foot high. These are sent to a line of wet-cutting diamond saws where they're rough-cut into 4½-in. square blocks, then sliced into brittle, 12-mil thick wafers.

After the wafers have been cut, the transformation really begins. During the casting process, the silicon is "doped" with small amounts of boron (about one part boron per 100,000 parts silicon). The atomic structures of these two elements are such that the resultant crystal ends up with a shortage of free electrons (free electrons are what make a conductor a conductor), and thus a slight positive charge. But like any DC generator, a photovoltaic cell needs both a positive and a negative pole. This polarity is built into the wafer by depositing a thin layer of phosphorous on one surface. The phosphorous has the opposite effect of the boron, giving the silicon an excess of free electrons. The phosphorous only penetrates the surface to a depth of about 3,000 angstroms (300 to 600 atoms), but that's plenty. When struck by sunlight, the excess electrons on the phosphorous-doped surface get agitated enough so that they begin looking for someplace to go.

Of course the electrons can't travel without a circuit. Positive and negative leads are formed by printing the front of the wafer with a metal screen and coating the back with a metallic spray. The gray surface of the wafer is then treated with a titanium-dioxide anti-reflective coating. In addition to helping it absorb more sunlight, the coating gives the cell its bluish tint. When the cell is connected to a load, the path of least resistance for the agitated electrons is to travel through the circuit to the electron-poor boron-doped layer. The atoms in the lattice never change position; they merely exchange electrons. Any electron given off by an individual atom gets replaced by one returning from the circuit. Thus the material never wears out. The physics is identical to what goes on in any semiconductor device. As Stephen Shea, a senior engineer at the plant told me, "electrically, a solar-electric cell is nothing more than a big, flat diode."

The finished cells are tested and sorted according to their power output. Depending on the quality of the initial silicon, each cell puts out around 1.6w, plus or minus 10%. A series of robots then assembles the cells into modules, solders the leads and encases each assembly in a protective frame. —C. W.

The Buzzards Bay House
Energy efficiency with style

by Peter Adrian Thomas

Every architect, in the course of a career, wishes for a client who would have him design and build a residence without restraints, and allow him to get away from humdrum ideas and programs. In many respects, the clients for a house I recently completed on Cape Cod, Massachusetts, were just such clients. But, to my surprise, soon after I delved into the preliminary design work, I discovered that the few prerequisites they gave me made for a more difficult challenge than I had anticipated. However enjoyable it was to travel, the design road turned out to be a long one for the very reason that the clients provided me with so little input. It wasn't long before I began to request from them the same restraints I had once hoped to avoid. But when the project was finally complete, I found this house to be one of the most satisfying I've done in many years of residential design.

An expanding program—Basically the clients wanted an extremely low-maintenance, energy-efficient house, and it had to take maximum advantage of a spectacular site on the scraggy, granite-strewn edge of Buzzards Bay, Massachusetts (drawing above). But as I prodded them for details of what they wanted the house to be, the program became more complex. My clients had lived in and loved England for a long time, and wanted characteristically English touches, such as a garden room off the kitchen for working with plants and a small greenhouse for cut flowers. They

also required maximum privacy from neighbors, quiet study areas for both of them and a separate wing for visits from their adult children. Details like heated towel bars were a must because the indoor wintertime temperature of the house would probably be kept in the low sixties because that's what the clients preferred. They also wanted a garage large enough to house four vehicles of their automobile collection.

The house had to reflect the owners' interest in conserving heating oil and their desire not to waste money on social ostentation. At the same time, I also had to struggle with the need for a passive-solar design and active-solar hot-water heating without making these obtrusive elements.

Drawing this page: Peter Adrian Thomas

A house shaped to the site—The building site is an exhilarating one, and in the beginning I visited it frequently at different periods during the day and at sunset to note how it felt. It was wonderful to see the different moods of the day that came and went over a period of 12 to 16 hours. Where the sun rose and set was extremely important to the solar orientation of the house. But the obvious way to capture the spectacular view—a long, straight, west-facing expanse of glass wall— would turn the view into something monotonous and predictable. So I generated a simple geometric footprint that had as its nucleus a living room facing the view (floor plan right). Skewing the master bedroom area toward the ocean, and the children's wing away from the ocean, gave those areas separate views as well as giving the house a more diverse and satisfying shape. It also solved the problem of segmenting the house into distinctly different—and private—areas for eating, lounging, studying, gardening and sleeping. Perhaps best of all, the shape of the house would provide enough south-facing roof area for solar water heating.

The house fits snugly into a natural embankment facing the ocean. The driveway winds down and around under the house to where the garage is tucked away, unseen as one approaches the house and the entrance motor court. The giant low roof and a massive central chimney convey the feeling of a very snug hideaway that really belongs on the site. The chimney is the bearing element that holds up this massive roof expanse, but it does more than that. In addition to housing the flues, it houses all the plumbing vents in order to keep the large expanse of roof free of ugly penetrations.

Natural browns and greys of the wood roof shingles are compatible with the lightly stained horizontal cypress siding, further softening the visual impact of the structure. The house is inoffensive, yet different from the predictable Cape Cod architecture.

A plan for privacy and views—The ocean views were broken up to provide exciting vistas from all areas in the house. Both wings exploit their views, though in different ways. The children's rooms open onto a long elevated deck; its height makes distant views feel closer. And being outside on this deck without being able to observe the living-room terrace increases the children's privacy as well as that of the parents. The master bedroom, on the other hand, is much closer to the ocean, and its large expanse of glass makes it possible to sit in bed and watch the nearby waves.

I separated the two bedroom wings by placing the public areas of the house between them, which resulted in plenty of privacy for children and parents. The living room, parallel to the coastline, opens out to a spacious bluestone terrace where one can sit and sun and enjoy the ocean rolling in.

Bathrooms, the greenhouse areas and the kitchen are oriented toward the street and entry side of the house. The natural topography

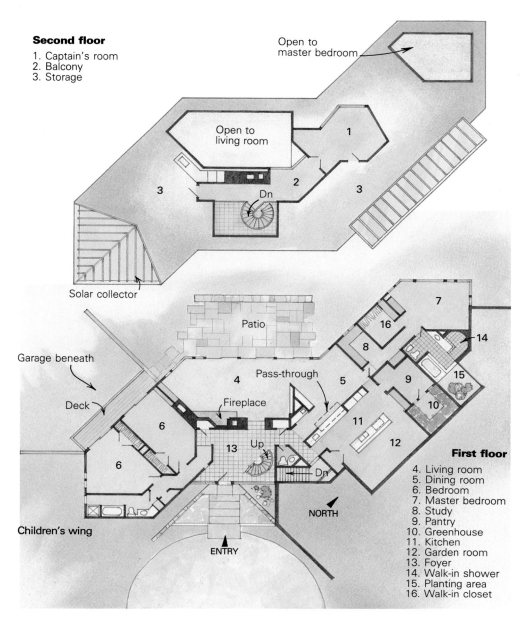

Second floor

1. Captain's room
2. Balcony
3. Storage

Open to master bedroom

Open to living room

Dn

Solar collector

First floor

4. Living room
5. Dining room
6. Bedroom
7. Master bedroom
8. Study
9. Pantry
10. Greenhouse
11. Kitchen
12. Garden room
13. Foyer
14. Walk-in shower
15. Planting area
16. Walk-in closet

Patio

Garage beneath

Deck

Pass-through

Fireplace

Up

Dn

NORTH

Children's wing

ENTRY

allowed me to bring the grade up under the eaves on this side of the house, further secluding the owners from street-side views.

Finding a focal point—I had very definite ideas about generating a focal point in the living room, and felt it should be a massive, earthy, masculine fireplace (photo following page). The random stone pattern that I had envisioned came to fruition, though not without a good bit of care and attention. I worked with the mason on and off for a few days laying up the granite. Putting the two-ton lintel into place was quite a chore, but it was made a little easier by using a wheeled hydraulic hoist. The hearth is nearly as massive, and though it looks like it cantilevers away from the fireplace, it is actually supported by unobtrusive steel angles set into the concrete foundation of the fireplace (bottom photo, p. 53). The stone we used, with its veins of russet browns and tans, echoes the outcroppings on the scraggy coastline nearby. The wall at the ocean edge of the terrace just outside the living room is of this same stone, and provides continuity from the living room out across the

terrace and down to the water. The cut bluestone of the terrace is quiet and unobtrusive, and its geometry contrasts with the bold, earthy wall.

Another dramatic focal point of the house rests within the entry hall (top photo, p. 53). Like a huge sculpture on display, a double-helix stair is revealed through large fixed windows at the front door. The stair was built and installed by Atlantic International, Inc. (1 Newburyport Tpke., Newburyport, Mass. 01950). It was designed and engineered on a CAD system, assembled by hand in the company's shop and then installed in sections shipped to the job site. The stringers and treads are laminated wood.

Sloped glazing without the chill—On the street side of the house, where it is bermed to the eaves, natural light floods into the rooms through a long expanse of roof punctuated with glass (photo, p. 54). Beneath the glass is the kitchen/greenhouse/plant area and master bath. Morning sunlight bathes these areas, and late in the day a softer top lighting makes for an atmosphere quite different from

that in the rest of the house. A glassed area for plants in the large kitchen was a primary requirement of my clients and reflects the great English love of plants, planting and gardening.

The long expanses of glass, however, offered the challenge of fending off cold winter air pouring down and hot summer sunlight overheating the rooms. I was afraid that 1-in. insulating glass would not be enough to chase the chill, so I devised a simple system to provide a third layer of glazing and a transfer of the cold air.

Six inches beneath the glazing is a ¼-in. thick sheet of safety glass, supported simply by wood trim fastened to the rafters. The lower end of the safety glass stops short of the wall, however (drawing next page). The result is essentially a glass plenum that gathers warm air filtering into the room through baseboard ducts and washes it across the insulating glass, and then guides it through screened vents into the attic. Once in the attic, the air is returned to the basement for redistribution throughout the house.

The system works quite well to keep the chills away, but there's not enough air flow to handle the heat gain in the summer. The problem was acute in the breakfast area because it did not have any openable vents (I had omitted them to gain a clean roofline). I was able to solve the problem simply by providing venetian blinds across the panels from top to bottom. By adjusting the blinds, it's possible to reflect the sun's heat away from the room without losing all the light.

Hot water from the sun—One priority at the beginning of this project was that the house be very energy efficient. I decided that part of the solution would call for a passive-solar design with active-solar hot-water heating. But the client wanted to avoid the clunky look many active systems have, with supply and return ducts scattered helter-skelter across the roof. My solution was to build everything *into* the roof, rather than mount it on top.

Just after the roof was framed, ¾-in. plywood was nailed to ledgers stretching the length of each rafter on the south-end hip of the house. Then ½-in. cold-rolled copper tubing was looped back and forth across the plywood and fastened with neoprene clips that lifted the tubing ⅜ in. above the plywood (the flexible clips also allowed the tubing to expand and contract freely). The rafters, plywood and piping were all painted flat black, and 1-in. thick insulating glass was installed over the top. Controlled by a thermostat, a pump circulates water through the system and into a storage tank.

The low silhouette of the solar panel was difficult to flash where the glass meets the wood-shingle roofing. The builder installed a slight curb flashed with lead-coated copper; I was afraid it would destroy the nice flat planes of the roof. But it looked fine and solved the flashing problem. The glass is not quite at the optimum angle to the sun, but

A laminated wood stair serves as a dramatic focal point in the entry hall. The mitered-glass eyebrow dormer above bathes the stair with daylight. Note the clean lines of the roof, including closed valleys (16-oz. lead-coated copper step flashing runs beneath). The siding is cypress with a light stain.

A granite fireplace surround stands as a focal point for the two-story living room (photo facing page). The massive stone lintel had to be lifted into place with a hydraulic jack. The hearth (photo right) is supported by steel brackets embedded in a concrete foundation wall beneath the fireplace. The slender air slot in the floor is just inside windows that face the ocean, and supplies heated or cooled air. An air slot for return air is tucked between planes of the ceiling (upper left in the photo, facing page).

A freestanding cabinet island (photo above) divides the kitchen from the garden room. The rooms face the street, so overhead glazing brings in light without sacrificing privacy. The glazing system functions like similar glazing in the bathroom (drawing and photo below). Though the house is fairly large, the clean detailing keeps it from being overpowering. Notice how the angle of the mitered-glass window (photo below right) is repeated in the floor register and in the soffit vent.

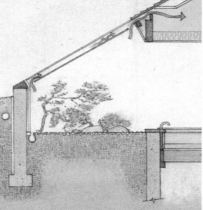

Planting indoors

To give the bathroom planter proper drainage and enough depth for roots, soil was trapped between the exterior foundation wall and a second poured-concrete wall (drawing above). With a system similar to that employed in the breakfast area, the small room is kept from overheating in the summer by translucent tempered-glass sheets mounted beneath the overhead glazing (photo left). Convection between the layers pushes overheated air into a vented attic. The system also reduces wintertime chills.

the system functions well. One thing I'd do differently next time, however, is line the roof cavities with black sheet metal, rather than black-painted plywood.

Prewarmed heat, precooled air—The design of the heating system for this house is not unique, but it's a little unusual. The basic system consists of two hot-air furnaces that continuously distribute large volumes of air at low velocity through a large duct encircling the house. We used two furnaces to provide two separate streams of heated air, but there was a cost advantage as well: two small furnaces were less expensive than one large furnace.

The air is distributed into each room through a continuous ½-in. wide slot in the floors, just inside of each window (photo below right, facing page). After air rises and washes the exterior wall, it circulates to the attic through ½-in. wide continuous slots at the angle between walls and ceilings. In the attic, the air blends with heated air coming from the glassed panels built into the plane of the south-facing roof. The attic air is then drawn through ducts back to the furnaces, and the process begins again.

There are a couple of advantages to this system. It's simple, for one thing. By prewarming the air fed into the furnaces, they don't have to work so hard, and that reduces the amount of fuel they require. The system has some aesthetic advantages, too. The thin lines created by the slots in the floor and ceilings are clean and unobtrusive.

Air flow entering through the slots in each room is controlled by motorized dampers, which are in turn controlled by a thermostat in each room. During the heating season, heated attic air is drawn down into the furnaces and redistributed by fans; the oil burners kick on as needed to reheat the air.

Though the house is not air-conditioned in the traditional sense, it is mechanically cooled. During the summer, the return-air duct to the furnace fans is closed by motorized dampers. Simultaneously, another damper is opened, permitting the furnace fans to draw cool air into the house through an outdoor grill buried in the hillside on the ocean side of the house. The cool ocean air is then distributed throughout the house.

When the temperature in the attic reaches 90° F, a 5,000 CFM fan goes into action, and draws any hot air out of the attic, exhausting it through a second underground duct buried next to the first one. At first my client wasn't too keen on having a large exhaust fan running often during the two summer months, figuring that the resulting energy expense would be high. When I explained what it would have cost to air-condition this house more traditionally, however, his objection faded quickly. □

Peter Adrian Thomas is an architect in Lincoln, Massachusetts. Photos by Paul Ferrino except where noted.

The eyebrow dormer

The clean lines of the roof are punctuated by three dormers. The largest of the three (photo below right) straddles intersecting roof planes to provide ocean views from the upstairs study. Mitered glass kept mullions or posts from obstructing the view. The framing here was extremely difficult because each of the intersecting roof planes is of a different pitch. The architect and builder puzzled out the solution on site.

The other dormers, one above the spiral stair and one above the living room (photo below left), were somewhat easier to frame (drawing below), and function more as hooded skylights than as dormers. After the rafters were headed off, diagonal runs of 2x stock were added to form the rough opening. The faces of this stock are plumb (like those of a ridge board), not square to the rafters, so that the well of each one is in the same plane as the glass; the result is an opening with clean, uncluttered lines.

The 2x stock that forms one side of the rough opening extends from a pair of rafters to a point just above the wall plate. This strengthens the opening and provides a rigid base from which to attach the cripple rafters that form the eaves. Carpenters framed an inverted V-shaped roof over the rough opening, then sheathed and shingled it to match the rest of the roof. A wood sill and mitered glass completed the dormer.

Dormer framing detail
The rough opening for each of the two smaller dormers is in some respects very similar to the rough opening for a skylight. To keep the top edges of the framing in line with the roof plane, each member of the doubled header steps down.

Sidebar photos: Staff

Expressing a Site

Materials gathered from the land
form a sophisticated, energy-efficient earth shelter

by Alfredo DeVido

From *Fine Homebuilding* (December 1991) 71:36-41

For six years, Richard Moore and his wife worked to change the face of their rolling, densely wooded land. They thinned out the underbrush and created a one-acre pond at the foot of a knoll. They set up a temporary camp and watched the land change over the seasons. And all the while they thought a good deal about what kind of house might fit both the land and their needs.

Then, in the fall of 1982, Richard asked if I would be interested in helping him with the design of the house. Having worked with him on other collaborative projects, I found the proposal quite appealing. Richard, his wife Noriko, and I had all spent a certain amount of time living in Japan and had a mutual admiration for the materials and craftsmanship of the Japanese house. In addition, the Moores had an appreciation of buildings made from unrefined local materials, a result of their visits to remote Himalayan villages. We agreed that this background would inform the design of the proposed house.

For and from the site—The site was tucked into the Connecticut foothills of the Berkshire Mountains, and the knoll it contained faced south. The Moores had decided, however, that the house was not to be *on* the knoll, but nestled *within* it (photo facing page). The prospect of doing an earth-sheltered house was of particular interest to me. I had designed passive-solar houses that controlled the flow of thermal energy into, through, and out of buildings by natural means. In some cases I employed direct gain; in others, glazed sunspaces or masonry Trombe walls. This would be my first chance, however, at making so much of so common a resource: earth. The precise site for the house was selected not only to preserve the character of the land but also to recognize sound energy-conservation principles. By fitting it within the terrain, the house would provide no exposure to the chill north winds.

As a result of years spent studying the land, the Moores knew that the property held a sufficient number of mature red oak trees to provide posts and beams for a substantial house. In addition, there was enough fieldstone nearby to surface anything we could think of. Because the use of natural materials was so important to all of us, the palette we finally settled on included stone facings and planters, oak posts and beams to support the roof loads, and sandblasted concrete to contain the hillside. Extensive stretches of south-facing glass would admit the winter sun.

Programmed for simplicity—After thinking of their house for so long, the Moores knew quite well what they wanted. The requirements included a combined kitchen/dining area, a living room, two modest bedrooms, two baths and a studio for weaving and graphic arts (floor plans, p. 59). A combination garage/workshop was "master-planned" from the outset;

A multipurpose roof. The sod roof imposed significant loading concerns. At the same time, however, it helps the house to blend with its site and moderates temperatures within.

planning for them early on would ensure a visual and structural fit later. As the plan developed, a screened porch became an important part of the program. All rooms would face south toward splendid views of the pond.

When we completed the preliminary design, there was enough of a plan on paper to allow a stand of oaks to be cut and taken to a mill for sawing into predetermined sizes. Blasting a notch in the hillside had already yielded additional stones (though most were unusable) to be used in the construction of the stone walls.

Cost-efficient planning—Custom houses, particularly unusual ones, are notoriously complicated to build. The pace slows as tradesmen struggle with convoluted designs and sheets of drawings packed with odd angles and non-standard dimensions. That, I think, is a costly way to build. Our firm works with a

system of construction that allows builders to put together one-of-a-kind houses at almost the speed of production houses. In order to do away with the time normally spent calculating heights, elevations and spans, the system offers a consistent set of heights for such elements as door and window lintels, and calls for plan dimensions based on a 10-ft. module. One advantage of a module is that it provides a regulatory device that gives order to the plan (top left photo, p. 61). But it also offers a means of communication within the design office, with the clients and, most importantly, with the contractor. This reduces job-site mistakes (mistakes cost money) because everyone knows that all dimensions are equal portions of the same module.

Another money-saving feature of the system is that the dimensions run from centerline to centerline. A window, for example, is placed

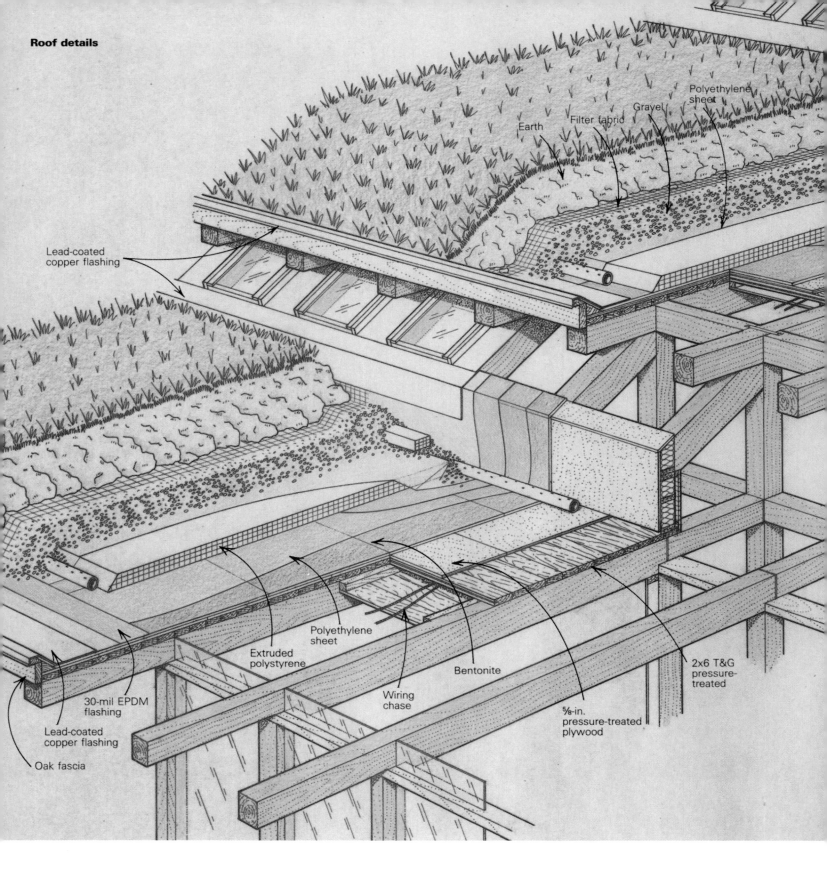

Polyethylene
sheet

Earth   Filter fabric   Gravel

Lead-coated
copper flashing

Extruded
polystyrene

Polyethylene
sheet

Bentonite

Wiring
chase

30-mil EPDM
flashing

Lead-coated
copper flashing

Oak fascia

⅝-in.
pressure-treated
plywood

2x6 T&G
pressure-
treated

on the centerline. This approach, in contrast to modular measurements that locate the edge of an object, allows the use of stock windows and doors. The expense of custom windows and doors is one that is seldom necessary.

Builders who have used our system claim it cuts down on job-site mistakes and enables the job to be explained quickly to subcontractors. We figure the system saves the builder 10% to 15% on construction costs.

As for the details, the basic 10-ft. square module can be subdivided into nine additional modules that are 3 ft. 4 in. square. Half of the smaller module (1 ft. 8 in.) can be combined with a full module to make 5 ft.; three of the smaller modules make 10 ft., a useful room dimension (floor plan, facing page). I have tried other modules, but found that they've resulted in rooms that were too small. Curved or circular walls are dimensioned from

points within the module. Angled walls are easily laid out in plan; rooflines in elevation are determined by the same basic grid.

The vertical module is predicated on the height of stock doors and windows and the precut stud, a standard in the American construction industry. In a further effort to make the builder's job a bit easier and eliminate misunderstandings, we call out rough openings of doors and windows on the plans.

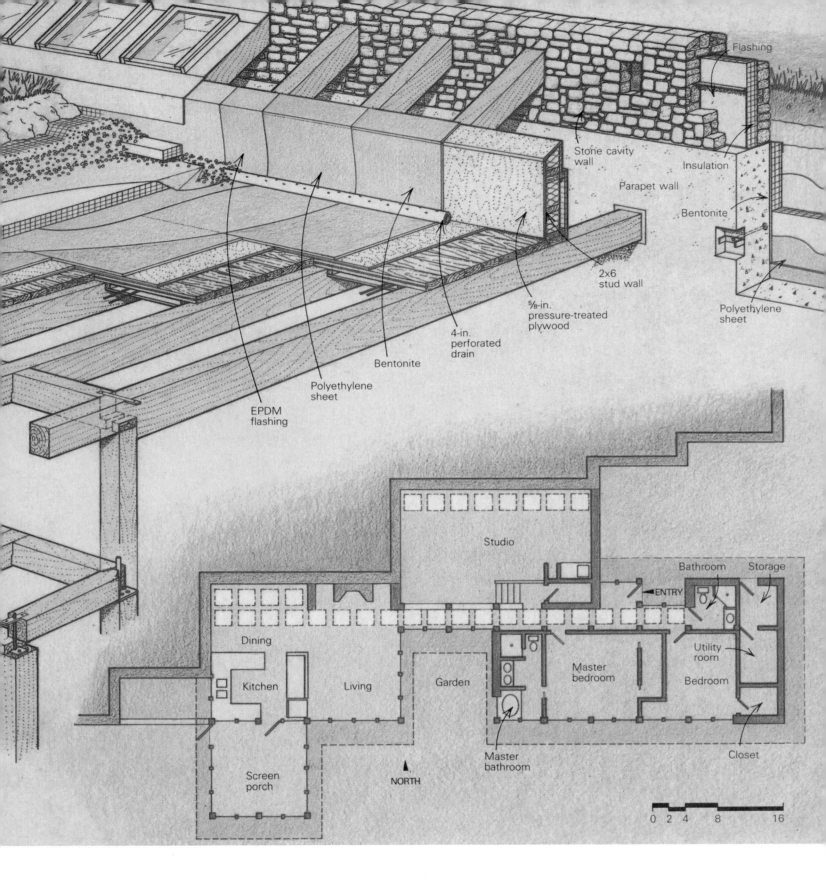

Flashing

Stone cavity wall

Insulation

Parapet wall

Bentonite

2x6 stud wall

⅝-in. pressure-treated plywood

4-in. perforated drain

Bentonite

Polyethylene sheet

Polyethylene sheet

EPDM flashing

Studio

Bathroom

Storage

ENTRY

Utility room

Dining

Bedroom

Kitchen

Living

Garden

Master bedroom

NORTH

Master bathroom

Closet

Screen porch

0 2 4   8   16

Resisting the earth—The structural aspects of an earth-sheltered house are not insignificant. Roof loads can add up to 250 lb. per sf, versus 35 lb. per sf for conventional construction (photo, p. 57). Shear stress (loads that cause a horizontal beam to break vertically) are a paramount consideration. Connections and bearing points that are commonly used in house construction are unacceptable: ordinary nails would bend and shear off, and bearing plates would deform. This would result in settlement cracks and ruptures in the joints between materials. And loads of this magnitude can pose a significant threat to the safety of the homeowner. In a house like this, with a number of short but heavily loaded beams, resistance to shear governs the design of connections, not flexure.

Accordingly, we turned the problem over to structural engineer Paul Gossen. He took into account the unusual loads and sized up the somewhat green lumber—the main structural members had been living trees only a year before, and green lumber isn't as strong as seasoned lumber. Structural joints requiring shear plates were designed to conceal the hardware as much as possible.

Another consideration of the earth-sheltered house is the problem of moisture. With the house buried in some places to the eaves, the

An orderly outlook. **Public areas of the house are separated from bedroom areas by a small garden area centered in the facade. The rhythm of support posts and ceiling beams visually ties a large screened porch (left side of the photo) to the more fully enclosed portions of the house.**

last thing I wanted was for the Moores to feel as if they had moved into a clammy basement. Much effort was spent on waterproofing and draining both the sodded roofs and the back of the house (drawing previous page).

Functional materials—Throughout the house, we attempted to use materials honestly and thoughtfully. That meant making the most of a given material's inherent characteristics. For example, concrete is an excellent material when it comes to resisting heavy loading, but with its excellent thermal mass it can also be used as part of a heating system. The Moore house is heated via hot air that's distributed through passages within the concrete slab floors. These passages terminate in floor registers in the central hallway, bathrooms, kitchen and at all south-facing windows. Concrete retaining walls exposed to the interior of the house were sandblasted to reveal the stone aggregate (bottom photo, facing page).

Over the radiant-heat areas, Richard laid standard rectangular slabs of grey flagstone, fitting pieces of natural cleft black slate between them following the module of the house. Slate was also used on both bathroom floors and as trim elsewhere. (For more on slate, see *FHB* #71, pp. 64-68.)

Though the textures of masonry and stone pervade the interior, the house is rich in the use of wood. In addition to the red oak posts and beams cut from the site, stock pine casement windows and trim were fitted between the posts, and the living/dining floor was laid in a parquet of cherry. Ceilings and some walls were surfaced with cedar. Walnut was used for the floor of a living-room alcove and for the entrance step, then repeated in the dining table and various other pieces of furniture.

Materials throughout the house are juxtaposed with each other. Oak is contrasted with the concrete and provides a psychological warmth (photos facing page). The flagstone and slate of the floor harmonize with the rugged texture of deeply jointed stone walls. Detailing was conventional in the sense that most exterior joints are lapped rather than separat-

Module made visible. The house, and all the elements within, conform to a modular plan. Aside from making the house efficient to build, the module left a visual record of its existence. Doors and windows line up with structural members, which line up with flooring.

Natural materials. To bring light deep within the house, skylights were placed in strategic locations. The natural light enhances the textures of wood and concrete.

A modest bedroom. Bedrooms reflect the owners' taste for simple spaces. For lighting, inexpensive porcelain fixtures were mounted in the ceiling; a drape of theatrical canvas softens the light.

ed with a reveal. This enables the builder to render joints more waterproof than with a butt joint or a reveal filled with caulk. At the same time, house maintenance is reduced. This is an attractive way of combining materials because flush joints are almost impossible to align properly.

Light and land—Although the house is earth-sheltered, generous quantities of light are admitted by the banks of south-facing glass, as well as by rows of skylights at the midpoint and back wall of the house. The Moores brought light into the same skylight areas at night with small low-voltage lamps located out of sight above the beams. For gener-

al lighting in each room, Noriko fitted strips of raw theatrical canvas between the beams to diffuse the light from standard porcelain fixtures (photo above). Theatrical canvas is treated for fire resistance, and lends a warm glow to the room when backlighted.

The house has been completed for several years, now, and performs very well. But this wasn't clear at first. Because of the high mass of the radiant floor, Richard found that turning off the heat during absences didn't do much to conserve energy. Now he leaves it on most of the time, using less energy in the long run.

The Moores have once again turned their attention to the land. Beginning with the installation of low fieldstone planters, they have

landscaped the area between the house and the pond. The numerous shrubs, trees and flowers that have been planted are nearly all native to the area, selected to preserve harmony with the surrounding landscape.

By day, this native oak and stone structure with its planted roof merges into the rolling landscape. Remarkably, it can best be seen as architecture at night, when the light from within silhouettes the rhythm of its structure, and the house glows like a welcoming lantern. □

Alfredo DeVido is an architect in New York City. He specializes in single-family homes. Photos by Joanne Kellar Bouknight, except where noted.

The Double Envelope

An architect applies the convection-loop concept with a simple, affordable design

by Joseph Burinsky

The concept of building a house within a house for the sake of solar heating and energy conservation has been called several things since it was introduced in the late 1970s. Terms like envelope, double-envelope, thermosiphoning convection loop and double-shell solar have all been used to describe this idea. All these names refer to the south-facing sunspace and the continuous plenum or airspace that wraps around the house's living space.

The double-envelope concept is based on convection—the natural rising and falling of an air mass as it gains and loses heat. By building two shells, one within the other (thus the double-envelope name), a continuous plenum is created around the house to contain the convective flow of air. During the day, air is heated by the sun in a sunspace on the south side of the house. As this air expands and becomes less dense, it rises into an attic plenum, moving toward the top of the house. As this air cools and is pushed by more rising sunspace air, it sinks down the plenum on the north side of the house, and then is drawn by negative pressure underneath the house and eventually back into the sunspace to be reheated. Along the way, it gives up some of its heat, transferring it through the inner shell of the plenum and raising the temperature of the storage mass beneath the house. At night, the convection loop reverses: Greenhouse air becomes chilled and sinks down into the basement plenum, forcing warmer air to rise up through the north plenum, the attic and back into the greenhouse.

There isn't always detectable air flow in the plenum, but this doesn't mean that the system isn't working. Even when convection slows or stops, the envelope of air that surrounds the inner house continues to buffer the living space from the temperature extremes outside the house.

In spite of the somewhat greater expense of building and insulating a two-shell structure, many people fell in love with double-envelope designs after reading about them in solar and building magazines. The idea of a usable sunspace and a naturally circulating, insulative layer of near-tropical air around the house was very appealing.

But as architects and home owners soon discovered, double-envelope houses don't always perform as they are supposed to. The sunspaces in many houses overheat severely in summer and can't be occupied. In other

The permanent shade hood above the sunspace gives this double-envelope house an unusual appearance, but it protects the sloped glazing and also prevents overheating in the summer. Telltale signs of double-envelope design aren't visible until you get inside the sunspace (facing page). Wood slats in the floor along the wall cover the opening that connects the plenum under the house with the sunspace. Air heated in the sunspace begins a convection current through the attic, down between the double north walls, under the floor slab and back to the sunspace, where the cycle repeats.

houses, daily sunspace temperature extremes during the winter range from below freezing to above 100°F. Insufficient convective air flow in the plenum because of poor loop geometry is another common problem.

Before developing my own double-envelope design, I studied the concept thoroughly, visited several double-envelope houses, talked with designers and owners, collected performance data and attended a number of solar conferences. What I learned was that double-envelope designs must be kept simple so that they can both function well and compete economically with superinsulated and single-wall solar designs.

The Kepner house, shown here, is a slightly modified version of my design study. Built between May and October of 1981, this double envelope is performing very well. The sunspace (photo facing page) is usable year round, and the convective loop has worked well enough to minimize the need for supplemental heat. With three bedrooms (one is still unfinished) and 1½ baths, it was built for around $29 per sq. ft. Even if you consider the good prices the Kepners got on building materials at the time, their house cost them quite a bit less than some of the superinsulated and double-envelope designs I'm now working on (they're closer to $45 per sq. ft).

Shortly after I met Frank and Tina Kepner, they bought land on the south slope of a ridge overlooking Berwick, Pa. This 6,155 degree-day climate has an annual average of only 49% of possible available sunshine (see *FHB* #21, pp. 60-61 for more on climate and site analysis). Frequently, during the heating season, there's even less sun available—about 20%. These conditions are far from ideal for a largely solar-heated home, so I knew at the outset that this would be a tough test for any double-envelope design.

The crawl-space plenum—Building this house didn't differ greatly from conventional stud-frame construction. As in many double-envelope designs, there are single walls on the east and west sides of the house. The south-facing sunspace windows are double glazed on both inner and outer walls. The north side of the house has double walls, and connects with the sunspace through an open attic space and a plenum beneath the house, which was constructed from 12-in. double-core concrete blocks that are stacked on end with their cores aligned north to south (photo bottom right).

Most of the builders I asked to bid on the house were apprehensive about constructing the plenum, the floor and the foundation that would surround it. Actually, it wasn't very complicated to build. Zane Parker, a local contractor, built the below-grade heat-storage mass with no problems greater than sore hands from lifting the plenum's 1,600 concrete blocks.

First, a concrete-block foundation was laid up atop a reinforced concrete footing. Then Parker installed a 6-mil moisture barrier over the compacted earth between the walls and laid down 2-in. thick extruded polystyrene insulation. A 2-ft. layer of crushed stone followed, and Parker compacted and leveled this heat-storage mass carefully, using a transit, a 28-ft. wood screed and power-driven tampers.

The concrete blocks for the plenum were set in place directly over the crushed-stone base. As shown in the photo center right, the blocks stop 12 in. from both north and south perimeter walls to connect the plenum's subfloor air passageways with the north-wall plenum and the sunspace.

Directly on top of the plenum blocks we poured a 4-in. thick reinforced concrete slab. This stabilized the block plenum and served as a base for the hardwood finish floor that was later installed over sleepers nailed to the concrete. We insulated the outside walls of the foundation with 2-in. foamboard. The boards are covered with parged-on acrylic cement that's reinforced with fiberglass mesh.

Some designers choose to link the below-grade heat-storage mass with the ground it rests on, tapping on the earth as a source of low-temperature heat (reliably 45°F to 50°F). This is certainly possible, but I feel that this same earth mass can act as an infinite heat sink, actually reducing the temperature of the concrete blocks through which the air circulates. So I chose to isolate the block, slab and stone mass from the earth beneath it with 2 in. of rigid foam insulation.

The double wall—The east, west and north exterior walls are all framed with 2x6s, 24 in. o. c. On the north side of the house, there is an inner 2x4 wall, which forms the 12-in. wide plenum at the back of the house. In theory, even a 2-in. wide plenum should allow for convection to take place. But a 12-in. wide plenum is far easier to build, and can more easily transport a large volume of very slowly moving air.

An important way to encourage convection through the plenum is to minimize barriers or points of friction in the airspace. This means that you don't want many windows or doors in the north side of the house, because the air turbulence caused by their heat loss will disrupt the air flow in the convection loop. I designed only two windows in the north wall of this house, and their jambs and sills are made of slats, rather than of solid wood (top photo, p. 67), so that air can pass through. The only other connections between the walls are four

attic floor joists and four second-floor joists that extend across the plenum to anchor the 2x6 outer wall. All mechanicals and utilities are inside the inner 2x4 wall.

The 2x4 inner wall had to be framed first, since nearly all the 2x10 second-floor joists would bear on it. The inner wall's bottom plate is anchor-bolted to the edge of the 4-in. slab above the block plenum. The 2x6 outer wall bears on the block foundation and was built after the inner wall, like a typical platform frame. As shown in the drawing, facing page, top right, the rafters bear on the outer wall's double 2x6 top plate.

The 2x12 rafters hold R-30 batt insulation between them, with the poly vapor barrier stapled to the rafters and then covered with ⅝-in. drywall. Since the attic floor represents the inner envelope in this design, it too must be insulated, in this case with 6-in. batts. The most important function of the insulation in the inner shell is to reduce night-time heat loss to the envelope.

To finish the walls, Parker and his crew started outside the house and worked inward. First they sheathed the 2x6 wall with 1-in. thick foamboard and nailed up the diagonal T&G cedar siding. Then they friction-fit nominal 6-in. thick fiberglass batts between the outer wall's studs and stapled a 6-mil vapor barrier to the inner face of the 2x6 wall.

Next, the plenum was lined with drywall. In double-envelope construction, the question of fire hazard is always troublesome. Conventional fire blocking in the plenum would destroy the convection loop. One sophisticated and costly approach is to install fire dampers in the plenum. These are fire-resistant flaps hinged and held open by fusable links that will melt at a specific temperature, closing the flap to delay the spread of fire.

Approval of double-envelope designs depends largely on the attitude of the local fire marshall or building inspector. In some instances, officials have interpreted the inner wall as the building boundary and the outer wall as part of the solar-mechanical system, eliminating the need for fire dampers. My approach was to cover the attic ceiling and the plenum walls with ⅝-in. fire-code gypsum wallboard, creating a one-hour fire-resistive wall. Smoke and heat sensors should be installed in the plenum to provide an added margin of safety.

The plenum's finished width of 12 in. allowed the crew a limited degree of maneuverability when positioning and nailing the drywall to the inner face of the 2x6 wall and the outer face of the 2x4 wall (photo top right). On the second floor, Parker left out alternate studs in the 2x4 wall so that material could be passed through more easily. These studs were toenailed in place after all the north wall's drywall was up.

Sunspace and shade hood—Since the sunspace drives the convection loop in a double-envelope house, it's design is important. Locating the glazing as low as possible in the loop improves convection, since solar-heated

Double north wall. The 12-in. wide plenum on the north side of the house is created by building two insulated walls. The vapor barrier is stapled to the inside face of the outer 2x6 wall, and the plenum will be lined with drywall.

The hollow-core slab. Concrete blocks, with their cores aligned north to south, form the plenum beneath the house, above. They are dry set between foundation walls on 2 ft. of crushed stone that's been leveled and tamped. Top, a 4-in. reinforced concrete slab is poured directly on top of the blocks. The blocks stop 12 in. from the north and south foundation walls, where the plenum connects with the sunspace and the north-wall space.

Photos this page: Joseph Burinsky

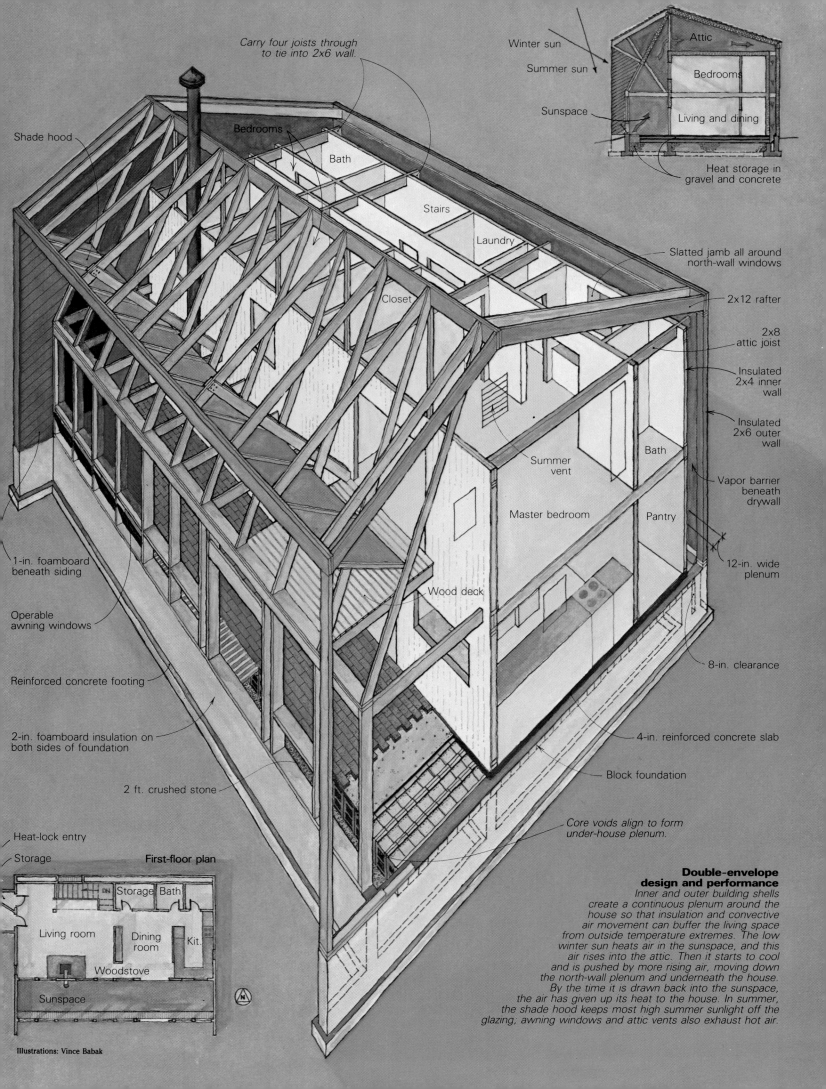

Winter sun

Summer sun

Attic

Bedrooms

Sunspace

Living and dining

Heat storage in gravel and concrete

Carry four joists through to tie into 2x6 wall.

Shade hood

Bedrooms

Bath

Stairs

Laundry

Closet

Slatted jamb all around north-wall windows

2x12 rafter

2x8 attic joist

Insulated 2x4 inner wall

Insulated 2x6 outer wall

Summer vent

Bath

1-in. foamboard beneath siding

Vapor barrier beneath drywall

Master bedroom

Pantry

Operable awning windows

12-in. wide plenum

Wood deck

Reinforced concrete footing

8-in. clearance

4-in. reinforced concrete slab

2-in. foamboard insulation on both sides of foundation

Block foundation

2 ft. crushed stone

Core voids align to form under-house plenum.

Heat-lock entry

Storage

First-floor plan

Double-envelope design and performance
Inner and outer building shells create a continuous plenum around the house so that insulation and convective air movement can buffer the living space from outside temperature extremes. The low winter sun heats air in the sunspace, and this air rises into the attic. Then it starts to cool and is pushed by more rising air, moving down the north-wall plenum and underneath the house. By the time it is drawn back into the sunspace, the air has given up its heat to the house. In summer, the shade hood keeps most high summer sunlight off the glazing; awning windows and attic vents also exhaust hot air.

Storage Bath

Living room

Dining room

Kit.

Woodstove

Sunspace

Illustrations: Vince Babak

Photo: Joseph Burinsky

air will have a good distance to rise, gaining velocity and creating strong convective flow. On a sunny day, you should be able to detect air movement in the plenum.

In this part of the country, there are many winter days when sunlight is more diffuse than direct. The sloped glass (its angle is 65°) performs particularly well on these cloudy or overcast days. Overhead glass also allows plants in the sunspace to grow up and not just out, as they usually do when you've got only vertical glass.

If you decide to build a sunspace with sloped glass, you've got to do something to prevent severe overheating during the summer. In this design, the south-facing roof extends over the sloped glass to shade it during the summer, when the sun is high overhead. My plans for a permanent shade hood caused no small amount of controversy when I was going over the design with the owners. Parker's estimate for extending the south roof, framing the overhang and siding the hood was $2,500. Without the hood, the owners would have to install a hand-operated curtain or awning system, which would cost $1,500 to $3,500. Considering the manual operation and shorter life of the latter option, the shade hood turned out to be a wiser choice. And since the house's completion we've found that its sheathed surface provides additional winter solar gain through second-order reflections off the snow.

The structural support for the shade hood

is provided by two X-shaped frames, which can be seen in the photo at left. One leg of each X is actually a 3x8 Douglas fir framing member for the sloped glass. It's fastened to the header above the sunspace's vertical glazing and extends all the way to the ridge, where it's nailed to the ridgeboard. The other leg of the X was made by through-bolting a pair of 2x8s scissors-fashion to the 3x8 with ½-in. dia. bolts. These twin 2x8s are bolted to the second-floor platform and extend to the 2x framing for the south-roof overhang, where they are also bolted in place.

The rest of the sunspace was framed with 3x8 Douglas fir. I designed both the vertical and sloped sections of the frame so that standard insulated patio-door replacement glass could be used for all sunspace glazing. Each tempered-glass panel is 46 in. by 76 in., so the finished opening for each panel should measure 46½ in. by 76½ in. This allows ¾ in. for bearing against stops and ¼ in. for expansion all around the glass panel.

Vertical-grain, all-heart redwood battens compress the ⅝-in. thick glass panels against glazing tape stuck to the redwood stops. The 1x3 battens are fastened with aluminum screws to the glazing stops, which are nailed down the middle of the 3x8 framing members. Sill battens and stops drain through weep slots cut before the wood was installed.

Just above the sunspace floor line and just below the fixed glass, operable awning windows were installed to bring fresh air into the sunspace during warm weather. Stormproof louvers in the attic are opened during the summer to exhaust rising sunspace air that would otherwise cause the house to overheat.

At right, the slatted jamb of this window in the master bathroom spans the north-wall plenum without blocking the envelope's convective air flow. The living room, below right, is framed with roughsawn beams and has a ceiling of tongue-and-groove pine boards. Behind the louvered doors, a wall of insulated glass separates the sunspace from the living room and the dining room.

Finishing up—On the west side of the house, there's a small heat-lock entry with an insulated 2x4 frame. It rests on an insulated slab. The heat lock has two weatherstripped doors—one leads outside and the other opens to the living room. When it's cold outside, very little warm interior air is lost, and not much cold air gets into the living space. Apart from conserving heat, the entry works well as a mudroom.

The owners are fond of roughsawn beams, and we used locally cut roughsawn hemlock beams in the living room (photo below right). Parker designed and built the stairway to the second floor from white oak. Finished flooring on the first floor is also oak. In the sunspace, bricks were dry set with tight joints directly over the concrete slab. A grill of oak slats was built to cover the plenum opening.

Performance—On an average winter day, sunspace temperatures typically range from 50°F to 88°F, while temperatures in other parts of the house are between 66°F and 74°F. This is with moderate sun and no supplemental heat (the house has a woodstove in the living room and electric baseboard heat). So far, the all-time low for the sunspace is 42°F, following four or five subzero days with almost no sun. The owners are both out of the house during the day, but often fire up the woodstove in the morning and evening. They use about 1½ cords of wood per year.

Because of the shade hood, daily highs in the sunspace during the summer average about 5°F lower than outdoor highs. Actually, the highest temperature recorded in the sunspace is 102°F. This occurred in mid-January of 1983, and was due in part to solar gain reflected off the snow. With the awning windows and attic louvers open during the summer, overheating doesn't occur.

It's always possible to improve a project, and if I hadn't been constrained by budget limitations I would have specified night insulation and triple glazing for north, east and west-facing windows. On current versions of this design, I'm improving wall performance slightly by using 1½-in. foamboard insulation against the inside face of the 2x6 wall and plywood underlayment just beneath the exterior siding. And an easy way to increase winter solar gain would be to paint the broad soffit of the shade hood white. In this part of the country, reflective gain off the snow and other surfaces can improve solar performance by as much as 45%. □

Joseph Burinsky practices architecture in Hazleton, Pa., and teaches at the Worthington-Scranton campus of Pennsylvania State University.

Seaside Solar

A traditional shape wraps around an energy-efficient core

by Peter L. Pfeiffer

In 1982 I was halfway through the Master of Architecture program at the University of Texas. I was studying solar design but was disturbed by the fact that most examples of energy-efficient architecture looked as if they had been designed by someone who never made it through freshman design studio. Just about the time I was getting desperate for a good thesis subject, I received a phone call in the middle of the night.

My brother was calling to say that our folks' house in Stone Harbor, a small town on a barrier island in southern New Jersey, had caught fire and was totally destroyed. Luckily, the house was empty and no one was hurt. I had many fine childhood memories from that Cape Cod style house and was heartbroken that it was gone. But the good news was that I had my first house to design. Now I could test my beliefs about combining energy efficiency with traditional design.

A coastal heritage—Cape May County, at the southernmost tip of New Jersey, is sprinkled with wonderful examples of Victorian-era sea captains' houses. I have always been taken with their bold and straightforward organization about a central stair tower, supported by strong columns that lead the eye up to an ornate cupola or widow's walk. A cupola at the center of a widow's walk acts as a skylight, flooding the center of the house with natural light. A cupola with operable windows also encourages natural ventilation by exhausting warm air.

These traditional seaside houses sacrificed a minimum of space to circulation, cooled themselves naturally, and were pleasant to live in. In addition, the design based on a square also made for a minimum of exterior skin in relation to the volume of space enclosed. High-school physics tells us that this is ideal for minimizing heat loss in the winter and heat gain in the summer. Operable transoms above the bedroom doors were another key feature of these homes. History had established both regional taste and functional design, and I thought that perhaps today's solar house designs should turn back the clock.

The town of Stone Harbor contained two other buildings that had impressed me since childhood. One was an old Coast Guard station set among the dunes at the end of the island. Attached to the station was a lookout tower that provided a 360° view of the Atlantic Ocean, the barrier island and the Jersey wetlands. The other buildings I've always admired are the local beach pavilions that still dot the coastline, with their simple square plans and hip roofs.

Neither of my parents were fond of the usual solar house, with its machine-like, Colorado ski-lodge look, and my mother in particular shared my enthusiasm for Cape May's architecture. This stylistic bent guided me through my first attempt at architectural design in the real world.

Sweating out the design—As one of my colleagues said: "You should always hold on to the drawings of the first project you did. Along with looking at yourself naked in the mirror, they're always good for a laugh." In the case of my first house this certainly was appropri-

With its weathering redwood clapboards, white trim and cupola ringed by a widow's walk, this seaside house fits the Cape May vernacular of the sea-captain's house. The traditional central stair and cupola provides light and ventilation and the sunroom, behind the windows at right, provides passive-solar heating. The trellised and latticed deck at left buffers the west dining room from winter winds and the setting summer sun.

ate. I dimensioned the house to the nearest quarter inch and drew 20 different types of foundation details. I called out the exterior trim as 2x4 smooth RSC, not realizing those initials stood for roughsawn cedar. I also drew up five alternate schemes for the mantel and hearth, each with accompanying details, and sent them to the construction manager, Robert C. Eldon, from the town of Cape May Court House. My parents and I couldn't agree on a scheme, so I passed the design back to Eldon, who selected a design and built it without further discussion. He and my parents, who acted as the general contractors, must have had the patience of Job to sift through those drawings.

My parents requested a 2,600-sq. ft. house with five bedrooms, enough space for themselves, and their seven children and an increasing brood of grandchildren, who visit mostly during the summer. The small corner lot (60 ft. by 100 ft.) dictated a compact footprint and tight plan, and the layout of the traditional sea captain's house suggested a plan based on the simple geometry of a square within a square. The bulk of the house consists of rooms fitted equally around a square stair tower (floor plans at right). Where extra space was needed—in the sunroom and living room, for example—appendages were pushed out from the main square. This design allowed the mass of the house to build up gently from the street corner (photo facing page) and the massing wouldn't obstruct ocean views belonging to the neighbors.

Although the previous house had been destroyed by the fire, its detached two-car garage escaped the blaze. While the design of the new house almost dictated a hip roof, the costs of re-shaping the garage roof from a gable to a matching hip would have been prohibi-

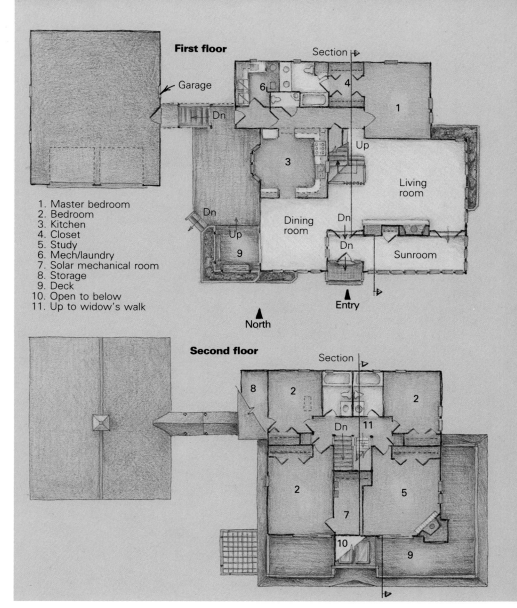

First floor

1. Master bedroom
2. Bedroom
3. Kitchen
4. Closet
5. Study
6. Mech/laundry
7. Solar mechanical room
8. Storage
9. Deck
10. Open to below
11. Up to widow's walk

Second floor

Section through house

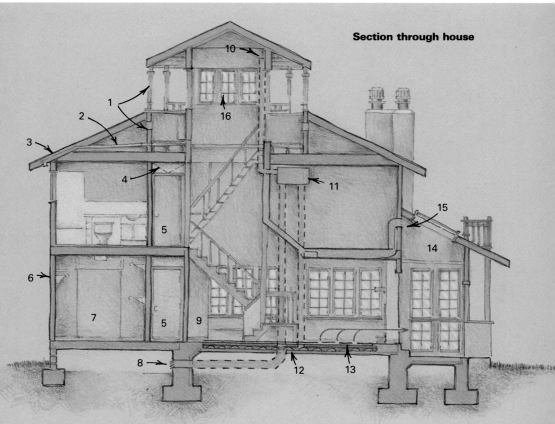

1. Roof vent
2. Drain pipe
3. R-38 roof
4. Transom
5. Hall
6. R-19 exterior walls
7. Closet
8. Crawl-space air intake
9. Living room
10. 8-in. dia. heat-recovery duct
11. Mixing box
12. Airfloor plenum in 5-in. concrete slab
13. Floor registers
14. Sunroom
15. One-way vent
16. Triple-glazed operable windows

Summer
On summer nights, the mixing box circulates cool air from the crawl space through the plenum to cool the slab. Excess heat from the sunroom is vented outdoors and most windows and transoms are opened. The heat-recovery duct in the cupola stays closed. During the day the cooled thermal mass of the concrete floor absorbs heat. Ceiling fans pull hot air up and out the cupola windows. The mixing box is off.

Winter
During winter days when the temperature in the sunroom reaches 78° F, a blower in the mixing box forces air from the sunroom and the cupola through ductwork to the plenum in the tiled concrete floor of the living room. The floor absorbs heat from the air and the cooled air is recirculated to the sunroom. At night, sunroom doors are closed, insulated window shades are drawn and heat radiates from the floor to the living space.

Drawings: Christopher Clapp

tive. So the garage was merely given a face-lift, and the two different roof shapes were left to co-exist with each other. As much as I struggled with this in the design development stage of the project, the result seems harmonious.

My first opportunity to negotiate with a building inspector came about because my parents wanted to attach the garage to the house. A local zoning ordinance, however, dictated that the existing garage could not be attached to the main structure of the house. I designed a covered walkway with a roof that cantilevers from 4x4 posts and hovers 6 in. over the garage roof. It provides a shield from rain, but it is not attached in any way to the garage and hence adheres to the letter of the law.

The existing garage also dictated the organization of the main floor of the house. The kitchen had to be close to the garage and the dining room close to the kitchen. This would allow the living room to be placed on the southeast side of the house to take advantage of the ocean views, and would grant easy access from the kitchen and dining area to a side sundeck between the house and the garage. While the afternoon sun was a plus for sunbathing, it would pose cooling problems for the dining room, with its large sliding glass door facing west. And the winter wind from the west could result in drafty dining on cold winter nights.

The solution was to shield the corner with an overhead trellis that was supported by 4x4 posts with lattice between them surrounded by a raised planter base (photo, p. 68). From the front of the house the planter would extend and reinforce the horizontal lines of the house while creating a private deck for enjoying the sunset. Flowering plants are now climbing the 1x2 cedar lattice, adding natural beauty and contributing to the windbreak. Bench seats are smooth redwood 2x4s that are bolted together; galvanized spacers between the 2x4s encourage drainage. The seats project

from the planter walls and take advantage of the cedar lattice for back support. The trellis also keeps unwanted solar gain off the dining-room tile floor, which would otherwise act as a heat sink just large enough to make summer dining an unpleasant experience.

Sources of energy—A gas-fired hydronic boiler on the first floor serves backup baseboard radiators, and a moderately high-efficiency central air-conditioning system provides backup cooling and humidity control in the summer. But most of the biggest heating and cooling demands are met by passive-solar heating, heat recovery, positive thermal storage, domestic hot-water preheating, nighttime thermal flushing, air-lock entries, and thermally induced natural ventilation.

The construction of the house provides a high level of insulation and infiltration control. Exterior walls are 2x6 studs with R-19 insulation batts and ½-in. rigid-insulation board, which was placed on the inside face of the walls. The second-floor joists and interior walls around the stair tower are insulated with fiberglass batt and rigid insulation, which serve to reduce heat loss from the first floor when the upstairs bedrooms are closed off from the rest of the house in winter.

An air-heated floor—Heating is provided by both direct and indirect solar gain. Heat recovered from the cupola combines with heat gathered from the sunroom to charge an air plenum cast into the tiled concrete floor in the living room and entry. The plenum (photo below) is formed in concrete by a network of interlocking metal pans called the Airfloor system, which was once manufactured by a company called Aircontrol Systems, Inc. (now made by Airfloor, 1442 W. Collins Ave., Unit P, Orange, Calif. 92667). This enclosed heat-transfer system avoids the drawbacks associated with tradition-

al rockbed heat storage, such as mildew and radon pollution, and its cost was comparable. The high water table on the island also made it seem best to avoid a rockbed.

The air-floor principle is nothing new: the bathhouses of ancient Rome were built on raised stone floors that allowed steam from natural springs to flow through and radiate heat into the structure. Aircontrol resurrected this idea for the development of post-World War II school buildings when the need arose for a system that could combine the advantages of radiant heating and cooling of concrete floors, but without the disadvantages of wet piping buried in concrete.

I found the system simple to build. Before assembling the prefab Airfloor pans, we poured a reinforced 3-in. concrete-base slab over rigid insulation (4 in. at the perimeter and 2 in. at the center) and a sand base. We purchased the pans from the nearest distributor of Aircontrol and had them delivered to the job site in the back of a small pickup truck. Each stamped sheet-metal pan forms two intersecting vaults and measures 12 in. by 12 in. by 3¾ in. high. Two of us spent a morning setting the individual pans out on the base slab and fastening them together with sheet-metal tabs provided by the manufacturer.

The voids between the pans were just large enough to hold electrical boxes for floor outlets, and electrical conduit and plumbing supply lines were easy to run in the channels formed by the vaults. We left a 3-ft. square void in the pans next to a supply duct in the wall. This void, which we formed with corrugated metal, would act as the manifold for supply air from a duct run in the wall between the mixing box and floor. We also cast in floor register openings next to the perimeter walls opposite the supply manifold.

After the pans were set, we poured a mesh-reinforced topping slab that came to 1½-in. above the top of the metal pans. Off-white ceramic tile was later set in a mortar bed on the concrete. If the design calls for it, the topping slab can be thickened to increase the thermal capacity of the floor system, thus allowing for a slower release of the stored heat.

How the whole house works—Heating the house by way of the Airfloor depends on the redistribution of warm stratified air from the cupola and the sunroom (bottom drawing, previous page). When the air temperature in the sunroom exceeds 78° F, a thermostat in the sunroom switches on a blower located in a mixing box mounted on an upstairs closet wall. The blower draws air from a heat-recovery duct located in the cupola (right photo, facing page) and from a one-way inlet in the uppermost part of the inside wall of the sunroom. The heated air is circulated through the Airfloor plenum, where heat radiates through the floor. After giving up its heat to the floor, the cooled air leaves the plenum through several floor registers, which deliver the cooled air into the sunroom via a one-way air vent low in the wall.

The Airfloor system consists of prefab metal pans joined into a network of ducts, set on a slab and topped with concrete. The three single pans at right will tie into living-room registers.

Photo this page: Peter L. Pfeiffer

The sunroom buffers the south side of the living room, providing enough heat for the rest of the house during most winter days. It also allows for an airlock front-door entry. An operable skylight vents the heat in the summer.

The central stair shaft and cupola provide a source of light, views and ventilation. Hot air is drawn through the heat-recovery duct at the cupola ceiling and forced downstairs. A standard stair connects first and second floors, and a ship's ladder completes the trip to a widow's walk.

As the floor gives up its stored heat to the living space at night, insulated window shades are drawn closed to retain the heat in the house. Heat-circulating fireplaces in the living room and bedroom provide a relatively efficient and romantic supplementary heat source. The living-room fireplace and both flues are surrounded by a high-mass stucco and concrete-block wall to add to the house's thermal mass.

In the summer, nighttime pre-charging of the floor plenum serves most of the cooling needs, too. By adjusting dampers in the mixing box, the system works in reverse in the summer to draw cool nighttime air from a vent that runs below the slab and into the crawl space under the remainder of the house. This cools the house for the next day. In the summer the heat-recovery duct in the stair tower and the sunroom air-intake duct are both closed; the crawl-space air intake has a dust filter and is opened for the warm months.

Air movement is enhanced by operable transoms above the bedroom doors and by ceiling fans, which siphon heat up the three-story stair tower and out the open cupola windows. Because of the broad overhangs on the cupola these windows can be left open most of the time—even in the rain. In fact, the roofed-over widow's walk surrounding the cupola is a fantastic place for views of the ocean and the island, especially as a storm approaches.

The overhangs at the sunroom, living room, and dining room shade the house during the summer months. The sunroom skylights have operable sun shades and can be opened to vent the sunroom continuously. The skylights also flood the entry with light (photo above left).

The house also employs indirect-gain solar preheating of the domestic hot-water heater during the peak summer months. A supply loop that runs in the topping slab (on top of the Airfloor) takes up heat from the plenum and further cools the floor in the summer. However, actual readings of incoming and outgoing water temperature lead me to conclude that this feature was probably not cost-effective.

Adding up the numbers—I kept tabs on temperatures and on the cost of running the house, which was built for $77 per sq. ft. of heated space. Under the extreme winter design conditions of a clear, cold night and a sunny day, the average temperature swing in the sunroom was from 41° F to 87° F, a difference of 46°. The living room, however, was well buffered from temperature extremes by the sunroom, so its temperature ranged from 57° to 70°, a difference of 13°. Insulating curtains also helped reduce temperature swings by almost 10° F. The backup baseboard heat is rarely used, so the total heating bill for a typical winter month—in a climate with 5,669 heating degree days—runs in the range of $20 to $30. Central air-conditioning was required for only two days in the sweltering summer of 1987. (My parents still aren't used to having a house with air-conditioning, so I turn it on during visits just to exercise the compressor.) Total 1986 electric consumption was 3,305 kwh, or $388.40; total 1986 gas consumption was 314 ccf, or $272.29. I analyzed utility records from 1986 and found that the household energy consumption was only 53% of the maximum allowed by the once federally mandated Building Energy Performance Standards (BEPS). Domestic hot-water heating is normally factored into the BEPS figure, but lighting, appliance and equipment energy consumption is not. But when I calculated the BEPS including these figures, the percentage dropped to 36% of the BEPS maximum standard. The BEPS standard was considered the mark of a very energy-efficient house, so this house works at least twice as well. □

Peter L. Pfeiffer is a principal in the Austin, Texas, firm of Barley, James & Pfeiffer, Architects, Planners and Energy Consultants.

Pennsylvania Snowbelt House

A passive-solar home on a less than ideal site

by Scott McArthur

The first time I saw the 20-acre property where I would later build for my in-laws, Harry and Margery McNaught, I was aware of how open and windswept it was. The land is located at an elevation of 1,700 ft. in the mountains of northern Pennsylvania's snowbelt and contains in its bowl shape the beginning of a watershed and a large spring-fed pond.

We wanted to put a passive-solar house and guest cottage where they would overlook the pond, and at the same time catch the full scope of the winter sun. The building site we chose was in a large, sunny field with hundreds of open acres to the northwest. It was easy to see that the drainage was not good here because it had not rained for about a week and my boots still squished in the saturated turf, and in some places I could even see standing water.

It was late winter in 1979 with two short months to design the buildings when I started playing with the idea of an envelope house. The concept of an elevated first floor with a crawl space underneath and a buffered "house within a house" seemed well suited to the wet, windy site.

In trying to simplify the shape and improve on the aesthetics over other envelope houses I had seen, I came up with a basic wedge, as if the front and rear roof lines of a New England saltbox continued to the ground (photos below). The 60° slope on the south side would provide a surface where two bands of large skylights could catch the sun, and the lower pitch of the north roof would deflect the wind. As a further buffer against the wind and to provide year-round protected access to the house, I designed an attached carport on the northwest corner, and backed both garage and house with a masonry wall that ran along the entire north side of the project.

Inside, the layout of this 1,563-sq. ft. house is straightforward (see the drawing on the following page). The living, dining and kitchen areas are on the south side, opening into the sunspace in order to take advantage of its light and warmth. On the north side of the house are the work area, the airlock entry, a laundry area and a bathroom. A loft above the kitchen and dining room holds a bedroom and an illustrator's studio.

The guest cottage, to the east of the main house, was designed as a simple well-insulated shed with a local Pennsylvania bluestone floor, laid in a grid pattern, to absorb and store the sun's heat.

A pole and concrete foundation—Knowing that frost can sometimes penetrate very deep in this part of the Northeast and that the soil at the building site was mostly clay, I designed the post-and-beam house to sit on a foundation of pressure-treated telephone poles in some areas, and reinforced concrete and cement block in others. The north corridor wall is 10-in. block with a 6-in. veneer of fieldstone gathered in the surrounding hedgerows. It sits on a 16-in. wide concrete stemwall. The southern sunspace stemwall is battered, and is also made from reinforced concrete.

The poles, which carry the rest of the house and garage, are aligned in rows spaced 8 ft. apart. The poles near the exterior of the house are set 6 ft. in the ground, about 3 ft. deeper than the interior ones, and sit on individual cylindrical pads of poured-in-place concrete. The forms for these pads are reusable, and

A solar wedge. Two bands of tempered glass bring light and warmth into the sunspace. A carport on the northwest corner of the house helps deflect the wind.

On the north side of the house, the roof, covered with Onduline panels, encloses a buffer zone formed by a partially bermed low masonry wall. A two-level deck is accessible from the sunspace.

From *Fine Homebuilding* (April 1988) 46:49-53

were made from 12-in. high rolled cylinders of sheet metal. The interior poles sit on continuous conventional footings. When the design work was complete, I dug into the construction with the help of my wife Susan and friends Taylor Oughton and Forrest Crooks.

Excavation consisted of rows of trenches for the round pads and the continuous footings and masonry stemwalls. The open site was first leveled with a bulldozer. That left about a 3-ft. change in elevation on the north side, where the block and veneer corridor wall would hold back the grade. After batter boards were set up, lines were drawn with lime to guide the backhoe through the maze.

Everything went well in the August sun, as we carved clean straight trenches in the hardpan. But on the last day of digging, a spring opened up in the northeast corner of the site. Water immediately started to flow down the east trench, turned a corner and continued down the south trench, where footings were to be poured. Meanwhile, the western sky was turning a mean dark grey, and a squall suddenly swept over us. We all scrambled for cover and watched the excavation turn into a soupy slop of wet clay. We had to clean up the muck with hoes and shovels to prepare for the footing pour. Luckily, the backhoe operator had completed the drainage outlet before the storm. That autumn was one of the wettest on record, with two drenching hurricanes, and the foundation proved to be the most difficult part of the entire project.

After positioning the round sheet-metal forms for the pads and forming up the footings, we wired up all the rebar. After the pour, we set 12-in. long lag screws in the wet concrete, heads down, where the poles would go. These threaded pins provided a simple mechanical connection of pole to footing when the poles were twisted into place. We braced them temporarily later on to prevent any backfilling from knocking them out of line.

A local contractor poured 32 yd. of concrete for the north and south foundation walls in a freak November snowstorm. As I embedded the anchor bolts in the top of the snow-dusted walls, I wondered how low the temperature might drop that night. We draped the walls with plastic in a desperate attempt to keep in as much of the heat as possible. As I watched the thermometer fall to 22°F that evening, I envisioned improperly cured walls, but the plastic must have helped—the walls are fine.

On backfilling day, the excavator's small bulldozer was out of commission, so he arrived instead with a monster dozer. By this time, the piles of earth that had been set aside for backfilling had a thick crust of ice on them. I anticipated toppled poles and cracked foundation walls, but the bracing held and the poles stayed in position. The only problem was that the bulldozer could not get between the rows of poles. Luckily, our neighbor had a small dozer that leveled out the earth just hours before winter's first deep freeze. After

weeks of hard labor, our work was safely buried underground, with only the tops of the poles and stemwalls showing.

Framing and sheathing—The sawmills in northern Pennsylvania cut a variety of hardwoods and softwoods, so I designed around full-dimension, locally available material. The construction lumber they supply is usually eastern white pine or hemlock, and at the time, it sold at a very reasonable price ($.25 to $.28 a bd. ft.). Despite the lower shrinkage rate of white pine, I ordered the hemlock for its greater strength and clearer appearance. In early spring all the framing lumber was delivered, and we stacked and stickered it to dry.

Our plan was to frame the main part of the house first, leaving the sunspace for later. Framing began in a typical July heat wave. The first

order of business was connecting posts to the poles. After marking a level line on all the poles with the aid of a bucket of pond water, a funnel and a garden hose with transparent ends, we cut and drilled them to receive steel pins to anchor the 6x6 hemlock posts that frame the house. We bolted 2x10 beams to either side of the posts with ⅝-in. dia. lag screws and common flat washers. The lag screws proved to be more economical than machine bolts and also remained tighter because the posts and beams shrank as they dried.

We connected the posts with beams on three levels. The first level was 2 ft. above the ground to carry the main-floor joists. The second level carries the loft floor joists, and the third supports the rafters. All of the roughsawn hemlock framing, except the wall studs, is exposed in the interior of the finished house to

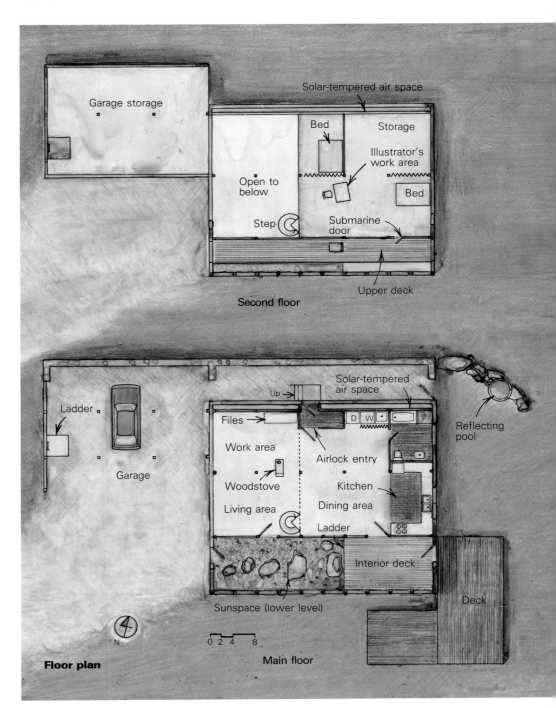

Second floor

Floor plan   Main floor

complement the smooth wall surfaces.

Purlins carry the finish roof surface of silver Onduline sheets (Onduline U.S.A., Route 9, Box 195, Fredericksburg, Va. 22041). These tough, corrugated asphalt panels are easy to align and nail down and also carry a lifetime guarantee for residential use. The 46-in. by 79-in. sheets come with either a smooth painted or granulated surface. We chose the smooth, but have discovered a couple of disadvantages. A violent hailstorm can remove paint in spots, and on very hot days, the material becomes too soft to walk on without deforming the corrugations.

Before the Onduline could be nailed on, 4 in. of urethane foam was sprayed between and under the purlins, which were raised slightly off the sheathing surface by ½-in. plywood spacers. Unfortunately, the weather during that November was too cold for us to be able to finish foaming the entire roof plane, so we had to batten down the roof for winter with a large sheet of polyethylene.

On the sidewalls, we covered the plywood sheathing with 1-in. thick boards of extruded polystyrene. This extra insulation provides a thermal break and also keeps the wall cavity warm enough so that condensation cannot occur either on the inside of the sheathing or in the 6 in. of fiberglass. The siding is T-111 plywood, with two coats of grey Olympic semi-transparent oil stain. The siding was nailed on through the 1-in. insulation board and into the studs with 16d galvanized ring-shank siding nails (W. H. Maze Co., Peru, Ill. 61354).

Interior work—With the vertical wall on the south side of the house covered temporarily with transparent plastic, we had a dry and weathertight space in which to work. We toe-nailed 2x6 T&G spruce to the hemlock joists to form both the first-floor ceiling and the loft floor. The smooth but unfinished spruce makes a simple, maintenance-free ceiling in humid areas like the bathroom and kitchen.

We framed the airlock entry and bathroom with 2x3s instead of 2x4s to cut down on wasted interior space. We then insulated the bottom of the rafters with 2 in. of foil-faced polyisocyanurate, taped the joints and nailed on a 1x6 T&G spruce ceiling. The result was a double-insulated roof with a 12-in. air plenum in between.

We hired a local artist, James Penedos, who did an excellent job on the drywall hanging and spackling. The 6x6 posts on the outside walls and the sloping sunspace rafters stand slightly proud of the drywall to frame white wall sections with blond roughsawn wood. To keep the look simple, no molding was used where the drywall abuts the rough hemlock, and no interior door or window casing was used either. Instead, the ¾-in. pine jambs and window frames protrude about ½ in. beyond the wall surface. To get a clean-looking shadow line between wood and drywall and to make the joint a lot easier to detail, metal corner bead was nailed around the edges of the drywall.

Usually when I design an industrial or architectural product, I try not to hide the mechan-

Industrial touches. In the kitchen (above), exposed electrical conduit doubles as a pot rack. Commercial rubber floor tiles and the 2x6 T&G spruce ceiling contrast with the drywall. No molding was used where the drywall meets the framing, and windows are untrimmed. A custom cast-iron woodstove (below) heats the house on less than a cord of wood per year. Nearby beams and the floor are protected in part by steel plate, and a circular register in front of the stove lets in combustion air from the crawl space below.

ics and fasteners. On this house, we finished all of the ceiling, floors and drywall work before doing any of the wiring. Surface-mounted switches and outlet boxes, connected by ¾-in. dia. metal electrical conduit, were screwed to the walls and ceiling joists. The exposed conduit snakes its way across a ceiling or down a wall, then through the first floor to the crawl space, where the conduit stops and the wiring continues to the circuit box. All of the exposed boxes and conduit bends were installed with care and take on a sculptural beauty. The conduit on the kitchen ceiling also doubles as a base for clip-on spot lamps, pots and pans (top photo previous page).

Other mechanical hardware that I designed to show rather than hide includes the metal ducts that move stratified hot air, and the white PVC plumbing vent stack. We installed a spiral staircase with steel step-plate treads that stands not too far from a woodstove with a matching step-plate as a hearth (bottom photo previous page).

The floors of the airlock entry, kitchen and bathroom were covered with solid rubber, raised-dot 12x12 tiles (American Floor Products Co., 5010 Boiling Brook Pkwy., Rockville, Md. 20852). This durable industrial flooring is usually found in high-traffic areas in public buildings. The texture is easy to clean with soap and water, looks interesting and feels good in bare feet.

The owners move in—With the floor finished but the sunspace yet to be built, the McNaughts moved into the house. That winter was the beginning of the fine-tuning process. The house proved to be extremely airtight. The entry door at this point did not have any latches; only its magnetic weatherstripping held it shut. When the kitchen stove exhaust fan was turned on, the woodstove would downdraft and the entry door would open. With a vapor barrier on the ceiling and walls, but not yet on the crawl-space floor, the house was like a heated plastic box, continually wicking up the earth's moisture. Condensation would show up at night on the inside window panes, and would drip until the puddled sills were ready to overflow. We were well aware that the house needed a ground moisture barrier and controllable venting to the outside.

Once the sunspace was completed, we let fresh outside air enter directly into the envelope through the sunspace and crawl space, where it would be tempered before entering the inner house through doors and floor vents. Excess heat can be exhausted through ceiling vents at the ends of the sunspace.

A three-level sunspace—We began framing the sunspace by doubling up and lap-jointing 2x8 hemlock to make the 24-ft. long rafters. A ratchet hoist was used to raise them to the house peak, where we bolted them between 2x12 roof rafters. Next, second-story floor joists were extended and bolted to the southern rafters at their midspan (photo below right). Like the roof rafters, the joists are 4 ft. o. c. and support the upper observatory deck (photo, p. 76). This deck is made from 2x3s nailed on edge with 6-in. pole-barn nails.

Below, at the first story, joists were extended out to support a spruce deck in the eastern third of the sunspace (photo below left). This deck, which is at the same level as the oak flooring inside, gives one the feeling of stepping outside. From the deck, one steps down onto a boulder leading to the ground level of the sunspace. Here a random line of large flagstones sits in a sea of 22 tons of bank-run river rock and pea gravel, which cover the entire crawl space and sunspace floor. The stones were all handwashed in order to remove dust and dirt that might later blow into the house and then were spread on a moisture barrier of 6-mil black polyethylene.

I had never worked with large double-glazed units before on a sloping face with an Onduline roof. I designed two horizontal bands of glazing running the 40-ft. length of the sunspace. The lower band consists of standard 46-in. by 76-in. units, and the upper band is a narrow ribbon of 46-in. by 46-in. units. The glass is separated top and bottom by silver Onduline roofing with shop-bent strips of aluminum flashing. The vertical battens were made from ¼-in. by ½-in. aluminum flat stock and attached with stainless-steel screws with neoprene washers.

I hired Creative Structures, Inc. (RD 1, Box 173, Quakertown, Pa. 18951), a greenhouse company located 150 miles away, to make up the double-glazed units and precut and drill the battens. I ordered all of the flashing from a local sheet-metal shop and the fasteners from Idea Development Inc. (P.O. Box 44, Antrim,

At left, the double-glazed sunspace extends the length of the house. Three steps below the deck on the east is a gravel-covered area that is open to the crawl space. Above, the doubled 2x8 loft floor joists extend out over the sunspace to support the observatory deck at the loft level. The metal cross bracing adds rigidity to the structure.

N. H. 03440). During installation, I was very pleased to see all the different glazing details come together in one hectic weekend.

Finishing details — With the building now sealed, I was finally able to devote time to some unique metal and wood details. The small doorway between the loft bedroom and upper sunspace deck was made into a capsule-shaped submarine hatch door, complete with a cast-iron porthole (photo right). The jamb was made from bending six sections of steel flat stock into individual C shapes and screwing them to the rough opening with countersunk woodscrews in rows, like rivets on a ship. A strip of black rubber garage-door gasketing creates a thermal break for the steel jamb and looks watertight. The door was made from a 20-in. wide standard hollow-core interior door. I cut it to shape, then glued in wood inserts to support the skin where necessary and trimmed those to fit the rounded shape. The final touch was a deep rust-red color and a large handmade steel latch.

For the two passageways between the main floor and the sunspace, I built spruce sliding-glass doors with comfortable vertical handles made from red enameled towel racks. On the other interior and exterior doors, I installed European-style locks with bright red, solid nylon lever handles made by Hewi Inc. (7 Pearl Court, Allendale, N. J. 07401).

All of the steel detailing in the interior is left its natural dark blue color with a light coat of linseed oil. The dark architectural metalwork contrasts with the rough barn-like framing and white walls.

Enjoying year-round efficiency — During visits with my in-laws, I have been pleased with the way that the house performs. The sunspace does not overheat too much in the summer, and the upper deck acts as a sunshade for the inside of the house. In the summer, when the hatch door is opened up to the vented upper sunspace and the lower north corridor entrance door is open, cool breezes circulate through the house.

With the drying effect of the moisture barrier topped with tons of river rock and large boulders, there is no condensation on the sloping skylights and interior windows. The humidity level and indoor air quality can be effectively controlled now through the introduction of outside air into the envelope. The only supplemental heat source is a cast-iron woodstove that I designed and made (photo, bottom p. 74). The McNaughts burn less than a cord of firewood per heating season.

In addition to the energy-efficiency of the house, another source of pleasure is the view. From the different levels of the house, one can see the pond and its constant activity. While sitting down for dinner, we have sighted ospreys smacking the surface for a fish, and blue herons landing among the cattails. □

Scott McArthur is a designer and builder presently living in New Hope, Pa.

The observatory deck above the sunspace is accessible from the bedroom by a capsule-shaped hatch door, built to resemble a submarine hatch.

Designing for a Temperate Climate

How a Maryland architect dealt with seasonal extremes using an arsenal of passive-solar and mechanical systems

by William Bechhoefer

Although cherry blossoms may come to your mind when you think of the climate in our nation's capital, for anyone who lives here, as I do, it's the extremes between summer and winter that are a strain on comfort and pocketbook. As a native of Washington, D. C., I can remember a few 0°F days each damp, gloomy winter, although temperatures in the 20s and 30s are the norm. Blizzards are unusual, but Washington does average 20 in. of snow each season. Houses need heating from October through early April, for an average of 4,300 heating degree-days.

I remember the summers as being even worse. People who could afford it sent their families to more pleasant parts of the country, away from the oppressive heat and sticky humidity. Cooling degree-days average 1,500, but with air pollution resulting from the high concentration of automobiles and very high humidity, comfort requires air conditioning

from June through September. In a poorly designed house, cooling can be even more expensive than heating.

As I was growing up, dealing with the climate meant applying liberal doses of cheap energy. But energy isn't cheap anymore, and finding economical ways to make houses more comfortable is one of my main concerns these days, both as a practicing architect and as a teacher helping students understand what design tools are available to them. Designing an energy-efficient building for a temperate climate is difficult because of the conflicting conditions each season presents. To cope with summer heat and humidity, you need shading and good air movement through the house. A lightweight structure is ideal for summer conditions because it doesn't hold much heat.

Winter requirements are just the reverse. The heating season demands that solar gain

be stored in the mass of the house, and that air infiltration be kept to a minimum.

There is a whole palette of energy strategies that can be used in this kind of climate. But their application must be carefully integrated with the peculiarities of the site and with a broad range of other concerns if the house is to become a home. I recently designed a house in Olney, Md., that is a good example of how workable solutions come from compromise, and from using a variety of cooling and heating schemes.

The site—The house was to be built on a 200-acre farm, on which cattle would be raised and a stable of horses maintained. My clients were a doctor, an artist and their four children. On the one hand, they wanted a working farmhouse that would fit in with the surrounding woods and pastures. On the other hand, they needed an efficient house they

Various heating schemes are evident in this view from the dining room into the kitchen. The return-air ducts behind the Kalwall tubes collect the stored heat and distribute it to all parts of the house. The woodstove on the right contributes supplemental warmth; the grate above it allows excess rising heat to be absorbed by the Kalwall tubes above. The floor plans, below, show how the house is divided into zones with the living areas on the south.

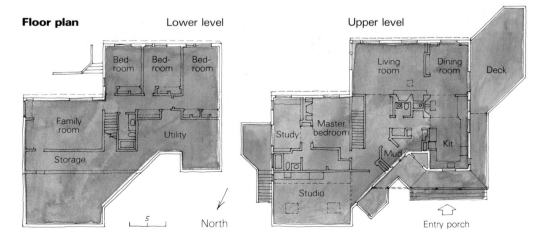

Floor plan Lower level Upper level

Bedroom, Bedroom, Bedroom, Family room, Storage, Utility

Living room, Dining room, Deck, Study, Master bedroom, Mud, Kit, Studio, Entry porch

North

5

could entertain in easily. They wanted good views to the outside, and good light within.

We surveyed possible sites for the house on horseback, a first for me. This gave us easy access to woods, pastures, creeks and ravines. Most important, though, the quiet and ease of horseback riding let us absorb the beauty of the land without distraction.

We rejected a dramatic site overlooking a creek because it was too close to the barns and exposed to severe northwest winter winds. There were several other nice sites, but they were too far from roads and utilities.

We eventually decided to build on a wooded knoll overlooking pastures and a creek. The views of the farm were great, and from an energy standpoint, the deciduous trees would provide vital shade in the summer. I sited the house just below the crest of the knoll to get some protection from winter winds. The views of pasture land were to the southeast, which is also the solar orientation I like best because it minimizes overheating in the afternoon, a problem in all seasons. It also squeezes out a little extra solar gain on winter mornings.

The owners had decided to dam the creek for a cattle pond (photo previous page). The pond would enhance the view, and would play a significant role in the energy strategy for the house. The approach to the house would be from the northwest under a natural arbor of trees. The road, which was almost half a mile long, would be easy to build since most of it was on a dedicated right-of-way.

What the clients wanted—Energy concerns are an important aspect of all good design, but are not necessarily the first needs to be addressed. I think that the design of a good home begins with the wishes of the owners and the requirements of the site. Since one of the owners was an artist, a large studio with good natural lighting was near the top of the list. They also asked for a separate living area for the children. The kitchen had to be large enough for several sets of hands to make dinner, yet compact enough to be used easily by one person. It needed to be open and informal, and still feel detached from the living and dining rooms when they were used for formal entertaining. Several rooms were to be trimmed out with black walnut that had been cut on the farm and air dried in the barn for over a year, and large expanses of wall were needed for hanging paintings.

How energy efficient?—My clients wanted an energy-efficient home. But they didn't want a house that looked solar. A greenhouse was out because they didn't want to grow plants indoors; furthermore, they didn't want anything obstructing their views. Nor were they interested in monitoring the temperature of the house and making daily adjustments. I certainly couldn't blame them for thinking that moving insulation into place in a large house would become an unpleasant chore in the winter, as would adjusting windows for precise ventilation patterns in the summer.

In short, my clients were not enthused by

Good natural light was important to the owners. Kalwall tubes in the open solar attic reflect and transmit light to all major rooms on the upper floor. The black walnut trim in the living room was cut from trees on the farm.

the dictum, "passive houses are for active people." I was not disturbed by this. There should be room for different degrees of concern about energy usage, and people have a right to expect technology to serve lifestyle rather than the other way around. Experience, too, has taught me that most kinds of movable insulation are not cost effective in a well-designed house in this climate with current energy costs. Where conditions are more severe, movable insulation makes better sense.

With all this in mind, I established the broad outlines of the house. First, I decided to take advantage of the slope of the site to make a two-floor house, with the parents on the upper level and the children on the lower, largely earth-sheltered level. On the upper floor, I placed the master bedroom, its study, and the living and dining rooms on the south side (drawing, facing page). On the north, where the light would be best for painting, is the studio. The kitchen, which generates heat, and the entry airlock and mudroom are also on the north. On the lower level, the bedrooms and a recreation room are to the south, and mechanical and storage rooms to the north. I think that this kind of zoning—dividing the house into southern living areas and northern buffer areas—accomplishes more than any other fuel-saving device.

Energy conservation—Along with the north-south zoning, the orientation of the house is the most important factor in energy conservation. Most of the glass is on the southeast, with overhangs calculated to permit both summer shading and the penetration of winter sun. I based my calculations on the sun-angle charts in Edward Mazria's *The Passive Solar Energy Book, Expanded Professional Edition* (Rodale Press, Emmaus, Pa., 1979), and shortened the overhangs somewhat because the site is so heavily shaded. While some sun does enter the house from late March through early September (when there is the greatest danger of overheating), it doesn't strike any of the heat-storage devices, and it just brightens the interior.

Earth-sheltering the lower level and siting the house below the crest of the hill provides protection from northwest winds. The roof is pitched to deflect these winds over the house.

Insulation is an important part of any conservation strategy. I used 2x6 studs 24 in. o. c. for the exterior walls and fitted them with foil-faced fiberglass batts. Including the exterior sheathing and cedar shingles, this gave us R-22 walls.

The roof was framed with 2x12 rafters, also on 24-in. centers, which allowed room for 9 in. of kraft-paper faced fiberglass and approximately 2 in. of airspace between the insulation and the sheathing. The roof is ventilated with soffit vents and ridge vents. Includ-

ing the extra-heavy asphalt shingles, the roof's insulation rating is R-33.

I did not use a supplementary vapor barrier. In the Washington area, condensation in the walls doesn't amount to much. While infiltration could be reduced with a polyethylene membrane, I don't like to seal a house too tightly because of interior air pollution. Most of my clients share this concern. Although construction is purposefully tight, I count on a little infiltration. If that sounds a bit casual, it's not. Last winter, the whole-house ventilator fan was turned on by mistake, and smoke began to fill the house immediately. It became evident that with the windows closed, the only available source of new air was a reverse draft down through the woodstove chimney. So the house is tight. It's just not too tight.

Heating—Heating is best approached in three stages: collection, storage and distribution. Collection was not a big problem in this house, because of its excellent orientation. The windows on the south admit all the solar gain needed. Heat distribution wasn't a problem either. Since most of my clients don't want to live with the temperature variations of a totally passive house, I usually provide backup heating and air-conditioning. The ducts and fan for these easily do double duty for the primary systems.

Heat storage was the greatest challenge. The choices are limited. Masonry floors and walls make an excellent heat sink. But because the house is wood-frame construction and all the floors were to be wood, the masonry was mostly below grade, in the walls of the lower level. The hollow block was filled with sand to increase its mass, and the walls were insulated on the outside with Dryvit. This

way, the heat-absorbing mass of the wall remains exposed inside the house.

I had drywall glued directly to the concrete block in the downstairs bedrooms, making it part of the mass and eliminating the usual air space that comes with mounting drywall on furring strips (which would have defeated the radiation of heat from the wall). This required that I use surface-mounted electrical outlets, so I designed a large base molding to cover them. This molding became a design element in all the downstairs rooms.

However, I needed a great deal more heat storage than the lower-level walls could give. I was intrigued by the aesthetic possibilities of water-storage tubes. Kalwall Sun-Lite tubes (Solar Components Corporation, P.O. Box 237, Manchester, N. H. 03105) have been used successfully for a number of years for solar mass. They are made of translucent fiberglass, and I was especially drawn to the possibilities of filtering and reflecting light into the rooms of the house with tubes located in the attic.

My calculations (see p. 81) showed me that 32 tubes 12 in. in diameter and 8 ft. high would give the house the mass it needed if they were incorporated in an open solar attic that ran through the center of the house. I designed the attic with large clerestory windows for heat collection. Light passes through the tubes into the studio and kitchen on the north side of the house. On the south side, light is reflected off the tubes into the master study and bedroom, and into the living and dining rooms (photo facing page). A return-air duct (drawing, top of next page) draws air across the warm tubes and distributes it through the conventional backup air system. This duct is automatically controlled, and doesn't open until the temperature in the solar attic

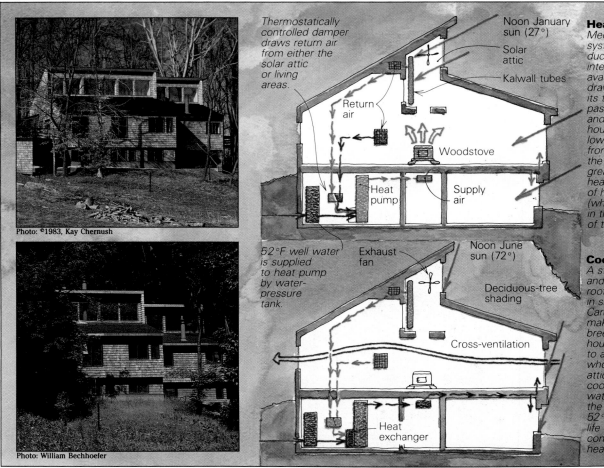

Photo: ©1983, Kay Chernush

Photo: William Bechhoefer

Thermostatically controlled damper draws return air from either the solar attic or living areas.

Return air

Heat pump

52°F well water is supplied to heat pump by water-pressure tank.

Noon January sun (27°)

Solar attic

Kalwall tubes

Woodstove

Supply air

Exhaust fan

Noon June sun (72°)

Deciduous-tree shading

Cross-ventilation

Heat exchanger

Heating mode
Mechanical and passive-solar systems are served by the same ductwork in an economical integration that makes use of available heat. Return air is drawn from the solar attic when its temperature is above 82°F, passed through the heat pump and circulated throughout the house. If the temperature is lower than 82°, return air comes from the living areas. It follows the same loop, but requires a greater contribution from the heat pump. Two other sources of heat are the woodstove (whose excess heat is absorbed in the attic) and the masonry of the lower walls.

Cooling mode
A stand of poplar, beech, walnut and hickory trees and calculated roof overhangs keep the house in shade much of the summer. Carefully planned ventilation makes use of southerly summer breezes in most rooms in the house. When temperatures rise to an uncomfortable level, a whole-house fan in the solar attic exhausts the hot air, and cool air is supplied by an air-to-water heat exchanger coil in the ducting that works off 52° well water. So far in the life of the house, the backup air conditioning from a water-source heat pump has not been used.

reaches 82°F. Since the attic acts as a plenum for warm air that rises into it by natural convection, little heat is wasted.

I began to think of the solar attic as a long core in the middle of the house, which could be used not only to collect heat and light for the entire structure but also to integrate the separate parts of the house. I used its walls as main structural supports for the roof and as dividers between major spaces. Bathrooms and closets fit in below it. So does the woodstove, which is adjacent to both the kitchen and dining room. Excess heat from the stove passes through a grill into the solar attic and further heats the tubes.

Finally, the solar attic provides heat for a domestic hot-water preheating system. Cold water is passed through three 29-gal. black-painted steel tanks on its way to the conventional water heater. The tanks replace three Kalwall tubes in the center of the attic, which is hidden from view. The system is virtually maintenance free and very economical.

There is significant heat loss from the clerestory windows in the solar attic. However, the entire heating bill for the winter of 1982-83 was about $400, very low for a 3,600-sq. ft. house in this area. Movable insulation can be added to these windows if rising energy costs warrant it.

Cooling—My cooling strategy for the house was quite simple. The shading from trees is very important, as is the earth-sheltering of the lower level. Except for two lower bed-

rooms, every room has cross-ventilation. The southeast orientation of the house opens it to prevailing summer breezes.

Excess heat rises naturally into the solar attic. The water tubes absorb some of it, preventing the air from overheating. Ideally, the windows in the solar attic would be operable to allow hot air to escape naturally. But that was rejected for its inconvenience and relative cost compared to fixed glazing. Instead, the excess heat is exhausted by a whole-house ventilator fan.

Well water provides another source for cooling. Air is passed over a heat-exchange coil in the ducts located in the basement utility room, which lowers its temperature and humidity. This air is then delivered to the house through the ducting system (drawing, above). The whole-house fan, natural ventilation, and the cool air from this coil were all that was needed to make the house comfortable during the summer of 1982. The backup air conditioning wasn't used at all.

Backup systems—My clients suggested a water-source heat pump for their mechanical heating and air-conditioning needs. They knew of several successful installations in the area, and asked me to gather some information on them. Water-source heat pumps (see *FHB* #14, p. 16) use water rather than air as a heat source. The advantage is that the water, which comes from a well, is a constant 52°F, whereas air temperatures can drop well below the minimum 26°F to 32°F required for a con-

ventional heat pump. The potential gains in efficiency are enormous.

The only data we needed was the rate of flow from the well. Twelve gallons per minute was the minimum requirement, and the well came in at more than 20 gallons per minute. Our mechanical contractor chose Carrier equipment because its quality is good and parts are always available. He downsized the system, recognizing that the house would get much of its heat from the sun, and that the heat pump would be activated only when the temperature in the solar attic dropped below 82°F. The idea of scaling down the size of heating and cooling equipment when it's to be used as a backup is a difficult concept to get across to most mechanical engineers.

Water taken from the ground must be returned there to keep from lowering the water table significantly. Since water passing through the heat pump is either warmer or colder than the original well water, it must be returned to the ground at some distance from the well to replenish the water table without affecting the temperature of the source well. The cattle pond proved an ideal spot, and we avoided the usual necessity of drilling a second well by using it.

The only other backup system is the woodstove. The wood box nearby can be filled from the outside. All wood is cut on the farm, which makes the stove very cost-effective. □

_____

William Bechhoefer teaches architecture at the University of Maryland.

Illustrations: Frances Ashforth

Working with Kalwall tubes

Kalwall Sun-lite water-storage tubes were an early entry in the explosion of solar products in the last decade. They remain popular because of the their effectiveness and simplicity. Made of translucent fiberglass .040 in. thick to transmit natural daylight, they are simply containers for one of the best mediums for heat storage—water.

Kalwall tubes come in a variety of sizes, with one closed end, and a friction-fit cap to seal the top against evaporation once they have been filled in place. They are easily installed and take 60% less space with 80% less weight than an equivalent rock or masonry heat-storage system. Even the largest tubes weigh less than 20 lb. empty.

The water can be dyed to increase solar absorption by up to 35% over undyed water, but light transmission is reduced considerably. The dyes available are black, yellow, bronze and blue. Even tubes with clear water will have some color due to the refraction of light. The tubes can also be used in applications where light transmission is not a factor, as in a Trombe wall or an enclosed solar attic. The chart below right gives the necessary design data.

Calculations—As with any form of heat storage, finding the compromise between too much mass and too little is important. Too much mass means that the material won't get warm enough to make much of a difference in heating the house. Too little mass, and some of the incoming solar energy will be wasted by overheating the air. As a result, the house will get too much heat during daylight hours, and not enough at night.

To determine the size and number of water tubes I needed in the house in Olney, I turned to Edward Mazria's passive-solar text. Using the tables, I calculated the amount of solar gain that would be available in the attic on Dec. 21, assuming clear conditions. I began with the square footage of clerestory glass and subtracted an allowance for shading by nearby trees and the house itself. Deductions were also made for transmittance of the wall of the water tubes. The final figure was 203,300 Btu/day.

I wanted to use 8-ft. long, 12-in. dia. tubes, since they best fit the space. Each of these would hold 6.25 cu. ft. of water, and have a heat capacity of 7,800 Btu, assuming that exposure to sunlight would cause a 20° rise in the water temperature. Simple arithmetic told me I'd need 26 tubes to heat the house. As a check, I used Mazria's rule of thumb for this climate, which calls for about 1 cu. ft. of water for each square foot of solar window. Figuring things this way, I would need 48 tubes to avoid overheating the air, but this would result in a rise in water temperature in each tube of only 10° or 11°, not enough Btus to heat the house.

Ultimately I compromised with 35 tubes. These would fit comfortably in the solar attic, and I would be able to get about a 15° temperature rise in the water without serious risk of overheating. By replacing three of these tubes with steel tanks for pre-heating domestic hot water, I reduced my order to a total of 32 tubes.

There are more precise methods for solar

Design specs for Kalwall tubes								
Diameter (in.)	Length (ft.)	Volume (gal.)	Weight (lb.)		Heat capacity (Btu) 20°F rise	Heat-storage capacity (Btu°F-sq.ft. glazing)	Floor loading (lb.)	
			Empty	Full			Per lin. ft.	Per sq. ft.
12	4	23.5	8	204	3,900	49 *	204*	260*
12	8	47	12	404	7,800	49 *	404*	514*
18	5	66	16	567	11,000	73.5**	378**	321**
18	10	132	19	1,122	22,000	73.5**	748**	635**

* Spaced 12 in. o.c. ** Spaced 18 in. o.c.

design than Mazria's, but I have found that his tables and rules of thumb are simple and reliable when combined with intuition and experience. Computer energy-analysis programs that are now becoming available make greater accuracy even easier to achieve for the designer.

Installation—The filled tubes are heavy. They can sit directly on a concrete slab on grade with no problem. However, if they are mounted above grade, you've got to beef up your floor construction.

The tubes are stable and stand by themselves. It's still a good idea to support them at the top in earthquake areas, or if they form a wall that people would be tempted to lean against. A wood or steel kickplate near the bottom to protect against impact also

makes sense where foot traffic is heavy. It is advisable to set the tubes in a pan or on a drainable waterproof surface, just in case they leak. In the house I designed in Olney, Md., I used an elastomeric membrane under the tubes with drains to the DWV system in the bathroom below.

The tubes should be unpacked and examined carefully upon receipt. According to the manufacturer, leaks are rare, and shipping damage is almost always the cause. Fill the tubes before you install them to check for leaks and to clean out any dust and dirt.

Once the tubes are in place, fill them with a garden hose. If you're not planning to use any dye, add a little swimming-pool chlorine to the water to inhibit the growth of algae. The friction-fit cap simply fits on top and completes the installation.   —W. B.

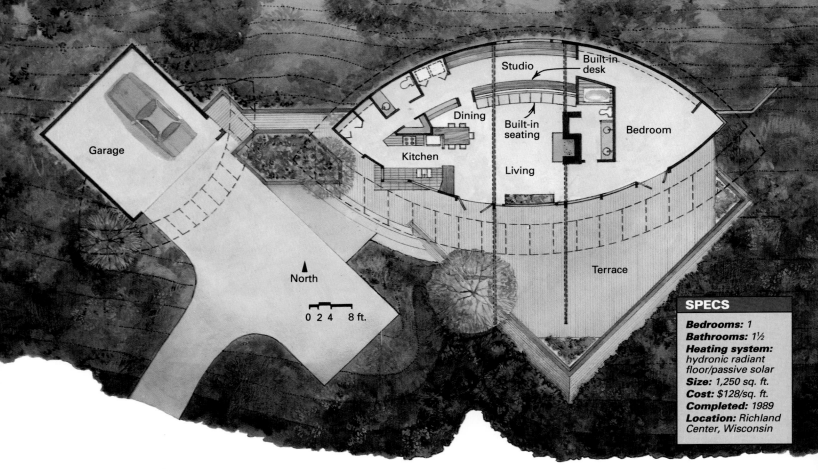

Garage

North

0 2 4 8 ft.

Studio
Built-in desk
Dining
Built-in seating
Kitchen
Living
Bedroom
Terrace

SPECS

Bedrooms: 1
Bathrooms: 1½
Heating system: hydronic radiant floor/passive solar
Size: 1,250 sq. ft.
Cost: $128/sq. ft.
Completed: 1989
Location: Richland Center, Wisconsin

An Arc in the Woods

A small, sun-tempered house for a retired couple

by Charles Miller

An article from the local newspaper in Richland Center, Wisconsin, eloquently told of the supposed inspiration for the curving form of the home in the drawing above. The writer explained that the architect, while visiting the site, found several pine cones scattered beneath the many trees. The architect, in turn, felt that the elliptical cones were a natural shape for this property and used them as the basis for his design. This is a wonderful story, but the architect, Arthur Dyson, assured me that many factors shaped the house—none being a pine cone. Dyson does appreciate the sentiments of the tale, however, because he considers the special qualities of the land, such as its topography, climate and vegetation, to be among the most important influences in the evolution of a building design.

Dyson, an architect based in Fresno, California, doesn't bring any preconceptions to a new project he's working on, and as a result all of his houses look quite different from each other. His rationale is simple enough: No two combinations of client wishes and site conditions are exactly alike. Therefore, no two houses should

be alike. What follows is the story of how one such set of priorities unfolded.

Bruce's dream—Bruce Barrett and Edith Tuxford had an attractive contemporary home in a beautifully landscaped part of Richland Center, yet they wanted to leave it. This puzzled Dyson at first, but as he learned more about Barrett and Tuxford, their reasoning was revealed. In the 40s, Barrett had studied architecture at Taliesin East, Frank Lloyd Wright's studio and school in Spring Green (near Richland Center). Among the projects then on the drawing boards were the Usonian houses—Wright's modest, open-plan homes that were designed to be affordable and in harmony with nature. The concept greatly influenced Barrett, and he hoped to build a home one day that embodied the same principles. He even had a particular kind of site in mind—one on a tree-covered hillside. Forty years later, he finally had the opportunity to look for such a site. He and Tuxford found it on the outskirts of town.

The building site is on a fairly steep hillside, within a typical southern Wisconsin pine forest.

The significant vista is to the south, where a view through the trees looks across Richland Center from the head of the valley. The eastern boundary abuts a vacant parcel that could be developed with another structure in the future while the western boundary faces the rear of an existing home and the street.

Into the contours—Winters can be severe in Wisconsin, so the northern exposure of the house had to be kept to a minimum. With that in mind, Dyson took advantage of the hillside by burying a portion of the house into it. At the same time, he gained southern views with a glass-curtain wall that opens onto a terrace (drawing right). Neither Barrett nor Tuxford wanted the house to tower over the ground, and they wanted to avoid cantilevered or above-grade terraces or balconies. So, in addition to minimizing the house's exposure to the icy winter winds, notching it into the earth emphasized its connection to the site.

To keep the cut into the hill manageable, Dyson placed the house where the grade is the

Drawings: Gary Williamson

Related roofs. Both the house and the garage are sheltered by gently sweeping arched roofs. Sited at an elevation close to that of the house, the garage screens a neighboring property from view and allows a path to the house without steps or a steep ramp.

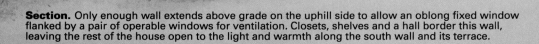

Section. Only enough wall extends above grade on the uphill side to allow an oblong fixed window flanked by a pair of operable windows for ventilation. Closets, shelves and a hall border this wall, leaving the rest of the house open to the light and warmth along the south wall and its terrace.

Beam bridges. A pair of beams extend like a pair of outstretched arms beyond the south wall and into the trees, linking the house with the surrounding forest. Inside, the beams cut across the living area, moderating the room's volume and directing the eye outward.

Double-duty window. The kitchen counter continues through the wall to emerge outside where it's used for buffets on the terrace. The window doubles as a pass-through for the dishes.

Storage wall. The nearly windowless north wall is lined with a row of closets and shelves.

shallowest. The soil from this cut was pushed downhill and compacted to support the terrace.

The house is laid out on an east/west axis to take advantage of the low winter sun. Dyson wanted the rooms to have as much exposure as possible to the sun's direct rays, an idea that suggested a wall curved in plan (drawing, page 82). After fiddling with various curves to suit the 30-ft. width and 70-ft. length of the house, Dyson eventually settled on a 47-ft. radius for the south wall.

Arched roof—The north wall of the house is low to the ground, rising only a few feet above grade to present minimal exposure to the winter wind. This created an arch in elevation as well as in plan, suggesting a curved roof to shelter the house. On the entry side, the roof nearly touches the ground where it comes to a point above a planter. The garage has a similar roof form.

The roof over the house is supported by wood I-beam rafters, chosen for their ability to span great distances and for their precise dimensions. The latter was especially important because the drywall ceiling is affixed to the underside of the rafters, and the kind of dimensional irregularities common to framing lumber could have shown up as humps and valleys in the ceiling finish. On top, the roof is covered with a flame-bonded, single-ply membrane painted silver.

On-site laminating—The strongest expressions of the curved roof are the fascias (photo, p. 83). They are compound-curve, site-built glulams made of 2x2 construction heart redwood. Builder John Karlstad fashioned the glulams in place, using the ends of the pressure-treated 2x10 outriggers to control their shape. The outriggers are 4 ft. o. c. and occur in pairs, sandwiching the ½-in. thick webs of every other I-beam rafter. Karlstad let the outriggers run long and plumbed up from the line of the foundation to get his layout marks for the overhang. Then he beveled the ends of the outriggers to match the radius of the foundation.

Working with 20-ft. long 2x2s, Karlstad began the fascias by screwing a single course into the ends of the outriggers, flush with their tops. Then he added succeeding layers from above and below, lapping the joints by at least 8 ft. The laminations are bonded with resorcinol glue and screwed to one another on 6-in. centers with 3-in. galvanized drywall screws. At the east and west ends of the house where the curved fascias adjoin one another, their laminations run alternately long and short, creating an interlocking finger joint. Karlstad used all 20 of his bar clamps to keep the pieces in plane with one another during glue up.

Open plan, carefully divided—On the one hand, Barrett wanted to be able to view the entire interior of the house from a single vantage point. Tuxford's concern for privacy, on the other hand, meant that they had to find a way to create private zones within the house without a lot of ceiling-height walls. To that end, most of the interior walls stop 3 ft. to 6 ft. from the ceiling. These partitions are placed to allow views of the ceiling from one end of the house to the other—in

effect sharing the ceiling with all the rooms. A lower wall screens Barrett's office from the living room. At 4 ft. tall, the wall is high enough to keep his files, worktables and shelves out of sight while still allowing him a view of the fireplace and the terrace when sitting at his desk.

Flanking the central living space are a sleeping area to the east and the kitchen to the west. The lower curve of the arched ceiling provides an intimate scale in the kitchen work space and in the bedroom, then rises to a generous 14-ft. height in the living area. Although Barrett and Tuxford requested a high ceiling in the living area, they didn't want a "gymnasium effect." So Dyson tempered the scale of the room with two parallel beams that reach out into the trees (top photo, facing page), symbolically tying the house to the woods and reducing the "high-sky" feeling on the terrace the same way the branches of a tree add a "ceiling" to a campsite. The beams are designed to carry removable canvas shades or wires for deciduous vines. Their ends termi-

nate at decorative finials that reflect the curved plan and sections of the house. The inner sphere of the finial is an 8-in. dia. shutoff-valve float from a cattle watering trough. It is circled by a 4-in. length of 14-in. dia. steel pipe on a threaded ½-in. rod. Strung onto each rod are a number of copper toilet-bowl floats, which only coincidentally resemble pine cones.

The kitchen counter continues right through the wall, extending the interior space visually. On the outside, the counter serves as both a plant shelf and a serving counter for summertime buffets on the terrace.

Closets and other storage compartments are hidden back in the northern depths of the house along a full-length corridor that connects one end of the dwelling to the other. Muddy boots can be parked in the small storage space off the entryway, and most of the time Barrett and Tuxford leave their shoes there and walk around the house in their socks. The floor is heated with a radiant hot-water system (Wirsbo, 5925 148th St. W., Apple Valley, Minn. 55124; 612-891-2000). Its tiny boiler is in the mudroom along with the shoes. Incidentally, the heating system is assisted by preheated water from a coil embedded in the chimney; the coil, in turn, absorbs heat from the fireplace.

This house is solar tempered, meaning it has insulated concrete walls and floors that are meant to absorb and hold the heat of the sun. It costs more to build such a house at the outset, but Dyson estimates that the extra expense will be offset in about three years by the lower energy bills. The fixed-glass windows are double glazed with argon gas-filled, low-e tempered glass. The glazing returns the long infrared waves of sunlight to the occupied space, reducing heat loss through the glass during winter. In the summer, the deep eaves on the south side shade the floors when the sun is high in the sky. Dyson used a sun chart to determine exactly how deep the eaves should be for maximum effectiveness.

Because of budgetary constraints, stonework was kept to a minimum and used for maximum effect. The limestone fireplace opens into the living and dining areas and can be enjoyed from the kitchen. Its stone backside forms a wall in the bathroom that has glass-shelved niches for displaying art or storing towels.

Legacy—In conceiving the form of this house, Dyson says he was seeking to make a living space that is both inspiring and refreshing. He wanted as well to bring indoors the kind of serenity tinged with excitement that comes on a walk in the woods. He says an open plan isn't the answer for everyone, but it suits perfectly Barrett's and Tuxford's needs. And it likely has the flexibility to meet its next challenge. Barrett and Tuxford plan to leave the house to the town of Richland Center so that it may be used as a library, perhaps, or as a kindergarten like the one attended by Frank Lloyd Wright, Richland Center's most famous native son. □

Charles Miller is a senior editor for Fine Homebuilding. *All photographs by Scot Zimmerman except where noted.*

Shingle Solar

Diverse styles shape a Colorado house that incorporates a Trombe wall and direct gain

by Jeffrey Ellis

Many solar homes are completely dominated by the solar aspects of their design, but that was not acceptable to my most demanding client—my wife. Linda's interest in our design partnership was the interplay of space, function, materials and style, and she had executive veto powers. My job was to subordinate the solar features to the living spaces and aesthetics.

Designing it—The starting point in our design process was a circular tower that would contain my office. We like circular spaces and shapes, perhaps because there are no corners to trap the eye and because the circle is a symbol of completeness and unity. Our 2,600-sq. ft. house was also planned to serve as a show-home. Our design and contracting company, Super Structures, was just three years old, and as designers without professional credentials, we needed to have a walk-in portfolio.

Stylistically, our major influence was the shingle style, popularized in the 1880s by such American architects as McKim, Mead and White, and by Henry Hobson Richardson, who

used cedar shingles to build playful, castle-like houses with turrets, towers, arches, eyebrow dormers and undulating roofs. The shingle style developed in part from the contact a few Victorian architects had with Japanese design concepts. The resulting designs are distinguished by pavilions, circular forms and openings, lattice screening and, above all, the thoughtful use of wood and the carpenter's art. We incorporated oriental elements into the interior trim, along with a tea room with *shoji*, a circular window, and a moon-gate entry.

Another design influence was the primitive architecture of 19th-century Colorado mining camps. Sheds upon sheds were haphazardly erected on steep, rugged slopes, complete with chutes, ramps, towers, booms and clerestories. These mine-shaft structures often achieved a functional beauty, and over the past ten years, they've inspired a regional style that I like.

Our floor plan (facing page) is unconventional. Three bedrooms, a playroom, a solarium and the tea room are all on the first floor, which is constructed much like a garden-level

The rounded forms of late 19th-century shingle style (a blend of Victorian and oriental features) and the contrasting masses and shapes of Colorado mining camps are integrated with the requirements of a passive-solar house. Extensive glazing on the south side of the house (top photo) is shaded from the high summer sun by arches. The north side (above) is low and mostly free of windows. At the northwest corner is a Chinese-style moon-gate entry.

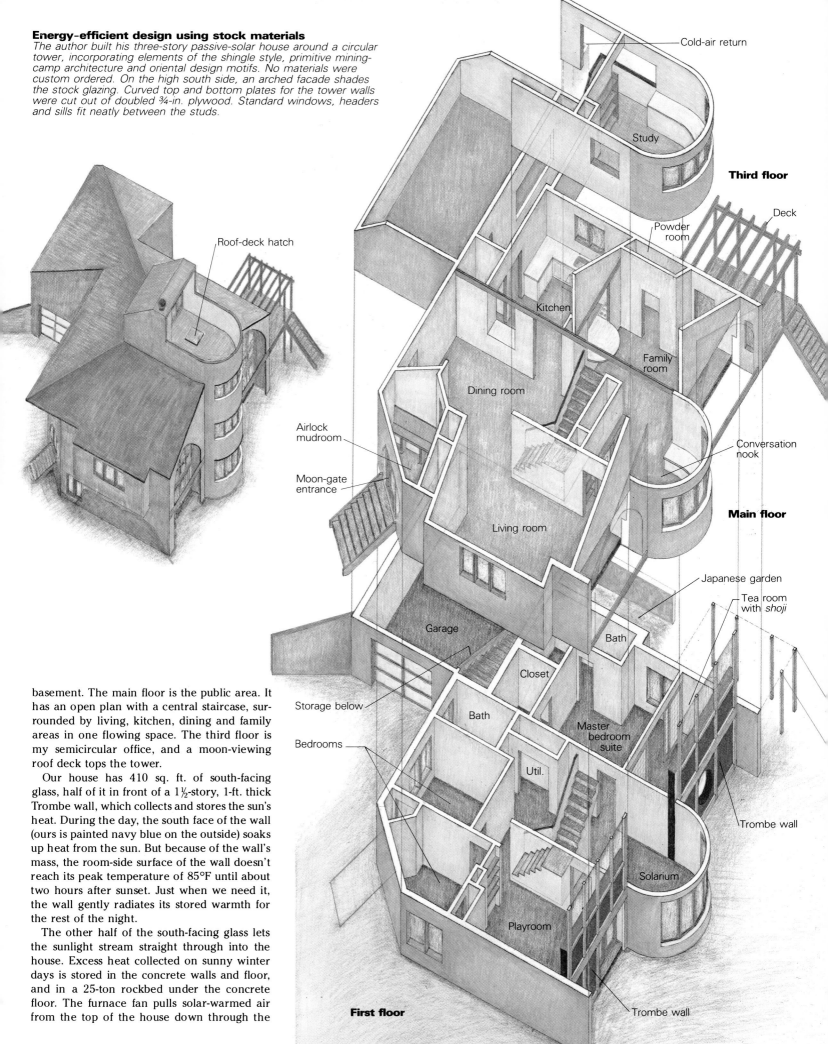

Energy-efficient design using stock materials
The author built his three-story passive-solar house around a circular tower, incorporating elements of the shingle style, primitive mining-camp architecture and oriental design motifs. No materials were custom ordered. On the high south side, an arched facade shades the stock glazing. Curved top and bottom plates for the tower walls were cut out of doubled ¾-in. plywood. Standard windows, headers and sills fit neatly between the studs.

Roof-deck hatch

Cold-air return

Study

Third floor

Deck

Powder room

Kitchen

Family room

Dining room

Airlock mudroom

Conversation nook

Moon-gate entrance

Main floor

Living room

Japanese garden

Tea room with *shoji*

Garage

Bath

Storage below

Closet

Bath

Master bedroom suite

Bedrooms

Util.

Trombe wall

Solarium

Playroom

First floor

Trombe wall

basement. The main floor is the public area. It has an open plan with a central staircase, surrounded by living, kitchen, dining and family areas in one flowing space. The third floor is my semicircular office, and a moon-viewing roof deck tops the tower.

Our house has 410 sq. ft. of south-facing glass, half of it in front of a 1½-story, 1-ft. thick Trombe wall, which collects and stores the sun's heat. During the day, the south face of the wall (ours is painted navy blue on the outside) soaks up heat from the sun. But because of the wall's mass, the room-side surface of the wall doesn't reach its peak temperature of 85°F until about two hours after sunset. Just when we need it, the wall gently radiates its stored warmth for the rest of the night.

The other half of the south-facing glass lets the sunlight stream straight through into the house. Excess heat collected on sunny winter days is stored in the concrete walls and floor, and in a 25-ton rockbed under the concrete floor. The furnace fan pulls solar-warmed air from the top of the house down through the

Illustration: Vince Babak

1½-in. rocks, which extract most of the air's heat. The concrete floor above the rockbed then radiates its warmth to the rooms above. There are over 150,000 lb. of concrete and rock in the house to store the solar heat. To retain this heat we used R-38 insulation in the roof and R-26 in the upper framed walls. The lower part of the house is also well insulated. It is bermed on the north, east and west. The overall shape of the shell was designed to withstand the hurricane-force Boulder gales (137 mph this year). Hip roofs slope up to the dominant southern exposure, so the house faces the sun and turns its back to the northwestern winds.

Building it—Because of its circular elements, this house proved as challenging to build as it was to draw. I had to find concrete contractors, carpenters, drywallers and other subcontractors who were not put off by the unconventional design. To compound the problem, we had only six months from start of construction until we moved in, and a budget that I knew was much too tight. If our deadline and budget were to be met, I knew I'd have to be at the site all day, every day.

I managed the construction, including scheduling, ordering, pricing, overseeing the tradesmen, paying bills and cost accounting, and was able to do miscellaneous carpentry and labor throughout the job. I found that it was easier to manage the tradesmen if my own hands were dirty. You can either work at the job site all day and solve problems when the workers ask for help, or schedule a visit each day, let them use their own ingenuity and then accept their solutions. A white-shirted supervisor peering over their shoulders all day understandably drives them crazy.

Our building philosophy is to use standard components and structural techniques in new contexts. There were no custom-ordered materials in this house. Using standard materials and on-site solutions can prevent delays and cost overruns but you have to plan carefully, supervise well and hire good tradesmen.

The circular features in the house were a challenge to the carpenters, and they were proud of the results. The 30-ft. high, 12-ft. dia. tower was a special adventure. Fortunately for us, the lead carpenter, Bob Helm, had had experience with large-scale circular jobs, and was undaunted. Each floor was platform-framed, using doubled ¾-in. plywood top and bottom plates, cut to the curve and overlapped, then nailed to 2x6 studs 24 in. o.c. We sheathed the walls with ¼-in. tempered hardboard. The windows were sized to fit in between the 24-in. stud spacing, so no unusual curved headers were needed. The symmetrical arches that flank the south window walls and block out the sun in the summer were also designed to save money. It is easier to build an arched facade than it is to custom-make arched insulating glass and curved window jambs and trim.

The building came in at $41/sq. ft. in 1980, well below the cost of a comparable custom home, even after adding a full design and contractor's fee. The solar features (Trombe wall, rock storage bed, fans, blowers, thermostats and so on) added about $6,000, with an estimated payback period of eight years with normal inflation and fuel cost increases, or four years with applicable tax credits.

Because this was our own house, we used many experimental construction methods that we would not have attempted on a job for someone else. Some, frankly, were less than successful. One of our disasters was the dyed concrete floor slab, which we had planned to

Facing page: The open and high-ceilinged rooms of the main floor—the kitchen, dining room and family room—are grouped around a central staircase that leads to the tower. Also on this floor is the low-ceilinged fireplace nook, a snug gathering place during winter storms.

score and grout like Mexican tile. We decided to pour the slab in two sections on successive days so that it could be scored before it cured. But the hot sun caused even the smaller volume of concrete to set up too quickly, and the workers had problems. So we let the concrete dry-cure, then scored it the next day with a concrete saw. This would have been fine, but the two slabs turned out to be ⅜ in. off. One worker spent a day grinding the floor level. Most of the scar is now hidden by an area rug.

The basic technique, though, results in a beautiful floor, and we've used it on subsequent jobs, pouring the slab all at once, and scoring it wet or dry depending on the temperature. The dark grey 1-ft. squares look like a cross between Mexican tile and slate.

Once the floor was done, we had to protect it during the remaining four months of the project. We taped down some rosin building paper. It worked well as a buffer between the floor and construction-related damage, but the tape permanently stained the concrete. We also found that the red chalklines we'd snapped on the floor were all but unerasable (blue was okay). Linda and I worked days on our knees, cleaning, grouting and sealing.

Living in it—This house makes us wonder at the power of the sun and the ever-changing Colorado weather. It is a live-in sundial, with daily and seasonal changes in the arc and angle of the sun through the windows and arches.

The central stairway, circular floor plan and soaring ceilings give the house a remarkably spacious feeling. Different areas appeal to us at different times of the year, and foster different moods. During winter storms, for example, the living area's high ceilings and uncovered window wall make us feel vulnerable, so we find ourselves spending a lot of time in the cozy, low-ceilinged fireplace nook.

The passive-solar system has worked well. We used only 56 Ccf (100 cu.ft.), or $22 worth of natural gas for auxiliary heat in January 1981. Public Service Company of Colorado has monitored this house for three winters, and they find that we use less than half the heating fuel other very well-insulated new homes (R-19 walls, R-38 ceilings, double-pane glass) require per sq. ft. of floor area. They also calculated the air infiltration with a blower-door test, sucking the air out of the house with a fan. The range of air changes per hour in tested solar homes was 0.5 to 3.0, with an average of 1.2. Our house was 1.0. (These figures should be used only to compare houses within the study.) It was interesting to discover all the places that weren't airtight and to stop them up. Recessed lights, elec-

At the top of the tower is the south-facing semicircular office. A trap door in the ceiling and a pull-down ladder lead to the moon-gazing deck on the roof.

trical outlets, the connection between the Trombe wall and the framing, and the roof hatch were all trouble spots.

Heating bills, however, reflect the habits and attitudes of the occupants as much as the construction of the house. If we insisted on 70°F day and night, our bills might double. Instead, on clear winter mornings, we put on sweaters and keep the thermostat down, because we know the sun will warm the house to 70°F by 10 a.m., and 80°F or so by noon.

In the summer, the house stays moderately cool. The arches of the south windows, the roof overhangs, and the night insulating shades on the east, west and north windows block the direct sun. The clerestory acts as a ventilation shaft, creating a strong air flow through the house at night when it's warmer in the house than it is outside. The house can get uncomfortably hot in Indian summer, because the sun is low in the sky, and the ambient temperature is still high.

Learning from it—Living in a passive-solar home has been invaluable to me as a designer and builder. Graphs, fuel bills and scientific papers outline the conditions, but don't convey the essence. Night insulation is a case in point. Everybody stresses the need for it, but most solar home builders seem to run out of money before they can install any over the glazed ares of the houses they build. We've felt the chilling effect of large expanses of bare glass on a frigid winter night, and I now realize that night insulation is essential to the success of a passive-solar design.

We have also experienced the dramatic difference in comfort between a tiled concrete slab floor with normal earth temperatures (where the tiled slab is at 45° to 50°F) and one with rock storage below it (65° to 75°F). We can actually sense the temperature differences at the edges of the rockbed with our bare feet. As a result, our current solar designs with tile on concrete floors all have solarium-heated air plenums underneath—6-in. concrete block laid sideways below the slab—to warm the floor.

Our monitoring of the intensity of the sun, our gas and electric use, and the ambient and house temperatures show that if we have a full day of sun, no matter how cold it is, there is no need for heat in the evening, and the temperature won't drop below 58°F overnight. If there is enough sun to cast a faint shadow, there is no net heat loss during the day, and auxiliary heat will be needed only in the evening. During a week-long winter storm when the house was unheated and unoccupied, it reached equilibrium at about 55°F.

Our most subtle learning experience was the realization that the amount of direct sunlight must match the function of each room. For example, working at my curved office desk under south windows is bearable in midsummer when the sun is high, but the low, penetrating winter sun is intolerably bright. Cheap translucent shades solve the problem, but it would have been better to control light architecturally rather than with add-ons.

Future plans—Because of our budget limitation, we planned from the start to build this house in phases. After two years we finally built a dining table, and we now use the dining area regularly for the first time. The solarium has evolved into a sewing and studio room with the addition of a combination easel and fold-down sewing center that we built in our spare time, over several weekends.

There were many solar innovations we did not use in 1979 (but have since) because their development was incomplete. A selective-surface foil glued to the concrete of the Trombe wall is one example. This special surface cuts radiant heat loss from the Trombe wall, increasing performance to nearly the level of night-insulated systems (see *FHB* #10, p. 51).

Other improvements to the house become more cost effective as natural-gas prices increase. We have added factory-made triple glazing panels to east windows, which have no night insulation, and to the south windows around the conversation nook. For less than $100, uncomfortable drafts off the cold glass have been reduced. We also plan to install insulating curtains on the south window walls, and add redwood planking to the roof deck.   □

Jeffrey Ellis is a builder in Boulder, Colo.

Linear Solar House
A patterned concrete floor and stick-built roof trusses accent a simple shape

by Don Parker

In 1984, Dan and Judy Reavis asked me to design a solar house. Their budget was modest, so we had to incorporate solar principles without all of the solar paraphernalia, such as roof collectors, pumps, fans, trombe walls, envelopes or excessive thermal mass. Their property in a south Denver neighborhood was 75 ft. by 125 ft.—large for the neighborhood, but still long and narrow. It was extremely flat and devoid of usable or attractive foliage. It had no view other than of neighboring 1950's ranch houses and a few 1920's bungalows of small size and utilitarian character. But there was plenty of sunshine available if we used the site properly.

Too often, designers and planners of high-density single-family neighborhoods are unable or unwilling (due to developer demands) to even recognize the direction of the sun relative to a single house. In this case, however, we allowed the sun angles, the narrow lot and the scale of the neighborhood to shape the house. The long dimension of the site ran east/west, which is perfect for taking advantage of the southern sun if the house is turned sideways to the street—not the traditional orientation. At 1,800 sq. ft., not including the garage, the Reavis' house would be larger than most houses in the neighborhood, so turning it perpendicular to the street would not only allow it to fit comfortably on the site, but also make it appear smaller.

After subtracting setbacks, we came up with a buildable envelope of 65 ft. by 105 ft. By pushing the house as far north (to one side of the lot) as possible, we could take advantage of the sun, have a usable south-facing yard and gain plenty of south-facing wall and roof area. An attached garage would fit at the east end of the house. A building footprint of about 23 ft. by 102 ft. could handle 1,800 sq. ft. of heated space plus a two-car garage.

Working out the linear scheme—Our long, narrow house was the ideal shape for solar applications. The way to get rid of the solar junkyard appearance would be to make the house itself a collector. It would have to be a

Each living space in this passive solar house abuts the wide sunlit hallway that runs the length of the south side. Painted waferboard and battens make a simple finish for the ceilings and walls.

simple direct-gain solar house that was comfortable enough to live in, and it would have to be easy to operate without too much closing, opening, switching, lifting and, least of all, monitoring of solar paraphernalia.

To allow for absorption of heat, we would need windows and a thermal mass. Every living space in the house needed to face south for heat collection, so I lined up these rooms on the east-west axis (floor plan facing page). The south wall would simply be a wall of windows, mostly casements. I tried to give the two bathrooms south windows, too, but I couldn't (because bathrooms usually generate their own heat, this wasn't much of a problem). A thick concrete slab would suffice as thermal mass. We would need a back-up heating system—a code requirement—but I hoped there'd be no need to use it.

The primary problem to this linear design was how to provide both circulation of people and privacy at the same time. A long, narrow house would most likely require a long hall passing each of the living spaces. There were two logical locations for this hallway: along the north side or along the south side. A hall on the north wall would make an excellent buffer from the cold for the living spaces on the south. But the only use for the space would be as a cold, dark hallway. And I believed that a

layer of closets along the north wall would make an even better thermal buffer. We agreed that placing the circulation path along the south wall would provide more flexibility (photo left).

Keep it simple—The premise of this project was not only simplicity of the solar design, but simplicity of structure and ease of construction. The Reavises hoped to carry out some of the work themselves; I helped out as construction manager. For economy, our objective was to make each process workable by no more than two people at once. We accomplished this in most cases. The concrete floor was manageable by two, and the long exterior walls were constructed in sections, set and braced easily by two people.

Dan didn't feel he had the skills to finish drywall, so the interior walls, dropped ceilings and covered beams would be finished with 4x8 sheets of ½-in. waferboard. He would cover the joints with battens, then paint. Even the roof structure was site-built of fairly short, easily handled members. The few steel members were small enough for three people to hoist in place by hand.

Building the roof—The 12-in-12 roof is gabled, with the ridge running the long direction. It breaks to a shallow 3:12 pitch over the walkway (drawing facing page). I angled the soffit over the south collector windows to approximate the angle of the sun at the winter equinox.

The structure of the long gable is exposed on the inside and stick-built of Douglas fir. Each 2x8 rafter is tied across the span with a pair of angled 2x6 collar ties, one on each side of the rafter (drawing facing page). Each pair of collar ties is fastened at the overlap through a decorative 2x6 spacer. Before the roof was built we stained the exposed rafters and collar ties with a coat of self-sealing cherry Minwax. We painted the collar-tie spacers a plum color.

Rafters on the north side bear on a 2x6 wall; on the south they bear on either built-

From *Fine Homebuilding* (February 1989) 51:72-75

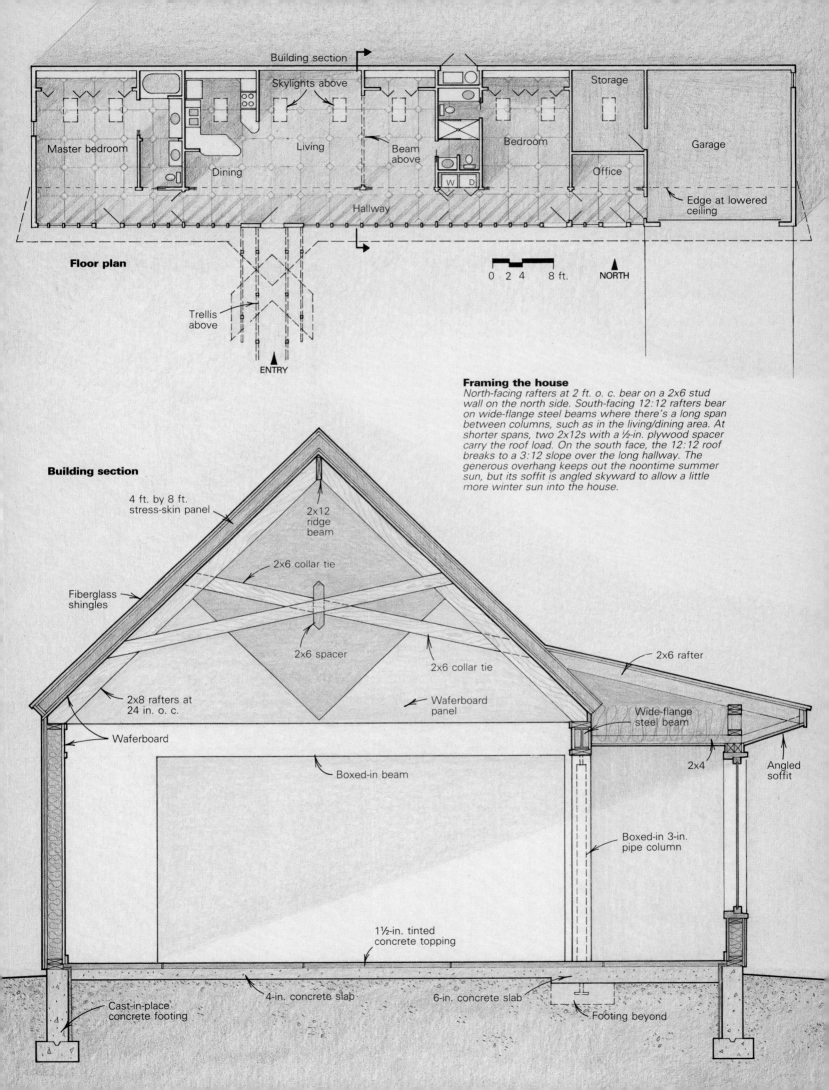

Floor plan

Building section

Skylights above

Master bedroom

Dining

Living

Beam above

Bedroom

Storage

Garage

Office

W   D

Hallway

Edge at lowered ceiling

0 2 4   8 ft.

NORTH

Trellis above

ENTRY

Framing the house

North-facing rafters at 2 ft. o. c. bear on a 2x6 stud wall on the north side. South-facing 12:12 rafters bear on wide-flange steel beams where there's a long span between columns, such as in the living/dining area. At shorter spans, two 2x12s with a ½-in. plywood spacer carry the roof load. On the south face, the 12:12 roof breaks to a 3:12 slope over the long hallway. The generous overhang keeps out the noontime summer sun, but its soffit is angled skyward to allow a little more winter sun into the house.

Building section

4 ft. by 8 ft. stress-skin panel

2x12 ridge beam

2x6 collar tie

Fiberglass shingles

2x6 spacer

2x6 collar tie

2x6 rafter

2x8 rafters at 24 in. o. c.

Waferboard panel

Wide-flange steel beam

Waferboard

2x4

Angled soffit

Boxed-in beam

Boxed-in 3-in. pipe column

1½-in. tinted concrete topping

Cast-in-place concrete footing

4-in. concrete slab

6-in. concrete slab

Footing beyond

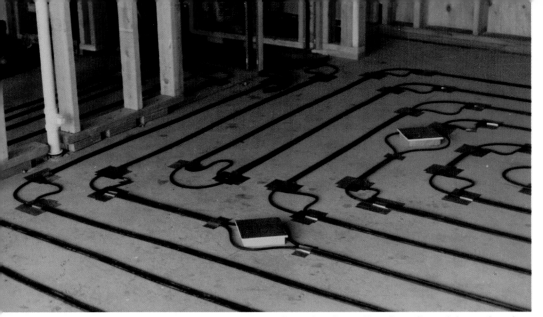

A 4-in. to 6-in. concrete slab was poured as a base for the radiant-heat floor (photo above). The owner then located accent tiles and laid double-tubed polybutylene pipe. A tinted 1½-in. thick concrete topping was leveled to the top of the lower sill plates and the tiles. Stick-built roof framing continues across the top of the 8-ft. partition between the completed kitchen and master-bedroom suite (photo below). The angle of the exposed framing is repeated in tile accents in the tinted-concrete floor and plastic-laminate cabinets.

up 2x12 beams or wide-flange steel beams, depending on the span (drawing previous page). Denver's occasional winds of 100 to 110 mph require that each rafter be tied down with some sort of hurricane clip. Here, we used pipe strap.

The rafters are spaced at 2 ft. o. c. to carry 4-ft. by 8-ft. stress-skin panels on the steep slopes. The panels are composed of ½-in. plywood sheathing, 3½-in. R-30 urethane insulation and ½-in. waferboard as the exposed inside face.

We thought that applying the roof panels would be the simplest part of construction, but that was not to be. Each panel weighed close to 100 lb. and was so awkward that it took three or four men to hoist one up to the roof. After dragging a few of these behemoths up the steep slope, the framing crew found that many of the panels were out of square and required jockeying for even a reasonable fit. It was tough to pound the 6-in. spikes with 1½-in. washers into the rafters without a few missing the mark. We had to cut off the errant spikes and patch the holes inside. Extra care was required to keep the interior face clean and free from tears.

We finished off with asphalt-fiberglass shingles. Since then, the Asphalt Roofing Manufacturers' Association has recommended that a ventilated air space be provided between asphalt shingles and an insulated roof deck. But Denver has a dry climate and low ventilation requirements compared to many parts of the country. Still, our struggles with the roof panels have led me to favor topping exposed rafters with decking, 2x6 sleepers, batt insulation (leaving room above it for air to circulate) and sheathing—then asphalt shingles.

A radiant floor—Because backup heat was required, it made sense to locate it at the source of solar absorption, the floor. We poured a 4-in. concrete base slab throughout most of the house. The hallway base slab along the south wall is 6 in. deep for maximum heat storage. At the winter solstice, the

The west-facing wall of the house (above) extends to form a fence along the street side.

Photos top left and bottom right: Don Parker

noontime sun penetrates approximately 20 ft. into the room, just about to the back wall. At the summer solstice, there is virtually no solar gain through the south-facing windows.

To add thermal mass, our choices for topping the slab were ceramic tile, brick or stone pavers or more concrete. We chose concrete for its relatively low cost. To make a more interesting floor, we tinted the concrete black and established a 4-ft. square grid of control joints; a 6-in. square white ceramic tile was set at the intersections of the joint lines (bottom left photo, facing page). I followed the suggestions for coloring and placing a concrete-and-tile floor found in *FHB* #11, pp. 46-50 (reprinted in *Construction Techniques 2*, The Taunton Press, 1986). Before laying out piping for the radiant heating, Dan set the tiles in place. He glued down a 2x block for each tile, then glued a tile to the block and taped the top of the tile. He then laid out the double-tube polybutylene (see *FHB* #22, pp. 68-71 and *FHB* #27, pp. 68-71 for details on installing radiant-floor heating). He placed the rows of piping at about 9 in. o. c. and fastened them with duct tape, splitting the double tubing at turns to allow the inside tube to make the curve (top photo facing page). The plumber completed the system by tying the piping into the manifold, pump, valves and gas boiler in the mechanical room.

Because of the polybutylene piping, we couldn't use a bonding grout over the first slab, which proved to be rough enough to hold the topping. Black pigment was added to the concrete batch while still in the truck, and it eventually cured to a pleasant shade of medium grey.

We repeated the diagonal motif of the floor tiles and roof trusses throughout the house. The cabinetmakers set a 4-in. square maroon tile in each cabinet door and filled the surrounding joint with grout. Grid lines in the cabinets were routed into the plastic laminate. I used more diagonals in cutouts in the fence and entrance structure (photo bottom right, facing page).

Operable windows—South-facing roof glass has always been a problem. Unless it is shaded inside or out, it can let in too much heat during the day and allow heat to escape at night. For this reason, we decided to omit south-facing skylights. We did, however, compromise a little on roof glass by installing nine 2-ft. by 4-ft. operable Velux roof windows along the north face of the gable, figuring that their ability to release heat during the summer outweighed any winter heat-loss problems. And Velux manufactures shades, awnings and blinds to reduce heat loss and gain (Velux-America, Inc., P. O. Box 3268, Greenwood, S. C. 29648). In any case, there would be little direct heat gain from the sun on the north side.

These units and the casement windows in the south wall provide the primary means of moving air in a low-to-high ventilation loop. As the hot air escapes through the skylights, it pulls a strong breeze through the house. Excessive heat or coolness can easily be controlled simply by manipulating skylights and casements, or the reflective mini-blinds on the casement windows.

Monitoring progress—There are many advantages to a linear solar house—some that

we foresaw and some that came as pleasant surprises. Aside from the advantages I've already mentioned—a big south yard, a short, swift convection loop and a simple structure—the slab-on-grade thermal mass provides easy access to elderly or disabled people. Many flat and narrow urban sites can accommodate a linear scheme where a more traditional configuration would seem crowded onto the site. And the simple roof has an ample south-facing surface to allow the application of any active solar equipment—either during construction or after.

With some owner labor, the Reavis's house cost about $50 per sq. ft., which is comparable to the cost of a mid-range builder home. Dan was able to do the electrical rough-in and lay the radiant floor, but couldn't find the time to finish the interior. The recent economic slump here has forced the Reavises to postpone the addition of Pella folding-wood walls between the hallway and the living spaces and to hold back on some details and the landscaping. But as they wait to complete the house, the interior makes a pleasant and low-cost retreat.

On cold sunny days the house heats itself quite easily, requiring slight adjustments to window openings and skylights. Aside from the concrete floor, there is no long-term storage facility, so some back-up radiant heat is required on cold nights. Dan and Judy carry out the performance analysis of their house in a most unscientific but accurate manner: They call me and tell me how comfortable they are. □

Don Parker practices architecture in Boulder, Colorado.

The south-side wall framing is built of exposed single and double 2x6s (photo above). The double studs act as door bucks, and the solo studs act as window bucks (drawing right).

Manufactured clad window

1x2

2x8 buck

Shim space

Caulk

Plan section through window jamb

A Little House with a Big View

Though heavily glazed on the north, it remains energy efficient and gets a third of its heat from the sun

by Bill Phelps

The proposal was simple enough. Could I design a small house with the feel of a cabin that would be energy efficient with heavy insulation and passive-solar gain; build it on a north-sloping site with magnificent views to the north, east and west; and do it on a budget small enough to overshadow every decision. Instinctively, and with the confidence of a builder looking for his next project, I assured Flicka Scott that I could build her dream. The next step, however, was to find design solutions. These didn't come as easily as my initial confidence had.

Flicka Scott's property is located about halfway up the north side of a butte just outside Jackson, Wyo., near Grand Teton National Park. The site (photo above) affords a panoramic view of two spectacular mountain ranges—the Tetons and the Gros Ventres—which converge to form the northern edge of Jackson Hole. For Flicka to enjoy this view,

Bill Phelps is a contractor and passive-solar consultant in Jackson, Wyo.

her house would need large windows on the north, east and west—an obvious obstacle to energy efficiency. Shading from the hill above the site to the south was another possible obstacle to the use of solar energy.

Solar calculations and thermal storage—
To evaluate the problem of shade on the site, I used the quick and reasonably accurate technique developed by Edward Mazria, which is explained in his *Passive Solar Energy Book* (Rodale Press, Emmaus, Pa. 18049; $16.95 paperback; $29.95 hardcover professional edition). With my transit and the sun charts in the book, I found that the top of the 18° hill behind the house was low enough that the sun just cleared it at the winter solstice on December 21. (For more on solar site selection, see *FHB* #5, pp. 52-53.)

As soon as I was sure that shading wouldn't be a problem, I began working out the best passive-solar strategy to use. I needed to decide two things: first, which collection and storage system would best suit the cabin; and

second, how much south-facing glass we would need to make this system work as efficiently as possible. Direct solar gain into the main living space would be the least expensive solution if I could come up with inexpensive thermal storage. A mass wall was too expensive, but a water wall solved all of our problems. It provided thermal storage along with some direct gain and daylight at a price we could live with. (For more on water tubes for thermal mass, see p. 81).

The next problem was how to support the tubes. We used tubes 12 in. in dia. and 8 ft. tall, and each tube weighs close to 400 lb. when it's full. Standard practice is to set them on concrete, but wood framing was a less expensive alternative for this house. So I built a 2x4 wall 20 in. inside the foundation wall and sheathed it with ½-in. plywood. Double 2x8 joists over the 20-in. span from that wall to the foundation wall at 8 in. o. c. carry the load, as well as the same subflooring and the finish oak strip flooring as the rest of the house (drawing, facing page). The tubes are

Photos, except where noted: D. J. Bassett

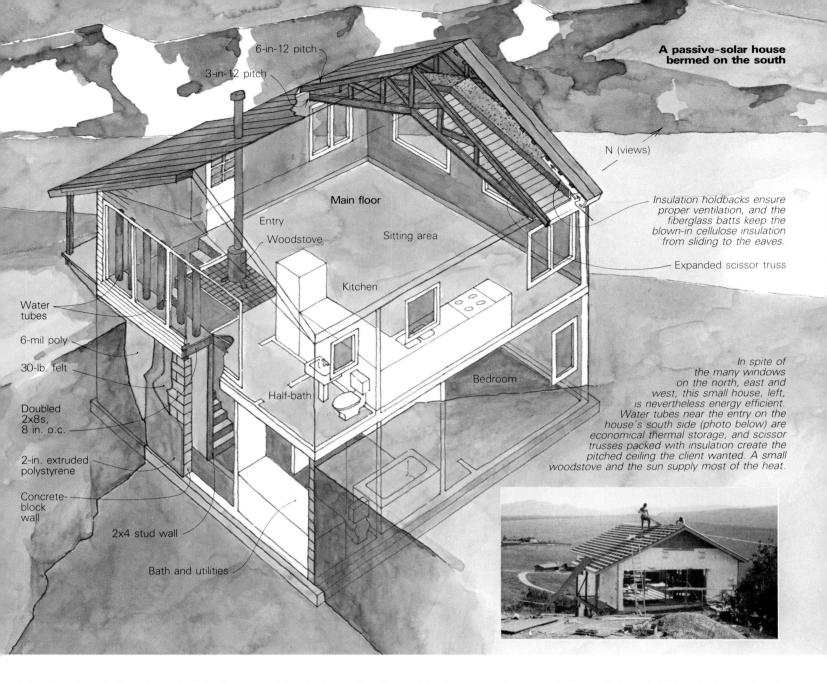

A passive-solar house bermed on the south

6-in-12 pitch

3-in-12 pitch

Main floor

Entry

Woodstove

Sitting area

Kitchen

Half-bath

Bedroom

Water tubes

6-mil poly

30-lb. felt

Doubled 2x8s, 8 in. o.c.

2-in. extruded polystyrene

Concrete-block wall

2x4 stud wall

Bath and utilities

N (views)

Insulation holdbacks ensure proper ventilation, and the fiberglass batts keep the blown-in cellulose insulation from sliding to the eaves.

Expanded scissor truss

In spite of the many windows on the north, east and west, this small house, left, is nevertheless energy efficient. Water tubes near the entry on the house's south side (photo below) are economical thermal storage, and scissor trusses packed with insulation create the pitched ceiling the client wanted. A small woodstove and the sun supply most of the heat.

Illustration: Frances Ashforth; Construction photo: Flicka Scott

doing fine, though I'm going to build a framework to stabilize their tops—right now, a large frisky dog might knock them over.

To calculate how much south glazing to add, I used the Solar Load Ratio (SLR) method, which is explained more fully in the sidebar on p. 97. This method lets you estimate the annual auxiliary-energy requirement of a passive-solar building. The key variable is the relationship between the building load, or heat loss, and the collector size, or solar energy gained.

We had a lot of heat-losing windows to bring in the view, and I'd decided not to insulate the basement as heavily as I could have (more about this below), so I knew we'd need a lot of glass on the house's south wall. We used four 46-in. by 76-in. patio-door replacement blanks for a collector area of just under 100 sq. ft. I used double-pane glass units rather than triple pane for greater solar-energy transmittance, and fitted each window with Window Quilt movable insulation to reduce nighttime heat loss.

The design—The shape of the house was determined by the client's budget. A simple rectangle 24 ft. by 28 ft. with a trussed gable roof provided an easy-to-build, no-frills structure with 672 sq. ft. on its main level. A full basement below fit nicely into the hill.

We had the building's shape, but the right floor plan did not arrive without a struggle. Flicka wanted a half-bath for guests, and a woodstove to keep the use of electric heat to a minimum, and she spent many hours shuffling scaled-down sofas, tables and stairwells around the allotted area of the main level. Her perseverance, and some timely suggestions volunteered by local architect John Breternitz, finally solved the puzzle. The stairwell, the woodstove and the half-bath were grouped together at the south end of the house, as shown in the drawing above. This left the north end open for furniture and kept the great views in front of the sitting and entertaining area.

Placing the stairwell below the south-facing windows worked out well because it opened a

path for sunlight to brighten the bermed end of the basement. The basement level was divided into two bedrooms on the north and a combination bath and utility room in the southeast corner. The remaining space adjacent to the stairs went for storage—always a real need in a small house.

Materials—Flicka wanted a metal roof. They have become very popular in our area because they're durable and don't hold snow. On the other hand, metal roofing is almost twice as expensive as asphalt shingles, and you still need ventilation from the eaves.

More important, though, is what happens when the snow slides off the roof. For personal safety, entries need porch roofs, and plumbing vents and chimneys must be positioned close to the ridge, or provided with a cricket (a small, wedge-shaped snow diverter that looks like a tiny gable dormer).

As the winter progresses, snow piles up against the side of the building—sometimes high enough to block the view from the win-

The main floor is one big room, with the entry, stairs, woodstove and water wall grouped at the south. The water tubes were an economical solution to the problem of thermal storage. The sitting area is near the view windows at the north. About ⅓ of the house's energy is solar.

dows. An infrequent but documented disaster can occur when a slab of ice and snow from the roof is released, strikes the mound of snow on the ground and is deflected back toward the building. This can shatter windows and glass doors. To avoid problems like this, I ran the ridgeline from north to south, protecting the solar glazing at the south and the patio door two stories down on the north.

The exterior of the cabin was sided with spruce and pine shiplap, which was about $500 cheaper than the cedar that is commonly used in this area. All of the siding and trim was back-primed before it was nailed up to prevent the cupping caused by uneven moisture adsorption.

Construction—Flicka wanted the walls and ceiling on the main level to be knotty pine, and the ceiling had to be pitched. We used 1x8 T&G boards to accomplish the first request. We also built the kitchen cabinets with pine, using the same boards for doors and drawer facing. That's a lot of knotty pine for some tastes, but the finish is light, the house is bright, and the effect is just what the client ordered—rustic and comfortable.

To create the pitched ceiling, we used a scissor truss. It has a 6-in-12 pitch on the top chord and a 3-in-12 pitch on the bottom chord. This puts the peak of the ceiling about 11 ft. off the floor. To allow for more space for insulation and ventilation where the truss sits on the exterior wall plate, our engineer used his computer to modify a standard scissor

truss design by adding a 2x8 block between the top and bottom chords where they intersect. This left a full 12 in. between the top of the wall and the top of the 2x6 upper chord at the outside edge of the wall. Two inches are used for ventilation at the eaves, leaving 10 in. for insulation.

Jackson Hole gets two frost-free months if we are lucky, and averages just under 10,000 heating degree days. It makes sense, in these conditions, to insulate a new house heavily. We insulated the ceiling to R-55 using blown-in cellulose over fiberglass batts. To add the cellulose, the insulation subcontractor had to crawl into the attic space through the hole left for a louvered attic vent and then make his way between the webs of the trusses, which at best gave him 2½ ft. of headroom. Before he arrived, we had installed insulation hold-backs to ensure proper ventilation at the eaves. We then stapled kraft-backed R-11 fiberglass batts between the bottom chords of the trusses to prevent the cellulose from sliding down the 3-in-12 ceiling pitch on the slick 6-mil polyethylene vapor barrier.

We triple-glazed the 140 sq. ft. of windows on the north, east and west sides of the building, but they still account for 27% of the total heat loss. Heat loss from the basement is about 30%, because we put only 2 in. of extruded polystyrene on the outside of the foundation walls. For a heated basement, 4 in. would have been more appropriate, but we decided against it for three reasons. First, the 2x6 wall at the main level could be cantile-

vered to cover the 2 in. of insulation, keeping siding on the exposed basement wall and the main level in the same plane. This avoided an awkward intersection, and the need for trim and flashing. Second, we felt that if the basement remained too cool or required too much electric heat, we could easily add insulation to the inside of the foundation walls in the future. Third, our client prefers a cool bedroom, so the heat loss from these rooms would be low, since the thermostat will be set way back. As for the rest of the downstairs, the guest bedroom will be used infrequently. The bath-utility room is insulated from the rest of the basement and benefits from the heat inevitably given off by the electric water heater.

I also added a de-stratification fan. It takes air from near the ceiling peak upstairs and blows it down into the bedrooms. It is used mostly to control occasional mild overheating upstairs on sunny days in the spring and fall, but it's also an easy and efficient way to carry some of the heat from the woodstove to the basement during the winter.

We sealed the basement walls below grade with two coats of plastic foundation coating, followed by a layer of 30-lb. felt. The 2 in. of extruded polystyrene insulation was installed next, and covered with a continuous sheet of 6-mil polyethylene. We backfilled with washed rock for better drainage, and a perforated drain pipe along the footing was run out to daylight where the grade dropped off.

The foot or so of exterior insulation that we left exposed above grade is protected with galvanized valley flashing. This is available in 50-ft. rolls, and it is simple to install. We nailed it along its top edge, which was then covered by siding. Before it can be painted, the exposed surface must be coated with vinegar. The acetic acid of the vinegar reacts with the zinc and etches the surface to accept paint. Two coats of paint from a spray can, and you have a durable and cheap alternative to parging.

Sealing against infiltration—The frame walls are responsible for the largest share of heat loss through their tiny lines of infiltration. The walls in this little cabin have several hundred feet of cracks. The junctures of floors, walls and ceilings and around the doors and windows allow most of the infiltration. Because twice as much heat is lost through infiltration as through conduction through the wall (27% of the house's total heat loss as opposed to 13%), it was important to use a wall system that has an unbroken air-and-vapor barrier, as well as sufficient insulation. Here's how we did it.

The 2x6 frame wall was insulated with unfaced fiberglass batts. We then stapled 4-ft. wide strips of 6-mil polyethylene centered

From *Fine Homebuilding* (June 1984) 21:56-59

over the junctions where the wall meets the ceiling and the floor. Inch-thick foil-backed polyisocyanurate foam sheathing was then added on the inside of the wall. We sealed all of the joints and any punctures with aluminum tape so that the foil backing could serve as a vapor barrier. We caulked the sheathing to the polyethylene strips at the top and bottom plates. Finally, we nailed horizontal 2x2 furring over the foam sheathing at 2 ft. o. c. to provide a 1½-in. chase for electrical circuits. The airspace in front of the aluminum foil adds a radiant-heat barrier valued at R-2.8. We added extra furring strips at the floor and around doors and windows for nailing baseboard and casing. We also installed a piece of polyisocyanurate foam between the interior-partition studs and the exterior wall when we were framing. This eliminated a common gap in the insulation and vapor-barrier envelope.

This system went on quickly and cost less than double-wall framing. It also allowed us to frame the walls and put on the roof in normal fashion before installing the insulation and the vapor barrier.

The second major barrier against infiltration that we installed was Tyvek. I really like this stuff. It is manufactured by Du Pont from olefin, a spunbound, high-density polyethylene fiber. It repels water and blocks air movement, but is highly permeable to water vapor, and allows moisture in the wall cavity to get to the outside.

Tyvek costs more than the usual 15-lb. felt or resin paper, which is generally stapled just underneath the siding. But it goes on so easily that you save the difference in labor expense. It comes in 9-ft. wide rolls, which are easy to handle and can cover a standard 8-ft. wall in one pass. One person walks around the house and rolls out the Tyvek, while a second follows along with a stapler. At window and door openings, we use a razor knife to cut an X across the opening. The four flaps that remain can then be folded in and stapled to the framing. When we install a window unit, we run a bead of caulk on the back of the brick mold to create an airtight seal between the window and the Tyvek. The brick mold on the windows we used on this house had been caulked to the window jambs at the factory. When they haven't been, we caulk there, too.

The low infiltration rate that results from sealing a house this tightly means that indoor air can get stale and humid. Engineer Jim Kleyman and I checked the house with an air door, and found that it got only .13 air changes per hour. The rule of thumb is that infiltration rates below half an air change per hour are unsafe.

The most efficient way to get fresh air in without losing heat is to use an air-to-air heat exchanger. These mechanical ventilation units use outgoing air to heat the incoming air without mixing the two. But they are expensive, and so, I regret to say, we decided not to install one.

To make do, the kitchen and bathroom exhaust fans (as well as the woodstove) exhaust stale and humid air. The fresh air that does find its way past the weatherstripping on the windows and doors and other unavoidable cracks turns out to be enough to supply the small woodstove, but not enough to feed the kitchen exhaust fan. When it is turned on, Flicka has to crack a window or the fan reverses the draft in the woodstove chimney, and draws smoke back into the house. She has learned to live with this inconvenience, but we will be installing a heat exchanger in this house soon. On future jobs, I'll insist on them more vigorously to guarantee a plentiful supply of fresh air.

The small amount of infiltration also caused some minor problems with moisture. Water vapor produced by people, pets (dogs produce an amazing amount of the stuff), cooking and bathing accumulates if not vented out. A little humidity is appreciated in a dry climate like ours, but excessive water vapor condenses on the windows. When the temperature fell to −30°F earlier this winter, some condensation occurred on the triple-glazed windows, and ice formed on the double glass on the south wall. That water eventually ends up pooled on the sills. Lowering the level of indoor humidity is the easiest solution to this problem. Again, an air-to-air heat exchanger would help.

Cost and efficiency—When we added up the bills at the end of the project, the cost for the house, excluding the septic system, well, and appliances, was $54,494. The finished living space is 1,344 sq. ft., which works out to $40.55 per sq. ft. Adding the nearly $5,000 we spent for the septic system and water, the cost increased to just over $44 per sq. ft.—still well below average around here. This was all the more satisfying since per-square-foot cost of a small house is usually so high and because we took the time and trouble to make this one so efficient.

If truth be told, I couldn't do this kind of job again for the price. I took on this project because I wanted to keep my crew working and because it was an especially interesting challenge. But another couple of bucks on the square-foot figure would bring in the kind of profit you need to run a business, and the price would still be good.

We are halfway through our heating season as I write this, and so far we have had about three weeks of sub-zero temperatures and at least eight weeks of cold, cloudy weather. From November through January, the house has used less than ⅓ cord of wood and about $50 worth of electric heat.

Flicka Scott is very happy with her cabin. She says she especially likes the daylight that floods in through all the windows, and the fact that this makes the room feel larger than it is. I am happy because we were able to show, in a small way, that the effective use of passive-solar techniques is not limited to perfect sites in sunny climates. This little house has 1½ times as much glass on the north, east and west as it does on the south, but thanks to lots of insulation and tight construction, it still gains about a third of its heat from the sun. □

Calculating solar contribution

The Solar Load Ratio represents the relationship between the energy that is lost by a building and the solar energy that is gained. The scientists at the U. S. Dept. of Energy labs at Los Alamos, N. Mex., have used complex computer simulations and data from actual passive-solar buildings to chart this relationship for 94 different types of passive-solar systems. The result is a comprehensive analytical procedure that considers location, weather, building characteristics and passive-solar system types, to predict how much auxiliary heat a building will require.

The accuracy of the method has been well documented. Experiments have shown the actual auxiliary heat used in monitored buildings to be very close to the predicted value. But the real value of the SLR method is not the prediction of energy use for a given year, but the weighing of the effects of different designs against each other to select the best solution for solar performance.

The computer—Although the method itself is complex, the calculations you need to do to use it have been simplified. You can, in fact, make a reasonable approximation of required yearly auxiliary heat by using the Load Collector Ratio tables. This method doesn't include as many building variables as the monthly SLR method. Both methods are explained in the *Passive Solar Design Handbook, Vol. II and III* (American Solar Energy Society, 1230 Grandview Ave., Boulder, Colo. 80302; Vol II is $10 from Superintendent of Documents, U.S. Govt. Printing Office, Washington, D.C. 20402; Vol III is $59 plus $2 postage, hardcover with Supplement; $45 plus $2.60 postage, paperback with Supplement; $25 plus $2.60 postage, paperback without Supplement).

To do the more accurate monthly calculations by hand is not difficult, but it is tedious and time-consuming. The value of time being what it is, they are therefore often left undone. Enter the micro-computer. The Solar Load Ratio method combined with the speed of a micro-computer has added a new dimension to the design of passive-solar buildings. It's quick and easy to run several building options to find the optimum mix. You can almost instantly compare variables like shading, orientation, passive-system type, number of glazing layers, and insulation levels to find out how they will effect the auxiliary energy required.

I use a program called Sunpas (Solar Soft Inc., Box 124, Snowmass, Colo. 81654). It has become an indispensable design tool for me, and it lets me show clients how much money and energy specific design approaches will save or use.

Sunpas is not alone in the field. You can learn more about micro-computer software for passive-solar design from the Building Energy Design Tool Council (W. I. Whiddon & Assoc., Inc., 4330 East West Hwy., Suite 914, Bethesda, Md. 20814). —*B. P.*

Superinsulated in Idaho

Lessons learned from an energy-efficient house

by Jonathan Marvel

Building sites in the old part of Hailey, Idaho, don't come up for sale very often. So when a corner lot became available in 1983, my wife Stefanie and I jumped at the chance to buy it. We had been living in Hailey for several years, and with two small children, we had decided that building in town would keep us near all the good aspects of small-town life. In the old part of town, the schools are close by, the wide sidewalks are busy and the 100-year-old houses dating back to the boom-town mining years contribute a sense of permanence to the neighborhood. Our site also had the advantage of being but a short walk to my architecture practice in Hailey's business district.

In the year and a half before we were able to build, I spent a fair amount of time considering the influences that would shape a house on our site. The lot is on the southwest corner of the intersection of what is basically a north/south, east/west street grid. A sun chart investigation revealed good sun exposure—even at mid-winter solstice with sunset at about 5 p. m. on December 21st. This underlines the wisdom of Hailey's settlers, as a narrow gap in the ridge to the west allows the sun to shine a little longer on the town. Here in the Wood River Valley, many homesites are shaded for long periods of the winter day as the sun sets early behind mountains that rise 2,000 ft. from the valley floor.

Good views to the west and north suggested a two-story house to take advantage of the scenery. A two-story plan would also leave more of the lot open for garden and play space for the kids. We didn't want our house to look out of place, so before I began designing, I spent time studying the aspects of the neighborhood houses that could be incorporated into a new house. Large porches, low fences, window bays, clearly defined entries, turrets and other Victoriana are all common parts of this townscape.

We chose to have a two-step-up transition at the sidewalk into the yard and another three steps up to the front porch to underscore the change from public to private (photo below). High awning windows on the street sides of the house balance the light indoors, while simultaneously providing privacy. But most of the glazing is on the southeast and southwest faces of the house to capture as much sun as possible (photo facing page).

L-shaped, with two stories—Our corner lot suggested an L-shaped house because its perpendicular wings would provide privacy for the backyard and offer the greatest exposure to the sun for the bedrooms and living rooms—an important consideration in a climate with a five- or six-month winter. The arrangement of rooms that we eventually settled upon places two bedrooms, two bathrooms and a small deck on the second floor (floor plan this page). The childrens' sleeping area is one large space right now. When they get a little older I'll give them each some privacy by dividing this space into two rooms.

On the ground level, a vestibule connects the front door with a wide hallway. The vestibule has a closet on one side and a row of coat pegs on the other. Beneath the pegs is a boot rack for the sometimes slushy footwear that crosses the threshold. Doors on the interior side of the vestibule help us to keep the arctic air out of the living spaces during the winter months.

At the south end of the downstairs hall are the kitchen, dining area and living room. While they occupy distinct corners of this wing, all three are open to one another (photo next page). A combination laundry room/pantry is adjacent to the kitchen. The other ground floor wing of the house is a studio/library of about 400 sq. ft. that has a half bath in one corner. This space doubles as a bedroom when guests stay over.

The first and second floors total about 2,400 sq. ft., which we felt would be the maximum size we could afford to build. For future use we decided to include a full basement which, at an estimated cost of $12 per square foot, we thought of as a bargain space. Any garage would have to wait for future prosperity.

Conservation measures—Skiers come from all over the world to enjoy the dry, powdery snow just up the road at Sun Valley. The snow is dry because it gets cold here, and stays cold. Ours is an 8,100 heating degree-day climate (about the same as Minneapolis). As a consequence, we spent a good deal of time considering construction details that would achieve maximum conservation of energy.

Fortuitously, as I began my design work I learned about the Model Conservation Standards (MCS) Program being sponsored by Bonneville Power (the public power supplier to much of the northwest U. S.). This program would subsidize construction of 400 houses that would meet or exceed the new construction standards for energy-efficient houses. We applied and were accepted as one of the houses to be built in Idaho. In return for the construction subsidy, which amounted to about $5,000 for a house the size of ours, we agreed to be monitored for energy use for two years without burning wood for heat. The house also had to be all-electric to qualify—although we eventually put in a gas range.

We settled on double-wall construction with a 6-mil polyethylene vapor barrier between the walls, (top drawing, p. 102). This detail allowed

Building on tradition. Symmetrical gables, horizontal siding, low fences and a broad porch are some of the traditional design elements used by architect Jonathan Marvel to fit his house into an established neighborhood (photo facing page). In the backyard the wings of the house come together at outdoor sitting areas on both levels (photo above).

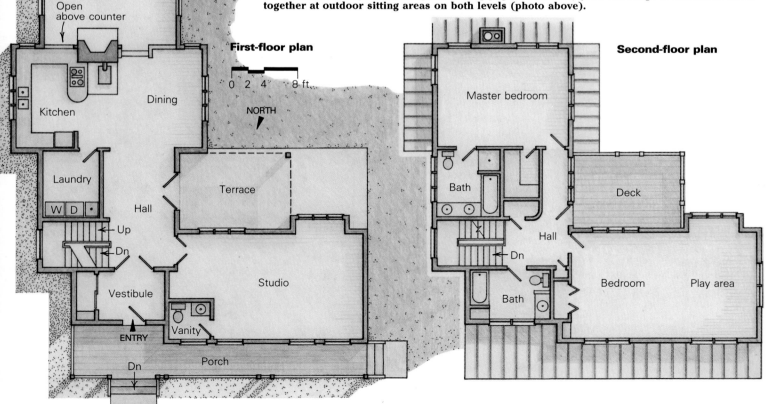

First-floor plan

0 2 4 8 ft.

NORTH

Living

Open above counter

Kitchen

Dining

Laundry

W D

Hall

Up

Dn

Vestibule

ENTRY

Vanity

Dn

Porch

Terrace

Studio

Second-floor plan

Master bedroom

Bath

Deck

Hall

Dn

Bath

Bedroom

Play area

Drawings: Vince Babak

us to use the interior wall for wiring and plumbing, without violating the integrity of the barrier. Stuffed with standard density fiberglass batts, the wall is rated at about R-30.

The flat-ceiling areas are insulated with R-60 blown-in fiberglass (Insulsafe from Certain-Teed, Box 860, Valley Forge, Pa. 19482; 215-341-7000). In cathedral-ceiling areas we have R-38 fiberglass batts with 1-in. polyisocyanurate sheathing over the plywood decking for a total R-value of 45. In the basement we installed 2-in. thick sheets of extruded polystyrene under the slab, as well as on the outside of the 8-ft. high concrete walls around the basement. Our long-term plan is to eventually furr out the basement walls with R-11 insulated 2x4 stud walls. We left the floor over the basement uninsulated during the monitoring period, as that permitted us to receive a slightly larger subsidy based on our gross heated area. Since then, we have added R-19 batts in the floor.

The program also required us to install a whole house air-to-air heat exchanger. The model we chose was an E-Z Vent #340 (Des Champs Laboratories, Inc., Box 440, 17 Farinella Dr., E. Hanover, N. J. 07936; 201-884-1460), which was the largest residential model we could find. On high speed, it provides 400 cfm.

For the windows I chose Pella clad-casements (The Rolscreen Co., 102 Main St., Pella,

Iowa 50219; 515-628-1000). The Pella design will permit us to replace the inner glazing panel at a future time with high-tech glass when the cost and heat-regulating efficiency of the glass improve. I did consider low-e glass but the expense did not appear to be cost-effective when we built the house.

At studwall corners we used drywall clips to eliminate the extra stud that is typically installed for drywall backing. Not only does this save some wood, but it also makes a little more room for insulation. And in the 2x6 exterior wall, we used 4x headers with 2 in. of extruded polystyrene insulation on the inside face of each one.

To protect the vapor barrier and roof insulation, I did not place any recessed lighting fixtures in exterior ceilings. And to cut down on convection currents in the walls, we kept plumbing penetrations through the top plates to an absolute minimum and sealed around the few that we made with urethane foam. In addition, wiring runs were routed to avoid passing through the top plates. We eliminated air infiltration at the rim joists by overlapping them with 2 in. of expanded polystyrene insulation.

According to our heat-loss calculations for the design area of 3,850 square feet (including basement), we would need 15 kw of electric resistance heat to keep the house at a comfortable temperature. In a somewhat experi-

mental solution I decided to install a 10 kw in-line duct heater (Delta-Flo Manufacturing Co., Inc., West Rialto Ave., San Bernardino, Calif. 92410; 714-888-3291). The fresh air that passes through the duct heater has already been preheated by the heat exchanger. I picked up the additional 5 kw of heating capacity with three baseboard heaters in the basement, which isn't served by the forced-air system.

Cost control—In an effort to balance our desire for some attractive finishes and details with our limited budget, we settled on some trade-offs. In the extra-expense column we installed a select-grade strip white oak floor in the downstairs living areas and hard maple for the kitchen countertops, window sills and baseboards (the maple actually cost somewhat less than the oak). At the heart of the house, we used Italian tile around the woodstove between the kitchen and the dining area, and around the fireplace in the living room. We also splurged in the kitchen and bought some high-end cabinets (top photo, facing page) called Opus One (Crystal Cabinetworks, Inc., 1100 Crystal Dr., Princeton, Minn. 55371; 612-389-4187). We decided to spend extra for cast-iron sinks and tubs in the bathrooms.

On the economy side we chose to use ½-in. drywall with a standard taped-and-light-spray finish. The ¾-in. radius BeadeX drywall corner

Around the stove. **The public spaces of the house are organized around a steel woodstove set against a tiled surround (photo facing page). Under the tile, a massive concrete-block chimney helps to retain the stove's heat. Cabinets finished with plastic laminate banded with white oak were one of a few carefully selected custom touches (photo right); drawer fronts are riftsawn white oak and the countertops are maple. The rounded drywall corners wrapping the window keep the trim to a minimum, yet maintain the rounded feel of the drawer and counter edges. Shelves normally used for clothes closets are an inexpensive and attractive way to organize dishware (photo below).**

beads (BeadeX Manufacturing Co., 833 Houser Way N., Renton, Wash. 98055; 206-228-6600) cost a little more than standard 90° corners. But we used drywall returns at all windows, so we saved the cost of extensive trim work and materials while maintaining the rounded softness at these edges afforded by the radiused corner beads.

The stairs and upstairs bedrooms were carpeted with a low-cost nylon carpeting (about $14 per sq. yd.), and we used sheet vinyl for the floors in the bathrooms and laundry/pantry. All the lighting fixtures were low-cost stock models from a local discount supply house or purchased by mail from Conran's Habitat (921 Eastwind Dr., Suite 114, Westerville, Ohio 43081; 800-462-1769). We have no upper cabinets in the house. Instead, we installed Closet-Maid open closet shelving (Clairson International, Inc., 720 S. W. 17th St., Ocala, Fla. 32674; 904-351-6100) in the kitchen (bottom photo) and pantry. The cabinets in the pantry-/laundry are low-end stock models.

Acting as my own contractor, I was able to maintain control over some of the costs of the construction as well as eliminate a contractor's fee. The final cost of the project amounted to about $59 per square foot for the 2,400 square feet of finished area. This excludes the subsidy—about $2 per square foot. Current construction costs would be about $70 per square foot.

Reading the meters—As part of the effort to quantify the study results, we compiled the costs associated with the extra insulation, the heat exchanger, the vapor/air barrier, extra lumber for the inside wall and labor costs, and came up with $1.75 per square foot of finished floor space—about $4,000. The calculated energy use for our house came to 3.73 kw hours per square foot per year; our actual measured use was about 15% less than this or about $500 per year at $.0412 per kw hour. According to BPA's research, this represents a savings of about 50% in energy use as compared with a typical house of similar size.

The air-to-air heat exchanger operated 24 hours a day during the heating season to ensure indoor air quality. Our indoor air was tested for formaldehyde gas (a typical outgas byproduct of many building materials, especially carpet backing and particleboard) and radon. Because I had specified low-fuming particleboard for all underlayment and because

The galley kitchen (above) features custom plywood cabinets and counters that are higher than usual. Cove lighting is built into the underside of the wall cabinets. The base cabinets (left) feature sliding trays for shelves.

cial place for myself. My architecture studio (photo at left, p. 66) on the clerestory fourth-floor loft has interior views to the spaces below and an exterior balcony, where I can "reign" over the farm as well.

Since the surrounding land is given back to the meadow, I designed five outdoor places for the house. In addition to the small decks off the bedroom, the architecture studio and the weaving studio, there is also a covered front porch complete with swing, which provides an exterior place protected from sun and rain. The major deck with built-in seating is to the south, and is off the main studio/living room. Much of the deck furniture we designed and built.

Building en famille—Our carpenter/builder son, Donn, agreed to build our house, with our family and his crew. The framing moved quickly,

and we had a real sense of accomplishment as the building took form, even though this four-story, nine-roof, five-deck building with the ceilings following the slopes of the roofs was not easy to build. But assembled section by section, with each section fairly simple to build, the whole came together without major problems.

I have always regretted that in usual building circumstances the designing must end before construction begins. But building our own house let me experiment with full-size mockups, and meant that I didn't have to make any decision until the hammer hit the nail. Even then, I sometimes changed things after they were built. This way of working was quite frustrating to the carpenters, but they understood the purpose of trying to achieve the best design, and made many valuable suggestions.

As the framing proceeded, masonry work began. The mason appeared one morning after the midnight shift in the factory and began the four-story chimney and fireplace. He found large stones on the farm for the front steps and hearth; these were hauled to the site and set. The call for brick, block and mortar continued for the next three weeks.

With the framing and chimney nearing completion, the windows and exterior doors arrived. The next three weeks were spent fabricating and installing the standing-seam galvanized roofing, which is common to the older homes of the area. There are no soffits at the overhangs and since most interior spaces have cathedral ceilings, ventilation of the rafter space was built in at the eaves, ridges and side walls. There are no gutters, so we installed a gravel strip with a French drain 3 ft. out from the building to receive the roof drainage. The siding is vertical roughsawn cedar. The windows and doors have Low-E glass, which reduces heat transmission.

The heating system is baseboard hot water fired by a water stove, with a pump and thermostat for each level. The 500-gal. water stove surrounding a wood/coal firebox has an auxiliary oil burner and a domestic hot-water coil. Separate ducted combustion air is provided directly to the stove and also to the fireplace. The house is heated with wood that is cut on the farm. We use about three cords a winter. Summer cooling is achieved by natural ventilation, with the "chimney effect" of the stairway drawing fresh air into the ground floor and expelling hot air at the clerestory loft.

A custom interior—Once the house had been closed in, interior work began. The wall finish is drywall. The interior trim, stairs, railings, floors and ceilings are clear southern yellow pine installed on site by the carpenters.

Peter Dillinger built all of the bathroom and kitchen cabinets (photo top left), and David East and Donn built the dining cabinet and closet shelf-cabinets. To express the nature of plywood, all edges were left exposed, which not only simplified the work but also, I believe, adds a richness of character. Making the cabinets and countertops on site saved us considerable expense, and allowed us to do some special things, such as building the heating into the cabinet base and making the countertops 2 in.

Three Sides to the Sun

Enough light to cast a shadow
can heat this house in the Montana Rockies

by Wink Davis

The realtor bounced us in his Buick to the crest of a ridge in the Montana Rockies, crunching the dry August grasses and wildflowers in our path. Gazing down into a gentle, bowl-shaped meadow, we found a site with everything we had hoped for—privacy, proximity to town, an open view and a plentiful supply of firewood. The south-facing slope allowed full exposure to the low winter sun, while trees and hills formed natural windbreaks to the east and west. It was the perfect site for the passive solar home my wife Nancy and I wanted to build. That was the summer of 1979. We tied up the deal that fall and stood watch on the land through the winter, evaluating the sun, snow, wind and shadows.

Before our move to Montana, I was a builder in Colorado, where I had worked on conventional homes for several years. We had lived in a house there with some solar features. It was properly oriented, with a bank of windows facing south, but lacked other elements necessary for an efficient solar-heated house. Impressed with the possibilities of solar heating, I read everything on the subject I could lay my hands on, and began to develop my own ideas and to work out plans for our new house. We knew that living in a passive solar home would be a new experience, so we discussed our needs, wishes and taboos. We both made concessions: Nancy agreed to hard tile floors and the necessity of operating shutters twice daily in winter, and I gave up dreams of an underground house with water walls everywhere. (I also gave up hope that the house would be an ever-evolving test facility for my solar ideas—Nancy would not live in a science experiment.)

Winter weather cycles in Montana begin with relatively mild temperatures (20° to 40°F), which almost invariably bring snow. When a storm breaks, it is followed by clearing skies and cold temperatures (−40° to 0°F), and frequently by strong gusty winds from the north, which drive the chill factor even lower. Cold, clear and windy weather gradually gives way to a warming trend, and the cycle begins again. During periods of extreme cold, the sun is generally shining enough to warm a house. Snow means cloudy skies but also brings warmer temperatures. Warm and sunny periods are infrequent and very welcome.

The site and the wind told us to keep the house low. I also wanted the winter sun to shine through the house onto the north wall, so concrete walls and floors would get maximum direct gain. These requirements call for a narrow house, long on the east-west axis. But a

Top, site-built rafter assemblies support the roof, providing long spans and clerestories for solar gain. The rafters were made by sandwiching a 2x8 between two 2x10s, using bolts and construction adhesive to secure the lamination. Above, the post between two windows is tenoned to fit into the laminated rafter. The slot cut into the rafter and the post will hold folding window-insulation boards.

28-ft. by 100-ft. rectangle is hard to work with, and not very pleasing in my opinion.

Our way out of rectilinear thinking came with a visit to the house of friends in Cody, Wyoming, one cold and windy day in December 1979. Their house, designed by architect David Wright, had very much the configuration, floor space and dimensions we had been working with. But the long rectangle was broken into three contiguous sections set at 30° to one another. This variation suddenly leaped out as the obvious solution to our problems with a long, narrow house. At once the unimaginative shape came alive with possibilities. Internal spaces related to one another in new ways, and sheltered alcoves were created at the junction of the angles.

In addition to these aesthetic advantages, the 30° angles solved a fundamental structural difficulty in passive solar houses. Because window space must be maximized, little room is left for diagonal bracing, and adequate rack resistance is hard to provide. In this design, the angles on the south wall transfer racking forces into the roof framing and ceiling decking.

The visit to Wyoming also confirmed the viability of heating with the weak winter sun in the northern Rockies. A cold front arrived about the same time we did, and with the outside temperature around −10°F, we sat down to tea in their warm, sunny living room. When the sun set and chilly air currents descended off the windows, beadboard shutters were put in place, and our host lit a fire in the potbelly stove just for ambience, as the outside temperature plunged toward −30°F.

The floor plan—Once we had located our building on the site and decided on the basic structure, we got together with a local designer and builder, Pete Stein, and produced a floor plan and construction drawings. We located spaces that need the first morning sun (the kitchen, dining room, office and sunroom) in the west end of the house, oriented 15° east of solar south (drawing, facing page). The living room and greenhouse face 15° west of south, receiving their best sun a little later in the day. The bedroom wing faces due southwest, catching the late afternoon sun almost directly.

The site plan revealed that the grade slopes mildly southwest and falls almost 5 ft. between the house's northeast and southwest corners. In addition, the natural grade line would be nearly level across the north wall of the east wing. Accordingly, we decided to sink the east wing into the ground 4 ft. and raise grade level 1 ft. at the southwest corner. This solution would keep the northern profile of the house low, helping to deflect winter winds, and providing relatively low-cost insulation for the areas below grade.

In solar houses I think it's important for the masonry or concrete mass to serve structurally as well as to store heat. The north wall in my design is poured concrete, which supports the roof, retains sheltering earth berms and collects heat from the clerestory windows. Interior mass walls, both poured concrete and cinder block, support the roof structure, divide the space and collect heat. Partition walls are 8 ft. high. The

spaces between the top of the walls and the ceiling are either open or glazed to admit sunlight into the northern rooms.

The foundation was insulated below grade with sprayed-on, high-density polyurethane foam, 3 in. thick at grade, tapering to 1 in. at the footing, where temperatures are less extreme. Z-shaped flashing protects the exposed edge of the foam. For insulation above grade, we used the Dryvit system *(FHB* #3, p. 8).

After the walls were poured, we screeded about 4 in. of sand to establish the sub-grade, covered it with 4-mil polyethylene for a vapor barrier and then laid down 3 in. of double foil-faced beadboard rated at R-10. Two-inch beadboard at the edges forms a thermal break. Next came 4 in. of sand, in which we laid plumbing supply pipes and electrical conduit. The sand, an excellent base on which to pour the 4-in. slab, protected the insulation during the pour, and increased the mass of the heat sink. The finished floor is Mexican terra-cotta tile in thinset and medium-grey grout. The dark red tile absorbs heat and provides good conductivity to the 8 in. of mass below.

The south wall is post and beam. We placed 4½-in. by 7½-in. select structural fir posts on 6-ft. centers along the south wall. These were tenoned at the top into the rafters, and notched to hold the double 2x4 top plate; we also grooved the posts along their full length to accept tracks for the folding, insulated shutters we were planning to add.

To expose as much mass as possible to the sun, we put the interior window sill only 8 in. above the finished floor. With the sill height established, the entire wall was sheathed with ½-in. CDX plywood. Window frames were fixed to the rough openings, allowing a ¾-in. by ¾-in. rabbet to project 1½ in. beyond the sheathing. The wall was then sheathed again in 1½-in. Thermax for an R-rating of 12, and finally with a layer of roughsawn cedar siding.

I had dreamed of timber-framing the house, but bowed to expediency and built the rafter assemblies on site by laminating three 2x planks. We bolted them together and also used construction adhesive for extra holding power. The two outside pieces of each rafter are 2x10s and the center is a 2x8, giving a 2-in. reveal below. This design allowed us to use standard lengths of lumber and to butt-join and splice them to get the 26 ft. needed for the long run.

The rafter assemblies are supported with 4½-in. by 7½-in. posts at various positions on interior walls. At the last moment, we decided to do away with a freestanding concrete mass wall at the back of the living room because it would constrict the space. But in doing this we eliminated the central support for the roof members in the living room; so I redesigned them and made king-post trusses to span the entire house. The rafter assemblies and trusses were lifted in place by hand; the north end bird's-mouths rest on the wall plates, and the south ends slipped down over the tenons to rest on both the posts and the top plates. Once the rafter assemblies were square and braced, we extended the roof planes with string lines to determine their intersections, and measured di-

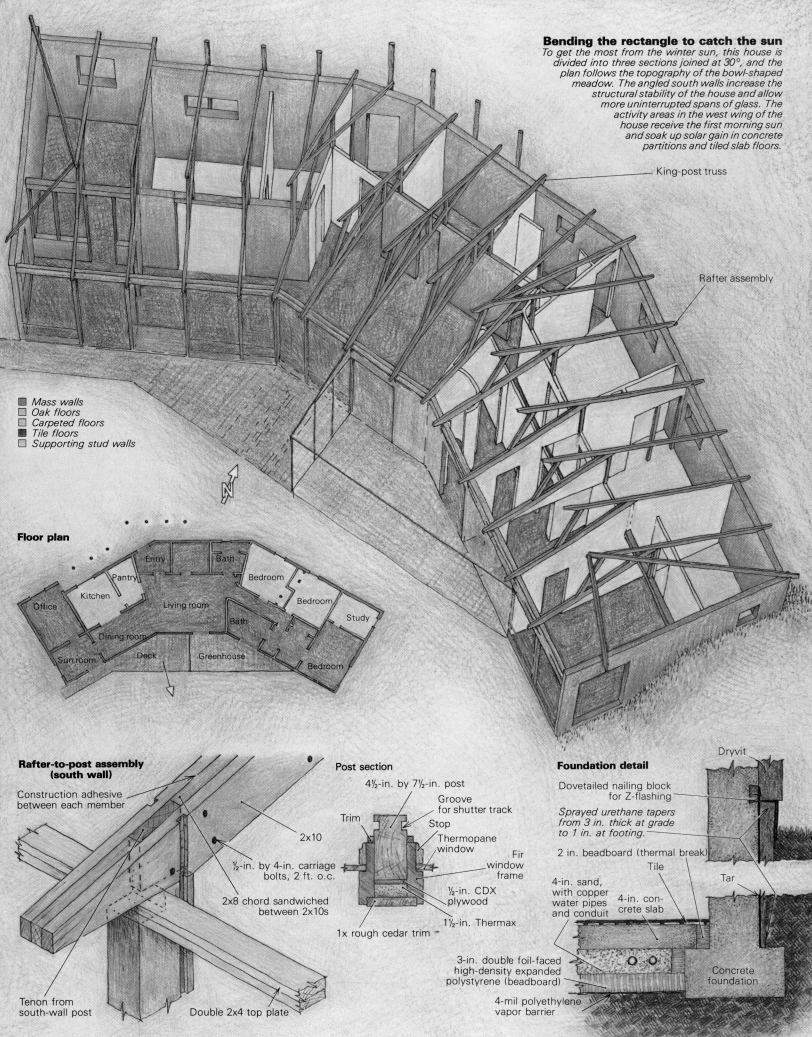

Bending the rectangle to catch the sun
To get the most from the winter sun, this house is divided into three sections joined at 30°, and the plan follows the topography of the bowl-shaped meadow. The angled south walls increase the structural stability of the house and allow more uninterrupted spans of glass. The activity areas in the west wing of the house receive the first morning sun and soak up solar gain in concrete partitions and tiled slab floors.

King-post truss

Rafter assembly

■ Mass walls
□ Oak floors
□ Carpeted floors
■ Tile floors
□ Supporting stud walls

N

Floor plan

Entry
Bath
Pantry
Bedroom
Kitchen
Office
Living room
Bedroom
Dining room
Bath
Study
Sun room
Deck
Greenhouse
Bedroom

Rafter-to-post assembly (south wall)

Construction adhesive between each member

2x10

½-in. by 4-in. carriage bolts, 2 ft. o.c.

2x8 chord sandwiched between 2x10s

Tenon from south-wall post

Double 2x4 top plate

Post section

4½-in. by 7½-in. post

Groove for shutter track

Trim

Stop

Thermopane window

Fir window frame

½-in. CDX plywood

1½-in. Thermax

1x rough cedar trim

Foundation detail

Dryvit

Dovetailed nailing block for Z-flashing

Sprayed urethane tapers from 3 in. thick at grade to 1 in. at footing.

2 in. beadboard (thermal break)

Tile

Tar

4-in. sand, with copper water pipes and conduit

4-in. concrete slab

Concrete foundation

3-in. double foil-faced high-density expanded polystyrene (beadboard)

4-mil polyethylene vapor barrier

Illustrations: Christopher Clapp

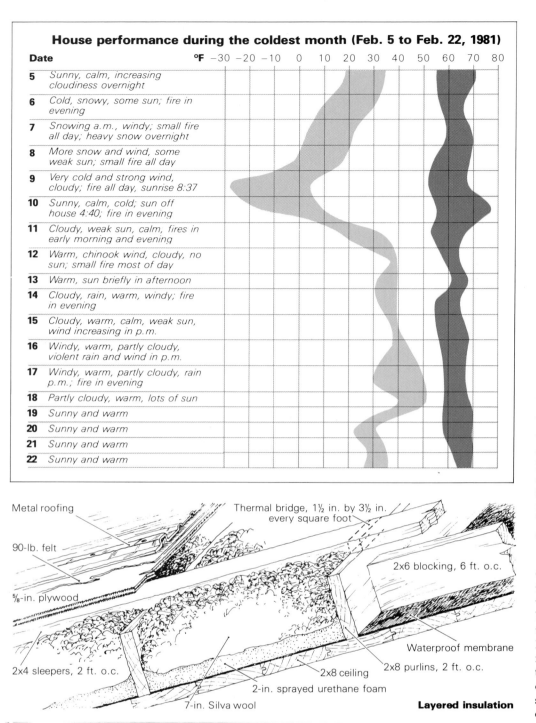

House performance during the coldest month (Feb. 5 to Feb. 22, 1981)

Date		°F −30 −20 −10 0 10 20 30 40 50 60 70 80
5	Sunny, calm, increasing cloudiness overnight	
6	Cold, snowy, some sun; fire in evening	
7	Snowing a.m., windy; small fire all day; heavy snow overnight	
8	More snow and wind, some weak sun; small fire all day	
9	Very cold and strong wind, cloudy; fire all day, sunrise 8:37	
10	Sunny, calm, cold; sun off house 4:40; fire in evening	
11	Cloudy, weak sun, calm, fires in early morning and evening	
12	Warm, chinook wind, cloudy, no sun; small fire most of day	
13	Warm, sun briefly in afternoon	
14	Cloudy, rain, warm, windy; fire in evening	
15	Cloudy, warm, calm, weak sun, wind increasing in p.m.	
16	Windy, warm, partly cloudy, violent rain and wind in p.m.	
17	Windy, warm, partly cloudy, rain p.m.; fire in evening	
18	Partly cloudy, warm, lots of sun	
19	Sunny and warm	
20	Sunny and warm	
21	Sunny and warm	
22	Sunny and warm	

Metal roofing

90-lb. felt

⅝-in. plywood

2x4 sleepers, 2 ft. o.c.

Thermal bridge, 1½ in. by 3½ in. every square foot

2x6 blocking, 6 ft. o.c.

Waterproof membrane

2x8 purlins, 2 ft. o.c.

2x8 ceiling

2-in. sprayed urethane foam

7-in. Silva wool

Layered insulation

Wink Davis

rectly for the two ridge/valley rafter assemblies. We bolted opposing pairs of laminated rafters together through the ridge and valley members and spaced the rafters 6 ft. o.c.

Originally I had planned to insulate the roof myself with a 7-in. blanket of Styrofoam, but to insulate such a large area (3,000 sq. ft.) we needed a period of dry weather. It was early September, raining and threatening to snow when we got to this stage, so I abandoned the first plan. Instead, I decided to hire a contractor to spray 2 in. of urethane over a waterproof membrane of polyethylene and then to add just under 7 in. of Silva wool (a cellulose product by Weyerhauser rated at 3.56 R per in.) to bring the R-value to 40. We toenailed 2x4 furring strips to 2x8 purlins to get the required depth and provide a nailing surface for the roof decking (drawing, left). With this system we waterproofed the roof in two days. The cost of the insulation and its installation was less than the price of the Styrofoam alone.

The project went well, and was finished in the allotted six months. The only delays were caused by rain and by the eruption of Mt. St. Helens, which rained ash across the landscape and brought a Governor's edict that outdoor work cease for several days. My role as owner-builder, for all its pressures and headaches, was very satisfying. Since I controlled the budget and schedule, I could simplify or complicate plans and procedures and save money as well as spend it. On-site changes are usually nightmares for a builder, but in this house I was able to experiment, and I welcomed new products. The house ended up costing $55 per sq. ft., including all materials, labor and utilities.

One year later—We've found that enough sun to cast a shadow can heat the house, although very little heat gets stored. On such days we build a fire in the evening, but we don't bother to bank it overnight because the mass hasn't allowed the living space to cool below 56°F. I monitored the performance briefly, and plotted the results for two weeks in February 1981, the coldest, cloudiest period that winter. Then I stopped, when the results (see chart, above left) confirmed what I suspected.

In that eight-month winter, we burned less than a cord of wood, about a third of it during the chilly, wet and cloudy spring, when the outside temperatures were generally above freezing but the sun refused to shine. In that kind of weather, heat loss is slight, and a small fire takes the damp chill off the air. We used no electric heat, and our monthly utility bills ran about $25.

The house is bright and pleasant, and the floor plan is convenient. Noise transfer, a familiar complaint of passive solar owners, is the only significant problem. Because we left the house open from one end to the other to allow

Insulating the roof. **Two-by-eight purlins, laid down over a vapor barrier and separated by 2x6 blocking, provide space for sprayed urethane foam and loose Silva wool insulation. The two-day job cost less than the original plan to use rigid foam-board insulation.**

When the owners decided to eliminate an interior wall, rafter assemblies over the living room, above, were transformed into king-post trusses. The open spaces atop the partition walls allow heat to circulate.

for heat circulation, noise carries freely. In an effort to remedy this, I installed fixed glass at the back of the living room, an expensive and not entirely successful solution to the problem. To this extent the house is still evolving.

Ironically, passive solar necessitates an active relationship. You must be prepared to light a fire, open and close windows and insulated shutters, put on a sweater when it's chilly and take it off when the sun comes out. We know when and where the sun rises at various times of the year, and we pay close attention to temperatures, precipitation and wind. We have to be acutely attuned to the changes of season. For me, the experience of being close to the natural forces around us is the most exciting aspect of our passive solar house. □

Wink Davis designs and builds passive solar homes in southwestern Montana.

A post-and-beam porch shelters the entry at the northwest corner. At grade level, Z-shaped flashing protects the insulated foundation. Metal roofing was chosen for its appearance, relatively low cost, longevity, fire resistance and its ability to shed snow. The material is quickly fastened with self-tapping, neoprene-washered hexhead screws.

'Imagine a simple greenhouse, attached to a living room, turned to the winter sun, and filled with shelves for flowers and vegetables. It has an entrance from the house—so you can go into it and use it in the winter without going outdoors, and it has an entrance from the garden—so you can use it as a workshop while you are out in the garden and not have to walk through the house.

'This greenhouse then becomes a wonderful place: a source of life, a place where flowers can be grown as part of the life of the house.

'For someone who has not experienced a greenhouse as an extension of the house, it may be hard to recognize how fundamental it becomes. It is a world unto itself, as definite and wonderful as fire or water, and it provides an experience which can hardly be matched by any other pattern.'
—Christopher Alexander, *A Pattern Language*

Sunspaces

A solarium specialist takes a close look
at the many factors involved in
designing a solar addition

by Richard MacMath

Many of us have imagined such a sunspace as Alexander describes, and yet truly successful sunspaces aren't that easy to find. The design factors that go into a good sunspace are fairly complex. We've learned that a careful evaluation of design goals and system components is crucial. The reward is, as Alexander says, an unmatchable experience.

Here at Sunstructures, we've completed dozens of sunspace additions, each one a bit different from the others. We classify our designs into four groups, according to glazing configuration: primarily overhead glazing, primarily vertical glazing, a combination of sloped and vertical glazing, and freeform solariums designed specifically for "off-south" applications (see the design portfolio that begins on the next page).

Defining design goals—Sunspaces can also be classified according to primary function. Some sunspaces are mainly living spaces—a rec room or living-room addition for a growing family. We use the word "solarium" to describe this sort of room. Other sunspaces are meant for plant cultivation. Those we call greenhouses. Sunspaces that are used for plants and living space are sometimes called conservatories.

Whatever the use or name, in northern climates these additions have another important function—to provide solar heat gain during the winter. These sunspaces generally employ the "direct-gain" concept of passive-solar heating.

Although there are many prefabricated sunspace kits available, we prefer to custom-design our sunspaces, using wood framing and standard glazing. With a custom-design service, we have the flexibility to fulfill the differing requirements of site, client and budget. We can also select finish materials that are compatible with existing finishes. As a result, most of the sunspace additions that we do don't look like additions after they're built.

All solariums have the same basic components—south glazing, ventilation units, thermal-storage mass, air-moving equipment and controls and (in most cases) back-up heating. Depending upon the type of glazing used, some solariums also require insulating shades or shutters for large glazed areas.

Glazing materials—The south-facing glazing can be any light-transmitting material—glass, fiberglass or various acrylics. Glass is usually the least expensive, regardless of the number of panes used (although some fiberglass products cost about the same). Where local codes require that all overhead glass be laminated, glass will cost about the same as acrylic glazing. Glass and acrylics are transparent, whereas fiberglass and other materials are translucent. With applications that require diffuse light rather than direct light (such as growing plants for food), or where privacy is important, translucent glazing may be more desirable than transparent glazing.

Two important considerations in selecting a glazing material are its transmissivity and its reaction to long-term exposure to direct sunlight. Standard glass transmits 80% to 85% of the solar spectrum (the remainder is reflected or absorbed), compared to 90% to 95% for special

"low-iron" glass. (Unlike ordinary glass, low-iron glass doesn't have green-colored edges.) Many fiberglass products, although translucent, claim a transmissivity of 90% to 95%.

Most non-glass materials suffer molecular deterioration under long-term exposure to the ultraviolet (UV) range of the solar spectrum. This means that after three or four years, many of these materials will begin to turn yellow, reducing their transmissivity and detracting from the overall appearance of the sunspace. When specifying any non-glass glazing material, be certain it is UV-resistant.

Most non-glass materials have the advantages of being shatterproof, lightweight and easy to cut and handle. Coefficients of expansion can vary, however, so you should check the manufacturer's specifications. Where storm damage or vandalism are a major concern, then these materials should be used, at least for the exterior pane of a double-pane unit.

New glazing and window products are now being introduced that will combine high transmission characteristics with high insulating values. Researchers at the Solar Energy Research Institute (1617 Cole Blvd., Golden, Colo. 80401) are developing glazings that can be programmed to regulate the amount of sunlight transmitted during summer and winter. SERI technicians have predicted insulating values in the R-10 to R-12 range. In the near future, an R-10 window with a transmissivity of 90% might be the standard.

For the last two years, we have been installing quad-pane units in most of our solariums (see *FHB* #20, p. 22). These units have two acrylic membranes sealed between two panes of 1/8-in. double-strength or tempered glass. The total thickness of the glazing unit is 1½ in. to 1¾ in., depending on the manufacturer. The transmissivity of the inner membranes is approximately 95%, giving the whole quad-pane unit a transmissivity of 65%, a little better than a standard triple-pane window. The three insulating airspaces give these units an R-value of almost 4. Quad-pane windows are comparable in cost to triple-pane windows, or double-pane windows with night insulation (either insulated shades or thermal shutters).

Orientation and tilt—For a solarium to provide a substantial amount of solar heating, its glazing should ideally be oriented due south. There are many instances, however, when this isn't possible. An orientation 20° to 25° off of true south will decrease performance by 5% to 10%. A solarium addition is usually constructed on the south wall of the home, although an addition on the east or west sides of the home can also have a large south-facing wall and roof surface. In the latter cases, the solarium "connection" to the home may not be as efficient as a south-side solarium.

The tilt of the glazing material is critical in providing a comfortable interior environment all year. Most solarium and greenhouse kits are designed with the overhead glass at a very shallow slope—about 20° (4-in-12 roof pitch). In northern climates, glazing sloped 20° will reflect most of the winter sunlight and transmit most of the summer sunlight—just the opposite of what

should occur. The optimum tilt from the horizontal for overhead glazing is the latitude of the site plus 5° to 15°. For example, most of our projects are built at a latitude of 40° to 45° N. Consequently, we install overhead glass at an angle of 45° to 60° from the horizontal. Anything below 45° slope at our latitude will cause severe overheating in the summer.

Most research shows that in winter, the solar heat gain through a vertical glazing unit is slightly higher than through a 45° tilt and only slightly lower than through a 60° tilt. In winter, therefore, there is little difference in solar heat gain with glazing installed anywhere from a 45° tilt to vertical. However, in summer, there is a major difference in the amount of sunlight transmitted through overhead sloped glazing and vertical glazing. For example, at noon on June 21 (summer solstice), sloped double-pane glass transmits 70% of available sunlight. Vertical double-pane glass transmits only 40% of available sunlight. This is one of the reasons why you may see solariums with only vertical glazing.

There is a qualitative difference between overhead glazing and vertical glazing. With overhead glass, you feel that you are more a part of the outdoors when you step into the space. You can look up and see the treetops and clouds during the day, and the moon and stars at night. With only vertical glass, even though it may be floor to ceiling, you feel as if you are still inside the house, rather than being out.

Passive ventilation—Although most of the glazing units can be fixed (non-operable), some operable units should be installed to allow natural ventilation in the solarium from spring through autumn. The two most effective means of passive ventilation are to provide cross ventilation (horizontal air flow) and stack-effect ventilation (vertical air flow) from the floor to ceiling or roof.

Cross ventilation promotes interior air movement by connecting high and low-pressure areas of the exterior: windows located on the windward and leeward sides of the room or building. Assuming the summer breezes are coming out of the west or southwest, operable windows or doors should be installed on the east and west walls of a solarium. If that isn't possible, operable windows located in the east and west ends of the south wall will also do, especially if these windows are casement windows.

Research has shown that better ventilation occurs when the air stream changes direction within the room, rather than flowing directly from inlet to outlet. Casement windows, when opened in the corners of the room, help create artificial pressure and suction zones along the south wall, thus promoting cross ventilation. Another advantage of casement windows is that their swing-out design gives them a clear opening area twice that of a comparably sized double-hung or sliding window.

Stack-effect ventilation occurs when warm air rises and is exhausted out of the room through a high opening in the ceiling, room or wall of the solarium. Again, assuming that the prevailing summer breezes are out of the west and southwest, vertical air flow is best achieved by a low

A design portfolio

The five essential solarium components—south-facing glazing, vent units, thermal-storage mass, air-moving equipment and backup heating—and one optional component—night insulation—can be combined in many different ways to produce a variety of solarium designs. Probably the most common type of solarium features sloped glazing. The solarium in the top photo at left is a good example. It's a simple 18-ft. by 10-ft. rectangular-plan addition, attached to the south wall of the house. The sloped glazing units are standard, double-pane, patio-door panels (46 in. by 76 in.), installed at a 45° tilt. Two south-facing awning windows provide ventilation, along with a door and windows located on the east and west walls. Thermal-storage mass is provided by a 6-in. thick, tinted concrete slab. Additional mass is provided by black-painted, 55-gal. drums filled with water. As the photo top right shows, this sunspace is primarily a greenhouse. Small fans above the glazing draw warm air from the solarium through ducts installed between the floor joists, warming the north side of the house. Chain-operated insulating shades over the glass reduce heat loss at night and on cloudy days.

In its simplest form, the shed roof for the solarium can be a continuation of the main roof of the house, as in the middle and bottom photos at right. Here again we used standard-size insulated glass patio-door units, but in two vertical layers. In the east and west walls and at both ends of the south wall, we used large casement windows for ventilation. One large, automatic insulating curtain, 20 ft. wide and 13 ft. high, covers all the south fixed glass at night. The roof shingles over the addition are as close a match for the original shingles as we could find, and the addition's finish siding aligns perfectly with the existing siding and is a good color match. The solarium looks very much a part of the house, and this is often an important design goal for us.

For one-story homes, or if it is

Sloped glazing is desirable for greenhouses because it maximizes solar exposure. The 18-ft. by 10-ft. addition shown above has low awning windows for ventilation and fixed, double-pane patio-door glass, angled at 45°. Inside, right, a tinted concrete slab and water-filled 55-gal. drums provide solar mass. *Vertical glazing* is better for solariums that are to be used as living space because there's less chance of overheating. Below, shed-roof additions can often be built as a continuation of the main house roof.

not practical to extend the existing roof, a hip roof or gable-roof solarium addition is often the best design solution. The gable-roof solarium addition shown in the photo at right is a good example of this strategy. Here we used primarily fixed double-pane glass on the south-facing gable, including some custom-made triangular units. Casement vent units are provided near the corners on the east and west walls. An operable east side skylight encourages stack-effect ventilation, and dark tiles over an insulated, poured-slab floor provide thermal mass.

Of course, many solariums employ a combination of sloped and vertical glazing. The photo below shows a food-producing greenhouse with a substantial amount of both sloped and vertical glazing. The house is connected to the solarium through doors and windows on the main level. The ground floor is used for plant cultivation, workspace and storage. Cross ventilation is provided by

Above, a gabled solarium is an alternative to a shed-roof design. Window-quilt insulation (below right) can be built into the framework. *Vertical and sloped* glazing are often combined in food-producing greenhouses like the one at bottom left. A *freeform* solarium is the only choice when the orientation and shape of the house make it impossible to design a full southern exposure. The quarter-round addition shown at bottom right spans between a southeast-facing wall and a southwest-facing wall.

windows and doors in the east and west ends of the south wall.

Occasionally, the part of the house where a client wants a solarium addition doesn't have walls that face within 20° to 25° of true south. To solve this problem, we're likely to come up with what we call a freeform design, like the one shown in the photo at bottom right. The owners wanted a family-room solarium near the back of the house, with at least some of the glazing facing true south. Our solution was a quarter-circle addition that connects a southeast-facing wall with a southwest-facing wall. This was the best way we could get most of the glazing to face within 30° of true south.

Ventilation is achieved with low awning units beneath fixed glass, with operable skylights in the solarium roof, and with high casement windows in an adjacent room. Obviously, this form looks different from the rest of the house, so it is finished in stained wood siding, with no attempt to match exterior finishes. —R. M.

opening on the pressure, or windward, side of the solarium, and a high opening on the suction, or leeward, side. The low opening can be awning or casement windows on the west or south walls, and the high opening is usually a north or east-facing operable skylight. A high window in the east wall or even a cupola would be just as effective. It is important to place the high opening on the leeward side of the solarium. If it is located on the windward side, the exterior air pressure will have to be overcome by the interior air as it is being vented from the room. This will reduce the velocity and amount of the air being ventilated.

In our sunspaces, usually about 80% of the south-wall glazing is fixed, and 20% of the south-wall glazing is operable. We install as many east and west vent units as is practical. We also include one or two skylights on the roof.

Thermal storage—To reduce the temperature fluctuations in the solarium and for storing heat into the evening hours, thermal-storage mass should be part of the solarium design. Masonry materials are the most common choices, but containers of water can also be used. Whatever mass is used, it should be located in direct sunlight for optimum performance.

The most common method of providing thermal mass is to install a well-insulated concrete slab floor. The slab should have a dark surface color, which can be achieved either by integral tinting or painting. A more expensive alternative is to install a dark tile finish floor over the slab. A rule of thumb is to use from 1 to 2 cu. ft. of concrete or masonry for every square foot of south-facing glass. In very sunny climates, we would recommend as much storage capacity as possible. In cloudy climates like our own (the Great Lakes region), we use about 1 cu. ft. of concrete or masonry mass per sq. ft. of south-facing glass. For direct-gain rooms, this usually means that we pour a 6-in. thick slab, with 2 in. of rigid insulation around the perimeter and beneath the slab. The quantity of heat stored in the slab is determined by the volume of storage mass, the amount of solar radiation transmitted, the absorptance (determined by color) of the surface, the specific heat and density of the material, and the rate of heat loss of the space.

Another method for storing heat in the slab is often called an "air-radiant system." Warm air, usually drawn from the highest point in the solarium, is circulated through tubes or ducts built into the slab. Heat is transferred to the slab, and the ducts return the air to a register near the south wall where it can again be heated (see *FHB* #30, pp. 50-54).

Air-radiant systems are usually more effective in preventing overheating during the spring and fall and maintaining even, comfortable temperatures all year round. This is because the heat is transferred from the air in the room to a large surface area of mass in the floor slab. For ductwork in air-radiant systems, we have used plastic drain tile, PVC pipe or a below-grade quality metal. Obviously, the metal ducts have better thermal contact with the concrete slab, but are much more expensive. Depending upon the desired air velocity and volume (cubic feet

In this solarium, a slab floor covered with tile and a brick chimney comprise thermal mass. An operable skylight promotes ventilation.

per minute, or cfm), the duct should be 4 in. to 6 in. in dia. To accommodate ductwork of this size and to provide enough thermal mass, air-radiant slabs should be poured at least 10 in. to 12 in. thick.

Air-moving equipment—The fourth important component for all solariums is some type of air-moving equipment. With the air-radiant slab described above, a thermostatically controlled blower draws the air from the solarium to the duct manifold in the slab.

Even in a simple direct-gain structure, some air circulation is desirable, both winter and summer. On clear winter days, it may be necessary to reduce the amount of heat gain in the solarium. This can be done with small, through-the-wall fans that distribute warm air to other rooms in the home, either directly or through ducts. We've installed conventional manually operated kitchen and bathroom exhaust fans, as well as special thermostatically controlled, reversible solarium fans for this purpose. Reversible fans enable you to push warm solarium air into the house, or move heated air from the house into the solarium.

On hot, humid summer afternoons with little or no breeze, an overhead paddle fan or an exhaust fan can circulate air and help to cool the space. We often install a 36-in. to 48-in. dia. two-speed paddle fan at the highest point in the solarium. The fan moves air in the space for summer cooling, as well as returning warm air to the floor level in the winter. A high-volume exhaust fan can also be installed to provide one

or two air changes every few minutes, but these are often unsightly and noisy.

If the solarium is to be used as a living space, you have to consider its heating system. The main-house heating system can be modified to serve the solarium, or an auxiliary heating system, such as a woodstove or electric baseboard, can be added.

With or without a heating system, controls are needed to modulate temperature, distribute heat and adjust ventilation. They can be as simple as manually operated vents or as complex as programmable electronic thermostats and motor-driven skylights and windows. In many of our designs, fans that move warm air from the solarium to other parts of the house are actuated by thermostats. When solarium air reaches a predetermined temperature, the fan comes on to distribute the heat. During the summer, exhaust fans can operate the same way, pushing warm air outside the living space.

Night insulation—We consider insulating shades or shutters an optional feature, depending on the type of glazing used. The insulating value for double or triple-pane windows will range from R-2 to R-3. With a good insulating shade, curtain or shutter in place, the total R-value will be in the range of 5 to 10, depending upon the particular product used and how well it is sealed around the edges. Night insulation can reduce heat loss by as much as 75%. However, if you analyze the performance of a double-pane unit with night insulation over a 24-hour period (assuming that the insulating shade is open eight hours on a clear winter day and drawn 16 hours that day), you will find that the average insulating value over the period (day and night) is approximately R-4 to R-5. The insulating value of quad-pane units is R-4. Therefore, if the cost is approximately equal, quad-pane glazing units preclude the need for nighttime insulating devices.

Costs—The cost of building a solarium will depend on many factors—its size, whether it is a plant space or a finished living space, the quality of the finish materials, who provides the labor, and its eligibility for local, state and federal tax credits. We have built solariums ranging in cost from $6,000 to $40,000. For estimates, we use a cost-per-square-foot figure, which includes all materials and contracted labor. For good-quality materials that will last the lifetime of the house and all labor costs, a finished, living-space solarium will average between $40 to $100 per sq. ft.

When discussing costs, we rarely dwell on payback calculations for a given project. It's certainly possible to design for maximum solar heating (and thus shorten payback), but it's wrong to define a solarium's benefits strictly in terms of money. If well designed and built, a solarium can be one of the nicest rooms in the house. On a sunny day in February, it's the warmest and brightest place to work, read, or just sit and watch the world go by outside. □

Richard MacMath is a builder and principal of Sunstructures, Inc., in Ann Arbor, Mich. Photos by the author.

Superinsulating the Non-Box

Truss joists and strapping create thick walls in a curved house

by Ed McGrath

Fairbanks, Alaska, sits just below the 65th parallel, and averages nearly 15,000 heating degree days a year. For obvious reasons, the area has long been an unofficial center for superinsulated building design. Mark Fejes and his partner Ellie Brown, the principals in a local design and contracting firm, are committed to superinsulated houses but don't like conservative, box-like structures. Their designs favor curves and structural post-and-beam construction, two features that can make it difficult to superinsulate.

After designing and building several unconventionally shaped houses, Fejes and Brown have worked out some solid construction details that enable them to superinsulate effectively and economically. They use prefabricated trusses to build a wide wall cavity outside of their post-and-beam frames. These Truss-Joist I-beams, or TJ-Is, can be ordered in various widths and lengths from most lumberyards. Incorporating them in a house design calls for some special detailing, especially with curved walls. Fejes has found that for building superinsulated walls and roofs, TJ-Is are faster and more effective than double-stud construction, even if the house is squarish.

Construction of a recent house began in the fall of 1981, after the firm acquired two acres of land high on a south-sloping hill north of town. For purposes of energy efficiency, the site was ideal, with more sunshine and warmer winter temperatures than in the valley below, where official weather data is recorded. Around Fairbanks, the air mass stratifies in deep winter, with the coldest air pooling on the valley floor, in the downtown area, and warmer, lighter air stacking itself on top. Thus Fejes used −50°F and 12,000 heating degree days in calculating heating requirements, rather than −60°F and 15,000. The soil on this hillside is also considerably warmer than in the valley. There is no permafrost (soil that stays frozen year round), and the hillside is well drained, with a frost line at about 4 ft.

Slab and frame—The plan of the house is based on an 8-ft. by 16-ft. grid, with joists spanning the 16-ft. distance, and 6x8 timbers making the 8-ft. span. The curved sections

Energy consultant Ed McGrath is the author of The Superinsulated House, *published by That New Publishing Co. (1525 Eielson St., Fairbanks, Alaska 99701).*

The vertical siding of this circular house hides a superinsulated wall built with Truss-Joist I-beams (TJ-Is) and 1x4 strapping. Alaska's harsh climate makes insulated sunspaces impractical, so the solarium is single glazed.

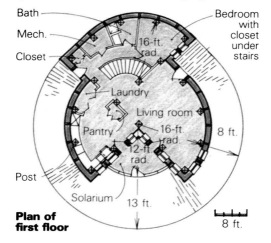

Plan of first floor

have a radius of 16 ft., conforming to the grid. Removing a south-facing slice from this circle made room for a wedge-shaped solarium with a 12-ft. radius (photo above).

Since the house was to have an insulated, concrete-slab floor, excavation at the site was minimal. Using a transit and a pocket calculator, Fejes and his crew located the structure's circular outline on the compacted ground and dug 4-ft. deep holes for the 19 poured-concrete piers that would support the major posts of the frame. All but two of the posts and their piers are located on rough 8-ft. centers around the perimeter of the building (drawing, above). The 8-ft. spacing between

posts meant no allowance had to be made at this point for framing in doors and windows.

Fejes built up the forms for the piers so that they would be even with the poured-concrete floor, keeping the bases of the posts above the concrete. The original plan for the house had been to pour the piers and slab before erecting the frame, but bad weather and highway load restrictions forced Fejes and Brown to reverse this order. Two ½-in. dia. pins were set into the top of each poured form to prevent the posts from twisting.

Except for several 24-ft. 6x12 beams of Sitka spruce that were brought in from the coast, Fejes built the entire frame for the structure from rough-cut local white spruce. Because this wood shrinks too much for traditional timber-frame joinery (up to ⅟₁₆ in. per inch of thickness), Fejes made structural connections between joining timbers with site-made joist hangers, and with homemade gusset plates of ¼-in. thick steel and lag bolts. A self-taught welder, Fejes fashioned angled gusset plates on site as they were needed.

Using the gussets, bents were assembled on the ground and then hoisted up on their piers and braced temporarily with diagonals. Most bents consisted of only four members: two perimeter posts located on opposite sides of the wall, and the ceiling and second-floor beams connecting them (photo, next page). After all of the bents were up, the crew nailed down a pine tongue-and-groove roof deck and installed the second floor. Metal strapping was nailed up diagonally to the outside face of the frame for racking resistance, and joist hangers were used to tie floor joists to horizontal 6x8 frame members.

The crew then began work on the radiant slab that would be the ground floor of the building. (For construction details, see the drawing on the next page.) First, 2-in. thick Styrofoam sheets were laid over 6 in. of compacted gravel, with an extra 2 in. of foam placed around the perimeter of the house. Then workers built circular forms to contain the poured slab.

About 1,500 ft. of ¾-in. dia. polybutylene tubing was placed on top of the blue Styrofoam. The tubing, which would later carry boiler-heated antifreeze through the slab, was laid down in a serpentine pattern, with both ends of six different lengths converging above final floor level in the boiler room.

After grading 2 in. of D1 gravel over the

The 6x6 posts of the completed frame sit on poured-concrete piers that extend below the 4-ft. frost line. Site-made steel gussets or angle braces are used at each connection of the post-and-beam frame. At this stage, the forms for the poured-slab floor are being built, and rigid foam insulation boards are being positioned inside them. The bases of the roughsawn spruce posts are temporarily wrapped in black poly to protect them from concrete splatters.

Construction details for walls and roof

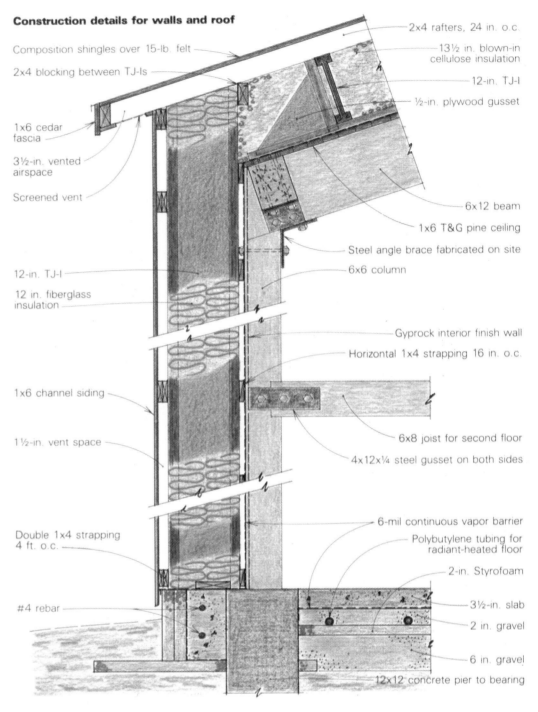

Composition shingles over 15-lb. felt

2x4 blocking between TJ-Is

1x6 cedar fascia

3½-in. vented airspace

Screened vent

12-in. TJ-I

12 in. fiberglass insulation

1x6 channel siding

1½-in. vent space

Double 1x4 strapping 4 ft. o.c.

#4 rebar

2x4 rafters, 24 in. o.c.

13½ in. blown-in cellulose insulation

12-in. TJ-I

½-in. plywood gusset

6x12 beam

1x6 T&G pine ceiling

Steel angle brace fabricated on site

6x6 column

Gyprock interior finish wall

Horizontal 1x4 strapping 16 in. o.c.

6x8 joist for second floor

4x12x¼ steel gusset on both sides

6-mil continuous vapor barrier

Polybutylene tubing for radiant-heated floor

2-in. Styrofoam

3½-in. slab

2 in. gravel

6 in. gravel

12x12 concrete pier to bearing

pipe, a 6-mil vapor barrier was laid down. Then the crew set up rebar and called in the ready-mix truck to pour a 3½-in. slab.

Constructing the cavity—At this point, the building's structural system was complete. Fejes' next job was to build, on the outside of this superstructure, a cavity for holding insulation, with a vapor barrier on its warm, interior side and ventilation beneath its outside face. The crew began by laying a 6-mil polyethylene sheet on the roof deck and backing every post and perimeter beam with a 2-ft. wide strip of the same material. The edges of these strips would later be folded and taped to the edges of the larger sheets installed beneath the gypboard interior finish walls.

The crew skip-sheathed the outside of the frame with 1x4s, which were bent to the curve of the house as they were nailed on 16-in. centers to the outside edges of the posts (photo facing page, top). This curved strapping served two purposes. Inside the house, both the poly vapor barrier and the gypboard walls were attached to it. Outside the post-and-beam frame, 12-in. deep TJ-Is were attached vertically to the 1x4s on 4-ft. centers. The 1½-in. by 2¼-in. laminated feet of the TJ-Is are connected with a central web of ⅜-in. plywood. The TJ-Is extend the full height of the building, creating a cavity that is filled with unfaced fiberglass batts.

This type of wood I-beam truss is usually used structurally, but in Fejes' design, it serves more as a spacer. The only load the trusses carry is that of the siding. Thermally, TJ-Is are a good choice, since the section of wood extending through the wall is just ⅜ in. thick, amounting to only 1% of the wall's surface area, compared to the usual 12% to 20% for standard framing. And the 4-ft. spacing between TJ-Is left room for doors and windows between framing members.

Next, the crew nailed a double layer of 1x4 skip sheathing to the outside face of the TJ-Is, bending the boards horizontally around the

house on 48-in. centers (middle photo, facing page). This time, Fejes found that while a single 1x4 thickness was rigid enough, the curve wasn't uniform where one board butted another. So another layer was added, its joints staggered over those of the first layer.

Rough openings for windows and doors were framed between the TJ-Is, and Fejes used ½-in. fir plywood to build the extra-wide jambs. Then the walls were insulated with two layers of 6-in. thick fiberglass. The crew staggered the courses so that cracks between layers wouldn't line up. Finally, local roughsawn 1x6 channel siding was nailed vertically over building paper for the exterior finish wall.

On the roof, TJ-Is were used again to create a cavity for insulation. The crew first nailed down 2x4s over the plastic vapor barrier covering the ceiling deck. The 2x4s were located parallel with the roof beams and on 4-ft. cen-

ters. This spacing allowed every other 2x4 to fall on a roof beam. The 2x4 furring allowed workers to walk on the roof safely and without damaging the vapor barrier.

The workers then nailed down 12-in. deep TJ-Is perpendicular to the 2x4s, on 4-ft. centers. To strengthen the upright position of the TJ-Is, Fejes and his crew used triangular plywood braces on every other 2x4, nailing each brace to both 2x4 and TJ-I.

Next, 2x4 rafters on 24-in. centers were fastened to the TJ-Is with nails and hurricane clips (bottom photo, facing page). Before the ⅝-in. plywood roof deck was nailed down, 13½ in. of cellulose was blown in between the TJ-Is. In this design, the trusses run perpendicular to the roof slopes and thus act as baffles, preventing the loose insulation from settling or slipping off the 3½-in-12 roof.

As shown in the drawing, the 3½-in. air-

Construction photos: Mark Fejes; Illustrations: Peter Jennings

Superinsulating with trusses. Top, with the ceiling and second floor done, vapor-barrier strips are installed against the outside faces of all perimeter posts. These strips will later be lapped against larger sheets that will cover the walls. The perimeter posts are then skip-sheathed with horizontal 1x4s on 16-in. centers. The 1x4s bent around the frame will serve as a nailing surface for the interior drywall. Middle, 12-in. deep TJ-Is are nailed vertically to the 1x4 strapping on 4-ft. centers, creating the insulation cavity that will be filled with fiberglass batts. The wall TJ-Is are then skip-sheathed with a double layer of 1x4s that serve as nailers for the roughsawn 1x6 channel siding. On the roof, which has a black vapor barrier, TJ-Is are installed perpendicular to the slope, on 4-ft. centers. As shown in the bottom photo and the drawing, facing page, 2x4 rafters are nailed on 24-in. centers to the tops of the roof TJ-Is to hold sheathing and shingles.

space between the rafters and above the cellulose was left open and extends from low eave to high eave. Screened vents in the soffits all around the house ensure adequate ventilation.

Once the roof was shingled, all that remained to complete the structural and thermal work was to build the solarium and install windows and doors. In most parts of Alaska, insulated sunspaces are impractical. The sun isn't out long enough to warm much of anything during the winter; and in summer, extended daylight (up to 21 hours) makes overheating a problem. Only during a few weeks of spring and fall does an insulated sunspace work as it's supposed to. For this reason, Fejes simply framed up the solarium with 2x4s and ordered single-pane glass for the openings. Generous double-pane glazing in the superinsulated walls backing the sunspace allow for some solar gain inside the house, and Fejes' strategy of using operable windows between fixed-glass windows saved money without sacrificing ventilation appreciably.

To keep the vapor barrier as tight as possible, Fejes used surface-mounted electrical outlet boxes on all exterior walls instead of conventional, flush-mounted boxes, which would have required cutting into the barrier. The plastic-sheathed cable was still run behind the poly, but at every outlet location, the cable was pushed through a small hole in the sheet and caulked in place.

The tightness of the house called for an air-to-air heat exchanger to push the building's air-change rate to a safe .5 per hour. But neither Fejes nor Brown could find a unit that they trusted to operate at extremely cold temperatures. Nevertheless, ductwork was installed throughout the house so that when a suitable heat exchanger is found, it can be installed easily. In the meantime, vent fans in kitchen and bathrooms and the operable windows provide adequate, though less energy-efficient, ventilation.

Happily for Fejes and Brown, the house was sold just as the interior finish work began. The buyer, an architect and facilities planner at the University of Alaska, was intrigued by the house's superinsulated circular design and excited about doing the better part of the finish work himself. □

An A.O.B. House
Meticulously finished, energy-efficient
and built to an Alternative Owner Builder code

by Timothy Clark

I still remember my anxiety on the morning the earth-moving equipment arrived. Until then, Greg and Nancy Kornbergs' new house had existed only on paper. I'm sure I didn't instill much confidence when I asked Greg, "You mean, you're really going through with this?"

After all, the house was unconventional in design and intricately detailed, and would be built primarily with the help of self-taught carpenters. From its terraced foundation to its furniture-quality roof, it would take years to complete. I knew, because I designed it.

Moving out—When I first met with Greg and Nancy, they were living with their two girls in

a small cabin in the coastal mountains of Northern California, well off the utility grid. Built during the early 1970s, the cabin had once served two comfortably, but a family of four was another matter. It was time to build a new house nearby and to convert the old one into a guest house.

Greg would be the contractor and foreman on the job. Nancy would be an experienced helper. Appropriately, the new house would be built in compliance with Humbolt County's "Alternative Owner Builder" (A. O. B.) code. An A. O. B. permit would not only allow more design flexibility than a standard permit (a critical element in this remote location), but

would also cut the cost of the permit itself (for more on the A. O. B. code, see the sidebar on the facing page).

A terraced plan—My first step in the design process was to commission a complete topographic survey of the building site. The survey showed the lay of the land and the exact locations of trees, boulders and other landmarks. Based on the survey, we decided to place the new house below the old one, on a 28% grade that levels out to a large flat area at its base. This would expose the house to spectacular views of the Eel River Valley and the Kings Range to the west, and preserve most of the

Drawings: Gary Williamson

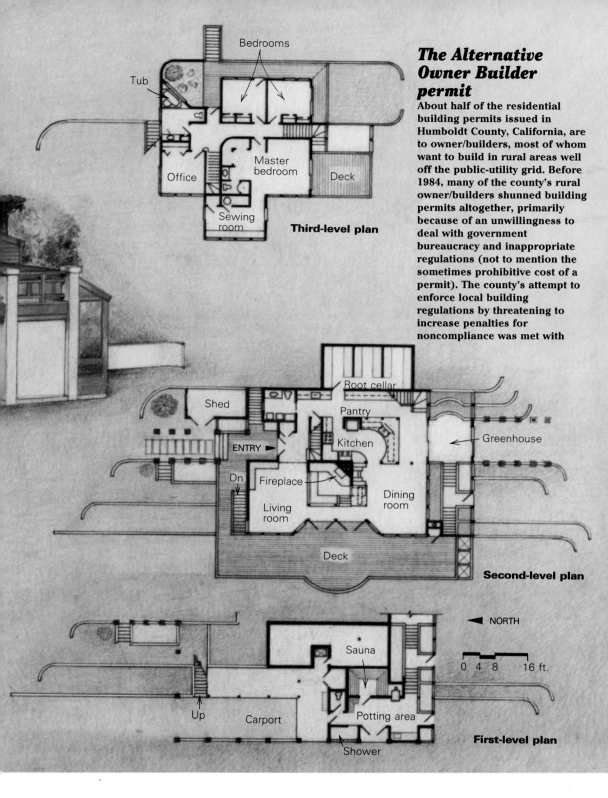

Third-level plan

Bedrooms

Tub

Office

Master bedroom

Deck

Sewing room

Second-level plan

Shed

Root cellar

Pantry

ENTRY ▶

Kitchen

Greenhouse

Dn

Fireplace

Living room

Dining room

Deck

First-level plan

◀ NORTH

Sauna

0 4 8   16 ft.

Up

Carport

Potting area

Shower

The Alternative Owner Builder permit

About half of the residential building permits issued in Humboldt County, California, are to owner/builders, most of whom want to build in rural areas well off the public-utility grid. Before 1984, many of the county's rural owner/builders shunned building permits altogether, primarily because of an unwillingness to deal with government bureaucracy and inappropriate regulations (not to mention the sometimes prohibitive cost of a permit). The county's attempt to enforce local building regulations by threatening to increase penalties for noncompliance was met with tremendous public opposit[ion?]. long series of meetings between county officials and a citizens' advisory group resulted in the adoption in 1984 of the Alternative Owner Builder (A. O. B.) permit.

Essentially an A. O. B. permit allows an owner/builder living outside the service area of a public water or sewer district to build any dwelling that does not abnormally endanger health or safety. The few rules associated with the permit govern only such critical features as fireplaces, sewage disposal systems and electrical systems. The regulations do *not* control design, structural standards, building materials or construction techniques. An owner/builder can obtain one A. O. B. permit every five years, and can construct anything from a mud hut to a mansion.

The only construction documents needed to obtain an A. O. B. permit are a site plan and a simple floor plan. The only inspections are for sewage disposal, plumbing, wiring and any conditions that directly endanger health and safety. Because of the limited structural requirements and few inspections, the cost of the permit is kept to a minimum (the permit for the house in this article cost about $200).

Since the county adopted the A. O. B. classification, more than 230 of these permits have been issued. There have been no apparent negative repercussions, and the resulting custom homes that I've seen are at least as well designed and well built as their standard counterparts. For more information on the A. O. B. permit, contact United Stand (a helpful citizens' group) at P. O. Box 2642, McKinleyville, Calif. 95521. —*T. C.*

level ground for a septic system, a garden and outdoor recreation.

Two conventional ways to build a house on a slope are to support the house on stilts or to carve a level space for it out of the hillside. I prefer to terrace the slope and the house itself, supporting the house on foundation walls that double as retaining walls. That way, each level of the house has direct access to grade and becomes an intimate part of the landscape.

The Kornbergs' house is divided vertically into three levels, each occupying its own terrace (drawings above). The main entry is on the north end of the second level. The fireplace forms the core of this level, around which are arranged the entry, living room, dining room and kitchen. Behind the kitchen, a 250-sq. ft. root cellar is built into the hillside.

The third level is the private one. It holds the master bedroom and half bath, the two girls' bedrooms, a full bath, an office and a sewing room. Each of the bedrooms has access to the outdoors.

The first level occupies the edge of the flat area, and holds a carport, firewood storage area, plant-potting area, and a sauna accompanied by a dressing area, toilet and a tiled shower that Nancy designed. An attached greenhouse steps up the hillside on the south side of the house, culminating in a 17-ft. high bar-rel-vaulted skylight that's aligned with the upstairs hallway. On all three levels, the foundation walls extend out beyond the house to support and define the terraced yard.

It took me a year to design the house and produce 28 sheets of working drawings. Meantime, Greg installed a spring-fed water system, an 1,800-gal. concrete septic tank and 400 ft. of leach lines.

The cooling tube—Once the heavy equipment started sculpting the hillside, my initial anxiety turned to excitement. It took only two days for a D-8 earth mover and a 3-yd. articulated loader to cut the three terraces. Excavat-

A polished ceiling. Befitting its Craftsman-style motif, the exposed redwood roof framing inside the house is enveloped in six coats of varnish (photo left). For contrast, the ponderosa pine ceiling was stained with boiled linseed oil tinted with yellow oxide, then varnished. During winter, the window wall in the left of the photo admits heat to the house from the adjacent greenhouse.

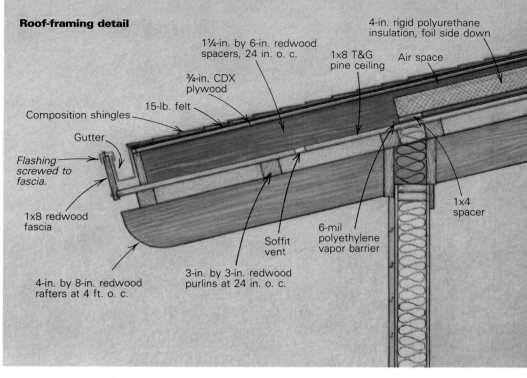

Roof-framing detail

4-in. rigid polyurethane insulation, foil side down

1¼-in. by 6-in. redwood spacers, 24 in. o. c.

1x8 T&G pine ceiling

Air space

¾-in. CDX plywood

15-lb. felt

Composition shingles

Gutter

Flashing screwed to fascia.

1x8 redwood fascia

1x4 spacer

6-mil polyethylene vapor barrier

Soffit vent

4-in. by 8-in. redwood rafters at 4 ft. o. c.

3-in. by 3-in. redwood purlins at 24 in. o. c.

ed earth was pushed to the ends of the terraces to form the parking area and side yards. Topsoil was set aside, and a temporary access road was built for each terrace.

With the terracing completed, Greg spent several weeks on his backhoe digging the foundation/retaining-wall footings and a trench for the cooling tube. The cooling tube is a 2-ft. diameter, 100-ft. long galvanized culvert pipe that's buried several feet in the ground on top of a 4-in. thick layer of gravel. One end of the tube pokes out of the slope on the north side of the house, and the other connects to the cooling/heating plenum inside the house. The cooling system is activated by simply opening vents near the peak of the roof. This exhausts warm air from the house, drawing earth-cooled replacement air in through the tube.

Greg used a cutting torch to put ½-in. holes in the bottom of the cooling tube so that condensation would drain out, and he screened the intake end of the tube to keep out rodents and insects. Later, he installed a rod through the kitchen floor (under the wood cookstove) and connected it to a damper at the plenum, allowing the cooling tube to be closed off easily during winter.

Stacking the foundation—About 2,000 concrete blocks, 200 yd. of concrete and 13 tons of reinforcing steel went into the massive foundation of the house. The footings range in width from 2 ft. 6 in. beneath 4-ft. high walls to 3 ft. 8 in. beneath 8-ft. high walls. Right-angled rebar dowels spaced 16 in. o. c. extend 24 in. out the tops of the footings. These and a keyway lock the footings to concrete-block foundation walls (drawing right).

The foundation walls are surface-bonded concrete block. With this method, the bottom course of block is leveled in mortar, and the rest of the blocks are stacked dry. The walls are then troweled on both sides with a mixture of portland cement and chopped fiberglass (for more on surface-bonded block, see *FHB* #12, pp. 34-37, or "Building with Concrete, Brick and Stone," p. 60, *Fine Homebuilding Builder's Library*, The Taunton Press).

We've found the surface-bonding method to be cost-effective because it requires only semi-skilled labor; with just a few hours of training, most people can stack several hundred blocks a day. The Kornbergs' house is designed on a 4-ft. module, so we used hollow-core "fast blocks" that measure 16 in. long instead of standard blocks, which measure 15⅝ in. long.

The walls were finished with a ⅛-in. thick coat of Surewall surface-bonding cement (W. R. Bonsal Co., Box 241148, Charlotte, N. C. 28224;

704-525-1621). We used standard grey cement on the backs of the walls and a factory-mixed, yellow ocher-colored cement on the visible areas. Immediately after application a large, wet paintbrush was used to smooth the trowel marks, creating a uniform texture.

Surface-bonded block walls are stronger than conventional block walls with mortar joints. Nevertheless, because this is a seismically active area and because most of these foundation walls double as retaining walls, we reinforced them horizontally and vertically with #4 rebar and filled each cell of the completed wall with concrete after the surface coating cured.

Where the block walls support the house, we placed anchor bolts 4 ft. o. c. to secure the mudsills, and leveled the mudsills in a ½-in. bed of mortar. The retaining walls outside the house were capped with Surewall cement only. Here, we put a nice round top on the walls using a curved trowel made of scrap plywood and sheet metal.

Once cured, the retaining walls were waterproofed on the backsides with two coats of foundation tar embedded in fiberglass reinforcement netting (the same stuff that's used to repair built-up roofs). Two layers of 6-mil polyethylene sheeting went over the tar. The polyethylene was extended under 4-in. perforated PVC drain tile at the bottoms of the walls (walls adjoining living areas received a 2-in. layer of rigid-foam insulation beneath the vapor barrier).

The polyethylene was protected during backfilling by a layer of ½-in. fiberboard. With one exception, the walls were backfilled with gravel and compacted soil. Because it would have been difficult to place gravel behind the uppermost retaining wall, we installed Enkadrain surface-drainage matting (American Enka Co., Enka, N. C. 28728; 704-667-7668) there instead. The matting looks like coffee-filter paper glued

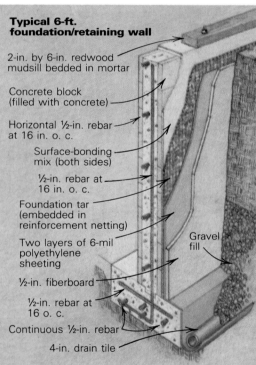

Typical 6-ft. foundation/retaining wall

2-in. by 6-in. redwood mudsill bedded in mortar

Concrete block (filled with concrete)

Horizontal ½-in. rebar at 16 in. o. c.

Surface-bonding mix (both sides)

½-in. rebar at 16 in. o. c.

Foundation tar (embedded in reinforcement netting)

Two layers of 6-mil polyethylene sheeting

½-in. fiberboard

½-in. rebar at 16 o. c.

Continuous ½-in. rebar

4-in. drain tile

Gravel fill

to plastic fencing that's been run over by a roto-tiller, but it works very well, resisting compaction while channeling water to the drain tile.

Milling around the job site—One of the benefits of the A. O. B. code is that it permits the use of ungraded lumber for framing. Greg produced almost all of the framing and finish lumber for the house (about 40,000 bd. ft.) on site, using a portable sawmill powered by a Volkswagon engine. He harvested Douglas fir for framing lumber and ponderosa pine for exposed ceiling boards from local second-growth forests. Redwood for trim, siding, decking and exposed framing members came from old-growth logs that were felled and left behind 30 years ago in a messy logging operation.

As Greg milled the lumber, he sorted it by quality and stickered it for air drying. The 1x6 siding and 1x8 ceiling boards were sent to a mill to be planed and tongue-and-grooved.

For the interior finish work, Greg bought some Indonesian mahogany from a sustained-yield plantation on the island of Java. It looks almost as good as Honduras mahogany, but with a fine-ribboned figure. He had also bought a koa log in Hawaii several years before, sawed it into 1x and 2x boards and stacked them in the corner of his shop for future use.

I should mention that my attitude toward using tropical hardwoods has changed a great deal. When possible, I now call for the use of local hardwoods harvested from well-managed, sustained-yield forests. I try to use redwood only in small amounts and don't deal with companies who harvest from old-growth forests. I also specify more patios and fewer decks, more stucco and less redwood siding.

Showcasing the roof—A crew of from two to 12 people worked for two years framing and finishing the house. This group was composed mainly of self-taught, apprentice-level carpenters and semi-skilled neighborhood friends. Greg saved a lot of the special jobs for me, though. When drawing the plans, I was sometimes unable to work out all the details of a particular feature. Like many designers, I figured the carpenters would take care of it. Greg would always find those trouble spots, like the laundry chute and numerous flashing details. "You drew it, *you* build it." It's a lesson they should have taught us in architecture school.

The framing is a combination of standard 2x6 stud walls and post-and-beam construction. The exposed redwood roof framing under a pine ceiling is perhaps the most visually outstanding element in the interior (photo, p. 118). The basic roof frame (top drawing, previous page) consists of prefinished 4-in. by 8-in. rafters and ridge beams, 4-in. by 10-in. hip rafters and 3-in. by 3-in. purlins. Rafters were lag-screwed to the top plates and hip rafters, and exposed screws were countersunk and plugged. The purlins were predrilled and nailed to the rafters except at the overhangs, where they were lag-screwed to resist high winds. We chose clear ponderosa pine for the ceiling because it contrasts well with the deep brown of the redwood framing.

After some trial and error, we devised an accurate method for cutting curves on the rafter tails, using a reciprocating saw. First, we drew the curves on both sides of the rafters with the help of a wood template. Then, while one person cut the curve, his partner steered the saw blade on the opposite side of the rafter using a scrap of plywood kerfed to slip over the back edge of the sawblade.

The roof was designed to be energy-efficient and beautiful. The top drawing on the previous page details its sandwich construction. The roof is ventilated by 1¼-in. soffit vents and continuous ridge vents linked by a 1¼-in.

Under the sky roof. **The upper level of the house, including the master bedroom, is daylit by a continuous "sky roof" at the ridge. The passage door in the bedroom has a koa frame wrapped around a dakua plywood panel. The closet doors are mahogany fitted with removable fiberglass "rice-paper" panels.**

airspace above the polyurethane insulation.

Upstairs, we installed an 8-ft. by 16-ft. "sky-roof" (photo above) made by Kalwall Corporation (P. O. Box 237, Manchester, N. H. 03105; 603-627-3861). I have used these energy-efficient (R-4.5) skylights in several buildings and am always impressed with their delicate beauty. They're great for covering large areas and are simple to install.

Watertight decks—Two of the exterior decks—the main one off the dining and living rooms, and the master-bedroom deck—had to be watertight. That's because the former sits directly over the lower level and the latter covers a portion of the greenhouse.

Our solution was a low-tech one. We cut sloping saw kerfs in the sides of the 2-in. by 10-in. redwood deck joists, slipped prefabricated 22-ga. galvanized sheet-metal panels into the kerfs, screwed the panels to the joists and caulked the top edge of the kerfs with polyure-

thane sealant. The sheet-metal panels are 22½ in. wide, or ½ in. wider than the space between the joists. This caused the panels to spring, forcing the edges into the kerfs and forming a trough to carry the water over the edge of the decks. The master-bedroom deck drains into a gutter at the edge of the deck; the main deck drains onto the ground below. The 2x6 redwood decking is fastened to the joists with galvanized bugle-head deck screws.

The installation went quickly and the design was cost-effective. There were only three leaks: two caused by the saw kerf passing through knots in the joists and the other due to poorly installed flashing where the main deck ties to the greenhouse. Next time, we might eliminate the saw kerfs altogether and install counterflashing over the tops of the joists.

A hanging stair—After three years of climbing up and down a ladder between the second and third floors, we were enthusiastic about building stairs to link the two floors.

The entry stair (photo top right) is an elegant symphony of hardwoods: koa, mahogany, kwila, alder and wenge. The entry floor is a mandala pattern composed of slate from the site, koa and wenge wood tiles, and unglazed quarry tile.

The kitchen stair (photo below right) is an open-riser affair that admits light into the kitchen from the adjacent greenhouse. The inboard ends of the risers are supported by a dadoed stringer, and the outboard ends by $\frac{1}{2}$-in. steel rods suspended from the kitchen ceiling. Greg welded a 10-in. long lag screw to one end of each rod, and a $1\frac{1}{2}$-in. dia. washer to the other end. The $\frac{1}{2}$-in. dia. lag screws allowed the rods to be screwed into a ceiling beam, and the washers support the treads. Each exposed section of steel rod is sandwiched between two routed pieces of 1x2 mahogany, glued together to form 2x2 balusters.

Handmade windows and doors — Building the windows was Greg's job. He made jambs, sills and mortised-and-tenoned frames for 27 fixed windows, 22 awning windows, 20 casement windows, one slider and two 8-ft. dia. true divided-light roundtop windows. The window frames are made of clear vertical-grain redwood and assembled with resorcinol glue and a finishing nailer. A dust-free paint room was set up in the root cellar, where the assembled jambs and frames were brushed with three coats of McCloskey's varnish.

To cut summer heat gain, we installed Heat Mirror glazing (a low-emissivity-coated polyester film stretched between two panes of glass) in all the windows. The glazing has worked better than I ever imagined. Despite the large number of west-facing windows in the house, no drapes or blinds have been needed to keep heat out during summer or in during winter.

All 52 doors in the house were built in Mick Burkholder's shop across the valley. Most of the exterior doors and frames were constructed of Indonesian mahogany with Heat Mirror tempered-glass panels. Interior doors have koa frames with dakua plywood panels (dakua is a Malaysian hardwood, the supply of which is becoming scarce; because of that, I'll never specify it again). My favorites are the numerous closet doors with their delicate mahogany or koa frames and fiberglass "rice-paper" panels (photos above and facing page).

The synthetic rice paper looks like the real thing, but is more durable and costs just $1 per sq. ft., as opposed to $1.50 and up per sq. ft. for authentic rice paper. The main drawback to the synthetic paper is that UV light from the sun causes it to yellow and become brittle. We bought ours from Japan Trading Co. (1762 Buchanan St., San Francisco, Calif. 94115; 415-929-0989). The doors were constructed with a removable wood grille should the material need to be replaced or repaired.

Most of the surface-mounted light fixtures in the house were designed and fabricated in our dining-room woodshop. We used scraps of koa and mahogany with fiberglass rice paper

The first impression. Awash in diffuse light, the main entry (top photo) plays five different hardwoods in the stair against a tile floor inlaid with a mandala of slate, unglazed quarry tile, and wood tiles. The stairwell is clad with koa panels and mahogany trim.

A suspended stair. The open-riser kitchen stair (photo above) lets light into the kitchen from the greenhouse. The inboard ends of the Douglas fir risers are dadoed into a stringer, and the outboard ends are supported by steel rods screwed to the kitchen ceiling.

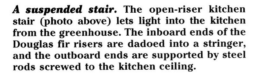

to make the wall sconces in the dining room and living room.

A finishing fiasco — Finding the right finishes to protect and enhance all the beautiful wood in the house involved a maddening amount of trial and error. We found that the claims made by many manufacturers were exaggerated at best. For the exterior redwood, we originally tried a two-part product from General Finishes called Seal-A-Cell and Armor Seal. It looked great at first, so we used a lot of it. Then it started to spot and mildew. After many calls to the manufacturer, we learned that though the product is a "tough exterior finish," it isn't recommended for areas that get very wet or are in direct sunlight. We used Petit spar varnish for the exterior redwood beams, rafters and fascia. Although it has held up well

under the eaves, it hasn't fared well on the south and west fascias. In some cases, six coats of spar varnish had to be removed.

The only exterior wood finish we've had any luck with is Sikkens Cetol HLS translucent wood finish (Akzo Coatings Inc., 1845 Maxwell St., Troy, Mich. 48084; 800-833-7288), which we applied in three coats to the siding. It only works on vertical surfaces, though; it doesn't hold up on horizontal surfaces such as decks and railings. We have yet to find a satisfactory solution for those applications.

The interior redwood beams and rafters were finished with two coats of Seal-A-Cell and two coats of Armor Seal before installation. Afterwards, they were finished with two coats of McCloskey's varnish. We stained the ceilings with our own concoction of boiled linseed oil tinted with yellow oxide, followed by two coats of McCloskey's varnish. The interior trim was finished with three coats of McCloskey's. For interior hardwoods, we were quite happy with General Finish's three-part "Royal Finish" (the company has since replaced this product with a similar one).

Home-based utilities — The A. O. B. code allows a variety of heating, cooling and electrical systems. The cooling tube handles the air-conditioning of the house during summer. During winter, a window wall between the greenhouse and dining room (photo, p. 118) is the main vehicle for transferring passive-solar heat into the house. The windows were designed with maximum vertical separation between the upper intake awning windows and the lower exhaust awning windows to encourage efficient heat exchange. Backup heat is supplied by a fireplace and by a propane-fired Lennox forced-air heater. Even the sauna is exploited for heat. On cold nights after it has been heated up, vents can be opened to duct heat into the greenhouse and kitchen.

Hot water is furnished by a propane hot-water heater plumbed to solar panels located on the south side of the dining-room roof. Water is also preheated by heat exhangers in the fireplace flue and wood cookstove.

Electrical power is generated in summer by twenty 12-volt photovoltaic panels and in winter by a small, 24-volt hydroelectric alternator. Power is stored by 12-volt batteries and converted to 110 volts by a Trace inverter. A propane-fueled Kohler generator provides backup power (for more on alternate power systems, see *FHB* #62, pp. 68-71). All of the alternative-energy equipment in the house was purchased from Alternative Energy Engineering (445 Conger St., Garberville, Calif. 95440; 707-923-2277).

Except for a little wiring work that the electrician has been promising for three years, the interior of the house is complete. But like most homesteads, there is always more to do. The entryway reflection pool and trellises are next. Then there's the landscaping, and stripping off that bad varnish on the fascias... □

Timothy Clark is a designer in Garberville, California.

Solar Adobe

A monster greenhouse and labyrinth of ductwork heat and cool a New Mexico house

by Benjamin T. Rogers

Sara and Ed Groenendyke had a site and an idea. The site in La Tierra, a semi-rural subdivision northwest of Santa Fe, New Mexico, was a beautiful hillside facing south, covered with pinyon, sagebrush and buffalo bunchgrass. Then there was the idea: the Groenendykes wanted a large greenhouse. Ed had been an orchid and tropical-plant grower in Tahiti and although he was no longer a commercial horticulturist, he needed a place to express his love of growing things. The site and the idea fused into the vision of a bermed house whose heat and hot water would be drawn from the greenhouse in the winter, with little or no need for auxiliary heat sources. This was a pretty tall order for a house located in this high-altitude, 7,000 + degree-day climate.

Summer cooling would be a lesser problem.

Massive masonry construction would be cooled by night breezes, then ride through the daytime heat without the big temperature swings that characterize lighter-weight construction systems. The greenhouse would cool itself by vents and shading devices, and a tower would provide evaporative cooling and humidity.

Earthwork and drainage—With basic requirements in mind, the Groenendykes retained Albuquerque designer Bryan Waldrip and Santa Fe builder Dietegen (Peter) Dominik to work on the project. The design stage was taken slowly in order to deal with many possibilities, beginning with Ed Groenendyke's first sketches and evolving through a stack of exploratory drawings. The design follows the Pueblo Revival style, with stuccoed adobe (and concrete-

block) walls with rounded parapets, colonnades *(portales)* and exposed vigas (see *FHB* #58, p. 85). The house would be set into the south slope of a low hill, with its north walls bermed high. To handle drainage along the bermed north wall, perforated pipe was buried at the level of the footings and covered with gravel. Window wells in the hillside were drained to the north slope of the berm. The foundation drainage system and patio drains and downspouts tie into a vertical 40-in. dia. steel pipe that acts as a culvert. Rains here are infrequent but heavy, so the culvert is flushed of any sediment coming from the foundation drains. A large drainpipe falls at a gentle grade of ⅛ in. per ft. until it sees daylight at the west.

Excavation for drainage, foundations and for an extensive below-grade ventilation sys-

All public rooms, including the dining/kitchen area, have at least one window and sometimes a door leading to the greenhouse (photo below). In winter, the owners open the windows to allow the heated greenhouse air to cycle through the house. The concrete-block and adobe walls between greenhouse and house can prolong the radiation of heat for up to five overcast winter days before one of the five fireplaces and three woodstoves are fired up.

tem made a big dent in the hillside (top photo). But the Groenendykes were insistent that the construction not run roughshod over the existing vegetation. During excavation, a number of existing shrubs and trees were removed, "parked" and returned to the land after earthwork was complete.

Heating and cooling—After design requirements had become sketches, I was called in as solar/thermal consultant. I calculated heating and cooling loads, sized ductwork and ran solar-performance estimates. I worked closely with Waldrip, who adjusted the size and slope of glazing areas and other solar features so the house could function properly without compromising the aesthetics. Most of this work was done on the computer, making it easy to play "what if" games in order to optimize solar gain, heat loss and insulation needs.

Hot air rises and cool air sinks, so we placed the greenhouse at the lowest level and stepped the rest of the house up the south-sloping hill (section drawing, next page). Each of the public rooms and the master bedroom overlook the greenhouse by way of operable windows or glass doors (photo left). The north walls are bermed up to 5 ft., with window wells cut down to 4 ft. We connected the north bedrooms to the greenhouse with a network of subterranean ducts (photo below right).

On a sunny winter day the doors and windows between house and greenhouse are opened, and doors between living areas and bedrooms are opened. The heated greenhouse air cycles through the house, falling as it cools. Solar engineers refer to this natural movement as a thermosiphon. No fans or other mechanical devices are needed; the sun does it all.

A common problem with a thermosiphon system is that rooms on the north side are often cold because the warm air doesn't reach them. In the Groenendyke house much of the air circulation flows through halls and doorways to the north bedrooms, where a critical portion of the air flow enters the 14-in. by 30-in. return air registers in the floor below the bedroom windows. From there it flows through 12-in. dia. polypropylene ducts to a central plenum room under the dining/kitchen area. From the central plenum, the air flows through a 36-in. corrugated metal pipe to a distribution manifold, which distributes the cool air to the southernmost glazing in the greenhouse. Here, the air is warmed by the sun and the cycle starts over. If the back bedrooms get too warm, the return registers can be adjusted or closed completely as the occupant desires.

This is the primary means of heating the house in the winter. South-facing skylights and clerestory windows provide daylight to some of the interior rooms and collect solar energy for heating in the winter.

In the summer the greenhouse is isolated from the house and is shaded and vented to keep it cool. On summer nights, which can be 30° cooler than the day, windows to the house are open and the whole house is cooled. In

Facing page and bottom photos: Benjamin T. Rogers

It takes digging deep to heat and cool a high-altitude house in northern New Mexico, where temperatures swing 30° or more from day to night. The black polypropylene ducts in the top of the photo above carry return air from north bedrooms, the coolest rooms in the thermosiphon loop. The 36-in. dia. metal duct will cycle the cool air to a distribution box, where smaller ducts complete the below-grade journey of the loop at the greenhouse. All ducts arriving or leaving the plenum are encased in pumice insulation and concrete (photo below); the 12-in. ducts make a cool wine cellar.

addition, the thermal mass of masonry walls remains cool throughout most of the day.

Part of the heating/cooling design includes a tower (drawing below). In winter, the bottom of the tower serves as the common return plenum for the ducts that cool and heat the entire house. The tower itself was designed to provide cool air during the summer to the greenhouse. A series of dampers at the top of the tower can be opened, drawing incoming air past a set of water mist nozzles; the cooled air would sink to the bottom of the tower, where it would be drawn into the greenhouse. But so far, the house has remained cool during summer, so the evaporative-cooling system hasn't been used.

Although the Groenendykes were convinced that the passive-heating design would work, they hedged their bets and provided a 15-ft. sq. space on the lower level of the house in the event that the house didn't perform as anticipated and we needed to install a boiler and baseboard heating system. After a few years the room was relegated to use as a wine cellar and storage area.

Building thermal mass—To help the house moderate temperature swings, all exterior walls and many interior walls are built from concrete block or adobe (top photo, p. 126). The standard concrete masonry unit used in the Santa Fe area is a pumice aggregate block that is lighter than a conventional concrete block. In the Groenendyke residence, all below-grade block work incorporated this lightweight product. Where block work continued above grade, higher-density concrete blocks were used because of their higher thermal mass. These were filled with a weak grout; it doesn't increase the R-value significantly, but does increase the thermal mass of the walls.

Adobe is hygroscopic, meaning that it readily retains water. Its R-value varies with moisture content, so for thermal purposes it is best suited for construction in climates characterized by low humidity. Stabilized adobe, produced by adding a small percentage (4.5%) of an asphalt emulsion to the mud mix, was used in this case. The asphalt adds strength and weathertightness to the brick. Stabilized adobe bricks were laid in portland cement mortar rather than the classical adobe mud because cement sets quickly in bad weather.

I think the asphalt emulsion compromises the thermal conductivity of stabilized adobe. In place, well-seasoned unstabilized adobe has an insulative value of about R-0.22 per in. and stabilized has been measured at R-0.15.

Adobe is normally laid flat with a 2-in. thick mortar joint, but I've seen loosely mortared adobe walls built with an occasional soldier course in earthquake-prone locations in China and Tibet. The vertical bricks can rock slightly without shearing the wall and the number of upright courses seems to correlate with the severity of the seismic threat. There is little seismic activity in the Santa Fe area, so the diagonally laid adobes in the entrance to the Groenendyke house are unconventional practice (bottom right photo, p. 126).

Most of the adobe walls and block walls are 10 in. wide, but the common walls between the house and greenhouse are 20 in. wide for more thermal mass. Both block and adobe walls are insulated on the outside with 3 in. of sprayed-on urethane foam, covered with 15-lb. building felt and chicken wire and finished with a three-coat stucco.

Brick and water Trombe wall—In a thermosiphon loop, the room at the lowest elevation tends to cool quickly after sundown. To offset this effect, we incorporated a southwest-facing Trombe wall into the lower guest

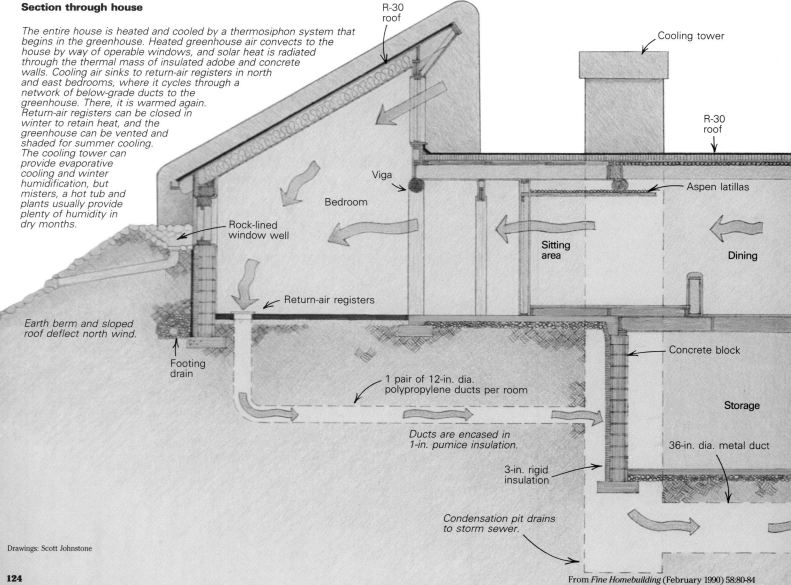

Section through house

The entire house is heated and cooled by a thermosiphon system that begins in the greenhouse. Heated greenhouse air convects to the house by way of operable windows, and solar heat is radiated through the thermal mass of insulated adobe and concrete walls. Cooling air sinks to return-air registers in north and east bedrooms, where it cycles through a network of below-grade ducts to the greenhouse. There, it is warmed again. Return-air registers can be closed in winter to retain heat, and the greenhouse can be vented and shaded for summer cooling. The cooling tower can provide evaporative cooling and winter humidification, but misters, a hot tub and plants usually provide plenty of humidity in dry months.

R-30 roof

Cooling tower

R-30 roof

Viga

Aspen latillas

Bedroom

Sitting area

Dining

Rock-lined window well

Return-air registers

Earth berm and sloped roof deflect north wind.

Footing drain

Concrete block

1 pair of 12-in. dia. polypropylene ducts per room

Storage

Ducts are encased in 1-in. pumice insulation.

36-in. dia. metal duct

3-in. rigid insulation

Condensation pit drains to storm sewer.

Drawings: Scott Johnstone

From *Fine Homebuilding* (February 1990) 58:80-84

bedroom. The classic Trombe wall depends on the mass of a masonry wall to store solar energy during the day and release it at night. Groenendyke built a single-wythe brick wall in an 8-ft. 4-in. opening in the outer adobe wall, placed water-filled Kalwall tubes (Kalwall, 121 Valley Rd., Manchester, Vt. 03103) on the outside of the brick (which is denser that adobe) and then glazed the opening (bottom left photo, next page).

A thick multilayered Mylar insulating curtain is drawn across the glass at night and during a heavy cloud cover, but when the sun shines, a temperature sensor triggers the motor-driven shade to open, exposing the water-filled tubes to the sun. When the curtain closes again at sunset or during heavy cloud cover, the stored heat is directed to the adjacent room from the brick and through several vents in the brick wall. The curtain, designed by a now defunct company from Snowmass, Colorado, provides an ingenious solution to the vexing problem of losing heat during the night or cloudy weather.

Big Fin—Hot water in the house is provided by a solar water heater on the south face of the greenhouse. Called the Big Fin (detail drawing, below right), it collects heat from

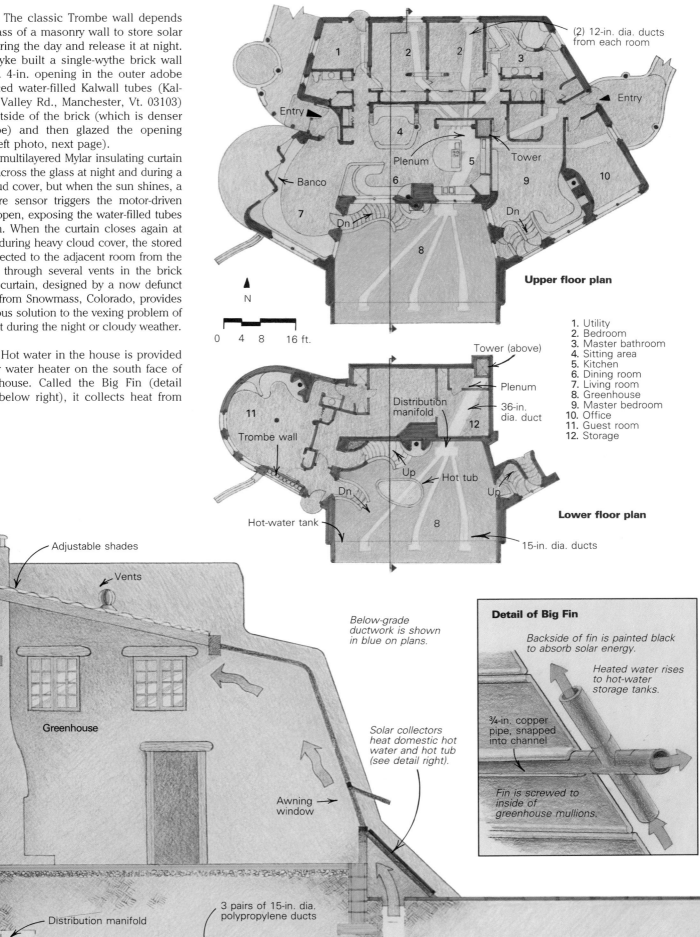

(2) 12-in. dia. ducts from each room

Entry

Entry

Plenum

Tower

Banco

Dn

Dn

N

0   4   8   16 ft.

Upper floor plan

1. Utility
2. Bedroom
3. Master bathroom
4. Sitting area
5. Kitchen
6. Dining room
7. Living room
8. Greenhouse
9. Master bedroom
10. Office
11. Guest room
12. Storage

Tower (above)

Plenum

Distribution manifold

36-in. dia. duct

Trombe wall

Up

Hot tub

Up

Dn

Hot-water tank

Lower floor plan

15-in. dia. ducts

Adobe

Adjustable shades

Vents

Greenhouse

Awning window

Below-grade ductwork is shown in blue on plans.

Solar collectors heat domestic hot water and hot tub (see detail right).

Distribution manifold

3 pairs of 15-in. dia. polypropylene ducts

Detail of Big Fin

Backside of fin is painted black to absorb solar energy.

Heated water rises to hot-water storage tanks.

¾-in. copper pipe, snapped into channel

Fin is screwed to inside of greenhouse mullions.

the sun on its long metal fins, which transfer the heat to ¾-in. dia. copper pipes. The hot water is collected in two tanks in the greenhouse. Big Fin (Zomeworks Corporation, P. O. Box 25805, Albuquerque, N. M. 87125) is one of many innovative solar products that have been developed by Steve Baer, a pioneer among the solar technologists (for more on Baer and Zomeworks, see *FHB* #26, pp. 52-57). The fins are extruded aluminum 8 in. wide, 4 ft. or 8 ft. long and just less than ¹⁄₁₂ in. thick. The aluminum can be left clear sat-

in or can be painted flat black or any custom color on one side. We screwed the fins horizontally to the inside face of the anodized aluminum greenhouse mullions, then snapped in the piping. This way, the collectors are located within the envelope of the greenhouse so they will not freeze (bottom photo). The 68° air in the convection loop, which passes directly over the lower surface of the fins, aids in tempering the Big Fin in cold weather.

Each 8-ft. fin provides 5.33 sq. ft. of collec-

tion surface. Zomeworks provides a long equation for figuring the number of fins needed for a household, but the general rule of thumb for the Santa Fe/Albuquerque region is four fins per person. We used 32 fins here, more than enough for the four occupants of the house.

To take advantage of natural convection, we placed the hot-water storage tank in its most cost-effective configuration: above the collectors. Otherwise, a pump must be added to the system. Potable water circulates by natural convection from the storage tank through the collector and back to the tank.

Half of the Big Fin system is dedicated to the supply of domestic hot water. The other half supplies a large hot tub in the greenhouse. In the winter an electric resistance heater is required to boost the operating temperatures to true hot-tub temperature (100° to 105°), almost doublng the monthly electric bill.

Performance—After the house had been occupied for about a year I asked Sara Groenendyke to tell me how the place was functioning. She said that on clear winter days she opens a few doors and windows to the greenhouse to allow additional warm air to flow indoors. She closes up the house at nightfall. There is little need for backup heat from the fireplaces or stoves. Heat stored in the massive adobe and masonry walls allows the house to store energy through about five days of overcast weather, and after that fires are in order. But Santa Fe seldom sees five days of overcast weather. □

Benjamin T. (Buck) Rogers is a consulting engineer. When he's not doing research in the field, he works from Embudo, New Mexico. Photos by Ed Groenendyke except where noted.

Adding mass to the thermosiphon loop are 12-in. concrete-block and 10-in. adobe brick exterior walls. As walls rose, windows were installed. Before placing the windows in the wall, a heavy mortise-and-tenon frame was slipped over the clad window. Once frame and window were in place, a massive pine lintel was lagscrewed to jambs and blockwork continued. The innermost layer of the Trombe wall, a single-wythe wall of yellow brick, is to the right.

The greenhouse, at right in the photo below, takes in sun year-round, unless exterior shades are drawn. The bottom of the greenhouse glazing is sloped steeply to make the best use of the solar collecting fins just inside the glass. Behind the tall window at the center of the photo are the water-filled tubes and brick wall that make up the Trombe wall in the guest bedroom.

Not the traditional bond pattern of adobe, this slanting wall is just an accent in the entry to the house. White portland cement was used in the mortar to accent the pattern.

Bottom photos: Benjamin T. Rogers

In the Solar Vanguard

In 1946, architect Arthur Brown used industrial components and a simple solar mass design to temper the desert climate

by Helen J. Kessler

Photo courtesy of Arthur Brown

Before Felix Trombe popularized his own mass-wall concept, a young architect in the Southwest was using interior walls for storing the sun's heat. Other architects were designing solar houses in the 1940s, but few did anything more than allow the winter sun to penetrate deeply into south-facing windows while overhangs kept out the summer sun. What is important about Arthur Brown's designs is not only that he stored solar heat in masonry mass, but that he also controlled this gain in a climate with wide daily temperature swings. The house he designed for Mr. and Mrs. George Rosenberg in Tucson, Ariz., in 1946 is an excellent example of how passive heating and cooling can use simple, inexpensive solar features that don't intrude on the aesthetics of the house.

The 3,200-sq. ft. Rosenberg house was built

The Rosenberg house, right, has over 100 lineal feet of floor-to-ceiling glazing. This 1947 photo shows the metal louvers at the eaveline (they were later removed). The use of a 12-in. steel I-beam (foreground) as a foundation, with spot footings every 8 ft., saved concrete when it was scarce after World War II. Above, the sun shines high on the block wall, which was originally painted a dark grey-green. It shields the bedrooms from direct solar gain, and heats the house at night by radiation.

Photos, except where noted: Helen Kessler

The low north side of the Rosenberg house faces the street, with jalousie windows for ventilation showing above the flagstone veneer. Evaporative coolers are hidden from view behind the chimneys. Another cooling measure is the white roof, which reflects the sun.

in the post-World War II era, which was marked by shortages of energy and building materials. Brown kept the cost of the house down by using a steel grade-beam foundation and factory windows—materials that were available and inexpensive because they had been part of the war effort.

The Rosenberg house is, in many ways, a classic solar design. It is long and narrow with all its rooms along an east-west axis to take full advantage of solar heating in the winter, and to avoid the summer sun (drawing, facing page). Running the length of the house is an interior, concrete-block wall that stores solar heat and stabilizes interior temperatures. The roof is a single shed with exposed rafters, purlins and decking. The 6½-ft. ceiling on the north side rises to 9 ft. on the south. The south wall, except for the garage, is floor-to-ceiling glass (photo, preceding page). This wall, which is

more than 100 ft. long, lets in a lot of sunlight, and gives the feeling that the trees and sky are an integral part of the house.

The north facade and entry are private by comparison. A bank of jalousie windows near the top of the north wall admits light and air. The wall, veneered with Grand Canyon flagstone, lends a maintenance-free elegance to the street-side entrance (photo above). The garage to the west protects the living space from the hot afternoon sun. The narrow eastern exposure of the house is windowless.

Solar beginnings—The idea for this house came to Brown after a commission from another client near Tucson. That client, in an attempt at daring decor, wanted the exterior walls of his house painted black. After some thought, Brown suggested that just the south wall be painted black. It would gain heat in the

winter, but not gain as much as the east or west walls would during the hot Tucson summer. The client agreed. When the house was completed, Brown inspected the south wall after sundown on a cold winter evening and felt the heat radiating from it as much as 5 ft. away. Standing there, he wondered why that same heat couldn't be captured inside the house, where it would do some good in the winter, yet be excluded in the summer. Thus, the passive-solar concept for the Rosenberg house was born.

Brown estimated that heat would move through the concrete at about one inch per hour, so he built the solar wall of grout-filled 8-in. block, plastered on both sides. This would allow the heat to begin to penetrate through to the north rooms of the house in the early evening, when it was needed.

Overhangs were designed to keep out the summer sun. In the high desert of Tucson, the

Photo courtesy of Arthur Brown

difference between the temperature in the shade and the temperature in the sun can be as much as 35°F at midday in the summer. The overhang at the sun porch once had metal louvers fixed at an angle 34° above horizontal to regulate the amount of sunlight entering the house during the hottest part of the year, but these were removed and replaced with a solid eave-sheathing so the owners wouldn't have to maintain the paint on the louvers.

With solar gain in mind, the concrete-slab floors were finished with a chocolate-brown pigment. The solar wall was originally a dark grey-green to absorb sunlight, but more recently has been painted blue. Every room in the house is adjacent to the wall. Rooms to its south—the sun porch, dining room and halls—take advantage of direct-gain heating from the sunlight that pours through the south-facing windows. The rooms to its north—the bedrooms, kitchen and living room—are warmed later in the day as the wall heats up.

Because it's on the south side of the solar wall, the sunroom becomes a living room in the winter. In fact, it gets so much sunlight on clear winter days that venetian blinds have had to be installed to control the heat. The north living room, which is cooler throughout the year, is used in the summer.

An unusual aspect of this solar heating system is that Brown used the space betweeen the glazing and the mass wall as a traffic area. There's a reason for this. Brown's clients were young and open to some design experiments, but aesthetic concerns were still paramount. The Rosenberg house doesn't assault you with the fact that it is designed to take advantage of sun and shade. The overall impression of the house is that it is comfortable. The solar features—south glazing, solar block wall, convection vents—don't look much different from the components in a more conventional house.

Architect Brown, now 82, believes in simple and pragmatic designs. Unlike many early passive-solar designs, the Rosenberg house does require some attention from its owners, but nothing more than opening or closing blinds and windows. The vents high on the south wall serve a double purpose. In addition to providing relief from warm air inside the house, they also serve as a raceway for electrical lines and conduits. When asked recently if he would change anything in the Rosenberg house if he had it to design over again, he replied that he might cut down the number and size of the openings in the solar wall to retain more mass; but on the whole, he is pleased with the house's design and performance. For more on Brown and his architecture, see pp.34-35.

Although records of the house performance have not been kept recently, the temperature readings (°F) below were collected by the owners in February, 1947.

	10 a.m.	2 p.m.	6 p.m.
Outside (north wall)	50°	62°	59°
Solar wall	94°	102°	81°
Living room	72°	72°	72°

These figures show how the solar wall keeps the temperature of the rooms behind it very

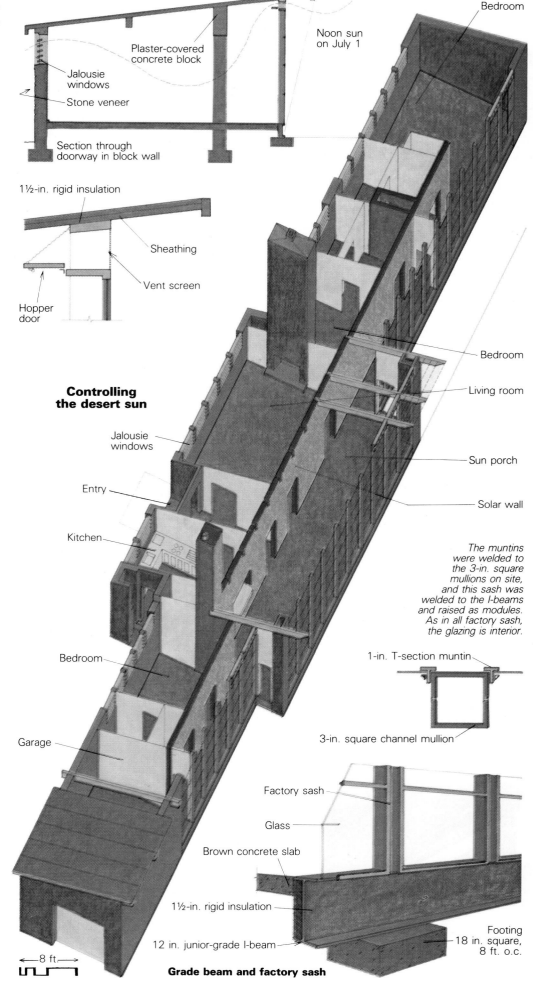

Summer ventilation

Plaster-covered concrete block

Noon sun on July 1

Jalousie windows

Stone veneer

Section through doorway in block wall

1½-in. rigid insulation

Sheathing

Vent screen

Hopper door

Controlling the desert sun

Jalousie windows

Entry

Kitchen

Bedroom

Garage

Bedroom

Bedroom

Living room

Sun porch

Solar wall

The muntins were welded to the 3-in. square mullions on site, and this sash was welded to the I-beams and raised as modules. As in all factory sash, the glazing is interior.

1-in. T-section muntin

3-in. square channel mullion

Factory sash

Glass

Brown concrete slab

1½-in. rigid insulation

12 in. junior-grade I-beam

Footing 18 in. square, 8 ft. o.c.

← 8 ft. →

Grade beam and factory sash

Illustrations: Vince Babak

The sunroom receives a great deal of winter sun, which can be controlled by adjusting the venetian blinds. The brown slab floor and solar wall (grouted blocks, plastered and painted blue) provide the mass. In the sum-

mer, the living-room jalousie windows draw cool air through doorways in the solar wall, right, from the north side of the house. By convection, hot air exhausts through vents high along the south walls.

In the summer, warm air escapes through hopper doors above the south-facing glass at the highest point in the house. The openings are screened on the outside, and the doors are easily opened and closed with a pole.

stable. Without the solar wall, the sun would shine directly into the living spaces, and the living-room temperature would fluctuate. The owners reported that they were quite comfortable through the late evening, and that the furnace came on for only about 45 minutes in the early morning on sunny days.

With the warm walls making for a high mean radiant temperature, swings in indoor temperature are gentle. The Rosenbergs felt that they were living in a healthier environment than one produced by a house heated exclusively with a hot-air furnace.

Cooling—In a hot, arid climate like Tucson's, the design for a house must take into account cooling as well as heating. Brown did this by placing vents at the highest level in the house, just above the south-facing windows. Combined with the low jalousie windows on the

north side and louvered doors in the openings of the central solar wall, the vents make for effective cross-ventilation. The area between rafters, normally filled by frieze blocks, is screened instead. On the inside of the south wall there are hopper doors of solid pine that match the exposed roof decking (photo left). Spring-loaded ring latches, which can be operated with a boat hook, drop these doors for ventilation. They are held horizontal by small lengths of chain.

The size and placement of the windows in the house give the rooms along the north side of the wall a different character from those on the south. The south rooms feel warm, airy and open because of the floor-to-ceiling glazing. The north rooms, on the other hand, feel cooler and more enclosed and secure. The jalousie windows contribute to this effect because they are small and set near the outside of this thick,

Solar heat makes its way through the concrete-filled living-room wall at the rate of 1 in. per hour. By early evening, the wall is warm all the way through, and will radiate its heat through the night. The jalousie windows are set in the stone veneer on the outside of the north wall, with hinged screens on the inside. The depth of these sills along with the sloping roofline give this room a feeling of being a haven from the summer heat.

stone-veneered wall. The top-hinged screens that cover the windows on the interior swing from 1x casings, with bookshelves below that project out into the room even further. This illusion of depth makes the rooms feel insulated from the outside world. Another thing that contributes to this feeling of enveloping coolness is the roof, which slopes down to the north wall (photo above).

During the summer, the natural convection cooling is supplemented by evaporative coolers, which Brown concealed behind the chimneys. The summer heat is also discouraged from entering the house by a white asbestos roof that reflects the sunlight.

A product of its time—The Rosenberg house was constructed during the postwar period, when conventional building materials were scarce. To build large houses, architects had to

be creative about the types of materials and the construction methods they specified. One of Brown's specialties was his ability to adapt components made for industrial buildings for use in well-designed, livable homes.

Two examples of Brown's use of industrial materials in the Rosenberg house are the window wall and the grade beam. The window wall is constructed of stock steel factory sash. Steel columns, made from two welded channel sections, are used as supports. A 1-in. T-section is used as a stop for the glazing. The foundation is built using spot footings and a 12-in. junior I-beam on the perimeter. This steel beam was then used as a base for welding the structure of the window wall. The I-beam also serves as a raceway for the natural-gas supply line. Steel pipe columns support the porch.

Despite its solid solar features, the Rosenberg house isn't built like an energy-conscious house

of the 80s. Although the roof and the edges of the concrete slab floor were insulated, the maximum amount used was 1½-in. of Celotex. All of its south-facing glass is single-glazed. Double glazing would have made a substantial difference in keeping in the heat in the winter, and keeping it out in the summer. Although jalousie windows are excellent ventilators, when they're closed they allow too much air infiltration by current standards. These criticisms are quibbles, aided by hindsight. We can learn much from Brown's experimental design, for it shows clearly that solar features need not be complex, expensive or obtrusive.   □

Helen J. Kessler is an architect who works with passive-solar design at the University of Arizona Environmental Research Laboratory in Tucson. She was once a student intern in Arthur Brown's office.

Cool Details

An energy-efficient infill house
inspired by Texas vernacular architecture

by W. Scott Neeley

Austin architect Lawrence Speck had several goals in mind when he designed his new house. The house had to be sturdy enough to withstand abuse from his two young sons, but elegant enough for entertaining. It had to have room for a future architectural office. It could not disrupt the neighborhood, yet it had to reflect Speck's architectural sensibilities (for more on those, see the sidebar on p. 135). The resulting design blends cement-board, slurried limestone and locally crafted custom metalwork into a house that solves a number of structural and aesthetic problems (photo above). It's energy efficient, too.

Suited to a T—The design took the form of two wings arranged in a simple T-shaped plan (drawing, p. 134). One wing is 18 ft. tall and encloses the living room, dining room and kitchen. Perpendicular to this space, a one-story wing holds three bedrooms (one of which can be used as an office), two bathrooms and

a utility room. Deed restrictions precluded a second floor in the house, but allowed a small loft over the kitchen. The house has 2,170 sq. ft., including the loft.

Speck's house extends to the minimum building setback on all four sides of the lot. The tall wing is positioned near the back, creating a large front yard for the kids.

Searching for bedrock—Construction drawings and specifications for the house were sent out for bid to three contractors whose work Speck respected. The bids were close, but Bill Dorman Construction got the job.

Construction started off slowly. Typical of the Austin area, the Tarrytown neighborhood is built on clay-based soils, which are notorious for expanding and contracting as they absorb water and then dry out. This movement can wreak havoc on a foundation. To minimize problems, most houses in the area are supported by a foundation of piers and grade

beams; the piers are poured deeply enough to resist expansion and contraction, and the grade beams are poured monolithically with concrete-slab floors.

For Speck's house, the structural engineer specified 18-in. dia. piers set on bedrock. Assuming that bedrock was no more than a few feet deep (also typical of Austin), Dorman hired an auger truck and began boring. He tried several locations without hitting bedrock, even when using the 10-ft. auger to its full depth. Another truck was ordered, this time equipped with a 20-ft. auger rig. Two more holes were bored, and still no bedrock.

The structural engineer provided an alternative foundation: 18-in. dia., 10-ft. deep piers with 30-in. dia. belted bottoms for increased bearing area (drawing, p. 135). Each pier is reinforced with four lengths of #6 rebar. Above the piers, 2 ft. to 3 ft. of the rebar were bent to a 90° angle for embedment into the grade beams. Two independent piers were also

poured inside the foundation perimeter to help support the loft and roof. Formed with Sonotubes, they extend about 8 ft. above the slab.

To ensure a stable foundation, it was crucial that the grade beams and slabs be isolated from the ground. Dorman poured the grade beams on top of corrugated concrete "void forms" (Harris Packaging Corp., 1600 Carson St., Haltom City, Tex. 76117; 817-429-6262). Made of a wax-impregnated fiberboard, these rectangular-shaped forms are designed to support concrete during placement, then deteriorate to create a void beneath the beams into which the soils can expand. The forms are available in stock or custom shapes and sizes, and the manufacturer ships them flat and pre-scored (for easy assembly on the job site) to any location in the U. S.

Void forms can also be used beneath slabs by placing the forms side by side. For Speck's house, however, Dorman poured the slabs over a minimum 6-in. thick layer of sandy loam, sufficient to absorb the minimal movement of the soil beneath the slabs. A 6-mil polyethylene vapor barrier between the loam and the slabs keeps the slabs dry.

A limestone sandwich—The 24-in. thick walls surrounding the living room were designed for energy-efficiency as well as for visual impact. They consist of an insulated 2x10 balloon-framed core sandwiched between two 7-in. thick layers of uncoursed limestone (drawing, p. 135). The framed core is sheathed on its exterior side with ½-in. water-resistant drywall. Taped and spackled, the sheathing prevents moisture from wicking into the walls through the highly porous limestone. A layer of 30-lb. felt over the sheathing adds extra protection.

Speck specified a "chiseled, slurried stone" for the veneer. He showed Dorman an example—the 150-year-old Arno Nowotny house located on the University of Texas campus. Its chiseled limestone is typical of that used for traditional Texas farmhouses, except that the mortar on the Nowatny house was slurried. Slurrying is a technique in which mortar is spread partially across the faces of the stones so that the individual stones are still visible.

The lead mason for the job, Don Cooper, is a third-generation stonemason and, coincidentally, a distant relative of Arno Nowotny. Cooper owns a quarry, where he quarried the Texas Cordova Cream limestone used for Speck's house. Abundant in the Texas hill country, the light-colored stone is relatively soft, but it holds up well in the gulf climate. The stone was cut using a gigantic circular saw fitted with a 6-ft. dia. blade that left a scarred face

Tall and bright. **The living/dining room is illuminated by ample glazing and indirect incandescent and fluorescent lighting. The lighting fixture at the east end of the living room (top left in photo) is notched into a soffit that houses the heating and cooling ducts. The truss-like metal webs at the peak are in fact simple collar ties that bolt to the ridge beam and to every third rafter.**

on the surface of the stone. One face of the stone was then machined with a hydraulic chopper to produce a *chopped* face (for a hand-chiseled appearance).

The hardest part of building a stone wall is controlling the appearance of the mortar joints. The slurried mortar technique made this easy. The joints were overfilled with a wet mortar, which was then rubbed with wet burlap sacks to spread it across the face of the stone. This blurred the distinction between stones, resulting in walls that look as sturdy as monolithic walls, but as singular as hand-crafted walls (bottom right photo, p. 136). The mortar was mixed with a reddish river sand, which adds warmth to the color.

It took two masons and two or three helpers eight weeks to lay the stone walls. They started at the back of the house, and their work improved steadily as they made their way to the front. The interior limestone, subject to the most scrutiny, was done last.

Dorman installed stock double-pane Marvin windows in the stone walls. The windows were ordered with standard jambs and no brick-mold, and then the frames were extended at the site. Jambs and sills were flashed with a garden-variety copper-reinforced plastic flashing purchased at the local building supply.

The stone walls are thermally responsive to the hot summers of central Texas. Most heat absorbed by the exterior stone is prevented from migrating inward by the insulated core. Meantime, air-conditioning cools the interior stone. Because cool masonry draws radiant heat from the body, the air temperature inside the house

feels about 10° cooler than a conventionally built house at the same temperature.

In two years, Speck's highest monthly electric bill has been less than $100. Electric bills for his fully insulated previous house ranged from $250 to $300, and that house was about 200 sq. ft. smaller than the new one.

Cement on the side—Speck called for the use of Pyrok Five Star Board (Pyrok, Inc., 136 Prospect Park W., Brooklyn, N. Y. 11215; 718-788-1225) as siding for the one-story wing and as paneling for the continuous fence surrounding the house. It's a cement-bonded particleboard that's been used in the U. S. in spray-on form as an acoustical and fireproofing material. In Europe, Pyrok has been used in panel form for everything from highway sound barriers to backer board for tile. Recommended for interior or exterior applications, it contains no asbestos or mineral fibers, is an excellent sound barrier, resists fire, moisture, fungus and insects, and can be worked with standard carpentry tools. It offers the rigidity of plywood and, in many cases, can be substituted for plywood as a structural wall sheathing.

The board was ordered in 4-ft. by 8-ft. by ⅜-in. thick sheets with shiplapped ends. Though the spray-on variety is made and readily available in the U. S., Pyrok panels are made in Wales and imported. Still, in late 1988, they cost a reasonable $32 per panel (they now cost about $48 per panel).

The panels were fastened to the stud walls with galvanized nails through holes predrilled on site, and to one side of the redwood fence

Floor plan

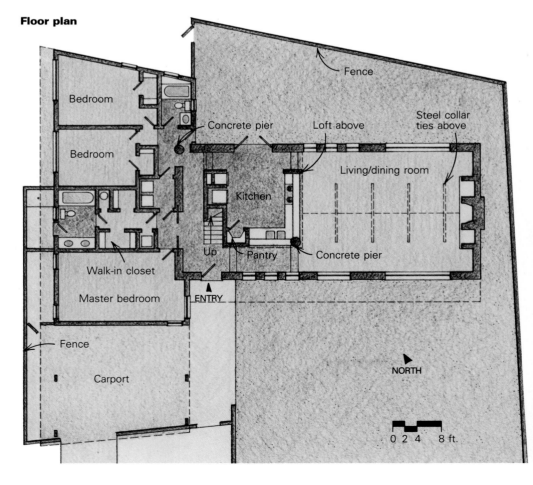

Fence
Bedroom
Concrete pier
Loft above
Steel collar ties above
Bedroom
Living/dining room
Kitchen
Concrete pier
Up
Pantry
Walk-in closet
Master bedroom
ENTRY
Fence
Carport
NORTH
0 2 4 8 ft.

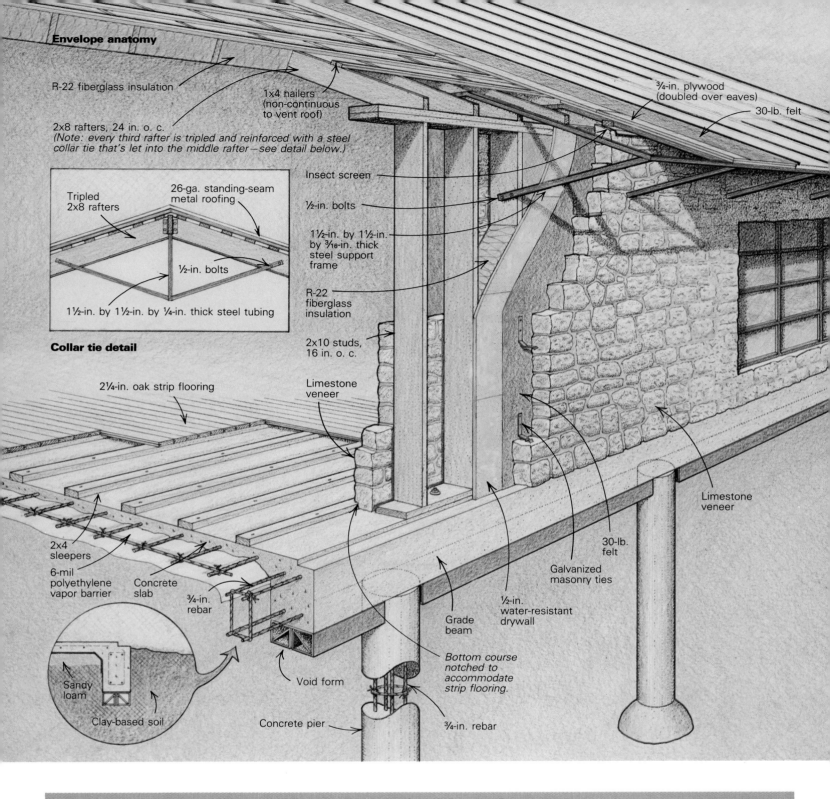

Envelope anatomy

R-22 fiberglass insulation

1x4 nailers (non-continuous to vent roof)

2x8 rafters, 24 in. o. c. (Note: every third rafter is tripled and reinforced with a steel collar tie that's let into the middle rafter—see detail below.)

Tripled 2x8 rafters

26-ga. standing-seam metal roofing

½-in. bolts

1½-in. by 1½-in. by ¼-in. thick steel tubing

Collar tie detail

¾-in. plywood (doubled over eaves)

30-lb. felt

Insect screen

½-in. bolts

1½-in. by 1½-in. by ³⁄₁₆-in. thick steel support frame

R-22 fiberglass insulation

2x10 studs, 16 in. o. c.

Limestone veneer

2¼-in. oak strip flooring

2x4 sleepers

6-mil polyethylene vapor barrier

Concrete slab

¾-in. rebar

Sandy loam

Clay-based soil

Void form

Concrete pier

¾-in. rebar

Grade beam

Bottom course notched to accommodate strip flooring.

½-in. water-resistant drywall

Galvanized masonry ties

30-lb. felt

Limestone veneer

Borrowing designs from the past

Of the architectural styles that inspired Speck's house, the most dominant is the traditional Texas farmhouse. Built by German immigrants who settled in rural Texas during the mid-19th century, these houses were inspired by the Neoclassic architecture of Karl Friedrich Schinkel, who had popularized in Germany the classical sense of proportion with a new starkness and simplicity of detail.

Texas farmhouses are characterized by heavy walls and lightweight roofs. Walls were usually made of hand-chiseled Texas limestone, and the roofs of galvanized metal. Speck translated these characteristics to the tall public wing of his house.

A second strong influence was the work of Frank Lloyd Wright. Wright often shunned embellishment, allowing building materials to speak for themselves. Speck's straightforward stonework and

choice of unfinished cement-board panels as a combination sheathing/siding material reflect the same concerns. Wright also stressed the importance of the horizontal line in architecture— "the line of man's tenure on earth." This inspired his Prairie style houses, as well as today's suburban ranch. On Speck's house, continuous horizontal battens on the cement-board panels tie the house to the ground visually.

Another influence on the house is the work of Mexican architect Luis Barragan. Barragan's houses combine rich materials and vibrant colors with almost primal simplicity. Speck is particularly impressed with the Prieto-Lopez house in Mexico City. That house has a huge window in the living room that, according to Speck, "eats the room." Speck's living room has a similarly large window, which measures about 11 feet square. —*W. S. N.*

framing with stainless-steel screws. Panel seams were caulked; then unfinished horizontal redwood battens were screwed to the panels on 16-in. centers. The battens were made by ripping redwood 2x4s at an angle through the center. The angled faces were mounted so that the battens slope for drainage.

Though Pyrok panels can be painted, Speck prefers the matte grey surface of unfinished panels. The only discoloration after two years is due to minimal bleeding from the battens.

In front of the house, Speck used Pyrok panels to create the parapet walls surrounding the carport roof. The columns that support the carport roof were placed at the 25-ft. minimum setback from the front property line. The roof is cantilevered 2 ft. beyond the columns, and the fence in front is set just inside the roofline. To avoid zoning problems, Speck incorporated the garage door into the fence (photo, p. 132), replacing the four lower door panels with Pyrok panels and removing the glass panels from the uppermost section to provide an open frame. A roof and fence were allowed this close to the property line, but not a carport.

Overhead steel—The living-room wing is capped by a cathedral ceiling framed with 2x8 rafters spaced 24 in. o. c. Every third rafter is tripled, and the four opposing pairs of triplets in the roof are stiffened with simple custom-made steel collar ties (detail drawing, facing page). Made of 1½-in. square steel tubing, the collar ties pierce the drywall ceiling to dramatic effect (photo, p. 133).

The rafters are topped with 1x4 nailers spaced 12 in. o. c., ¾-in. plywood decking, 30-lb. felt and, finally, reflective 26-ga., standing-seam metal roofing. The 1x4 nailers aren't continuous, so they allow fresh air to circulate through the roof between soffit vents and ridge vents.

On the south side of the house, a 4-ft. deep eave provides summer shading. Speck designed a metal frame to support it. Made of ³⁄₁₆-in. thick by 1½-in. by 1½-in. square steel tubing, the frame is a continuous rail with V-shaped brackets welded to it on 24-in. centers (bottom right photo). Each bracket is bolted to a rafter (the rafters are cut off at the plates) and to either a stud or a 2x block between two studs. The stone wall is mortared around the brackets where they penetrate the veneer.

The bracket system and the collar ties were delivered primed, and were later painted a deep red. For added stiffness at the eave, Dorman substituted a second layer of plywood decking for the 1x4 nailers. The open soffit was finished by attaching metal sheeting over 30-lb. felt to the underside of the decking.

The roof over the one-story wing is supported by prefabricated roof trusses sloped ¼ in. per foot away from the adjacent stone wing. The trusses are topped with ¾-in. plywood and a 4-ply built-up roof.

Finished for durability—Indoors, hard-working materials keep maintenance to a minimum. The living/dining-room floor was finished with 2¼-in. wide T&G red oak. The oak

Low-maintenance kitchen. The kitchen cabinets have flush-mounted, painted plywood doors and drawer fronts, plus plastic-laminate countertops. A small pantry substitutes for upper cabinets. The floor is Mexican porphyry, an igneous stone that's similar in texture to granite. It's sealed with an alkyd-resin product that requires little maintenance.

Railing in steel. The entry stair is patterned after a famous stair in Mexico City. The treads and risers are made of red oak, and the rail is square steel tubing.

Soffit support. A custom-made steel frame supports the 4-ft. wide eave on the south side of the house. "Slurried" mortar gives the limestone walls a monolithic appearance.

was nailed to 2x4 sleepers that were nailed with a powder-actuated hammer and glued with construction adhesive to the concrete slab. For a clean joint at the stone walls, the flooring dies into a channel at the base of the stone wall.

The floor in the entry hall and kitchen (top photo) is Mexican porphyry, a reddish-black igneous stone, similar in texture to granite. The stone was thickset in a mortar bed over the floor slab and grouted with a mortar colored to match the stone. When the grout was dry, the floor was cleaned with tri-sodium phosphate and thoroughly rinsed. Then, a mixture of one part boiled linseed oil to one part Thompson's Water Seal was applied. The floor was finished with two coats of Spark's Stone

Glamour (Spark's Southwest Inc., 1804 Industrial Blvd., Colleyville, Tex. 76034; 817-488-6585), an interior/exterior alkyd resin that seals, waterproofs and requires little upkeep.

The stair to the loft is stark and dramatic. The treads and risers are made of 2x red oak, nailed and glued together. Though Speck originally wanted to dispense with a handrail, Dorman convinced him that he'd regret it. So a one-piece metal handrail was fabricated as a simple, stepped series of horizontal lines (left photo above). The handrail is fastened with screws to the stair and to a wall up top. □

W. Scott Neeley is a designer and builder in San Francisco, California. Photos by Bruce Greenlaw.

Southern Comfort

Ample ventilation
and heat-shedding
construction details
in a passively cooled
south Florida home

by Ted Hutton

Several years ago, officials at Florida's major power company looked around at the hundreds of new homes going up each day and saw a sea of refrigerated concrete boxes. With the hum of air conditioners in their ears and the prospect of more to come, the people at Florida Power and Light decided to seek out new building techniques that could help reduce reliance on mechanical cooling and heating. The Passive Home Program, which was started by FPL in 1983, has brought needed innovations to an area of the country that had lagged behind the rest of the nation in energy-efficient home design.

Many of the technical details incorporated in the Passive Home Program were provided by

the Florida Solar Energy Center, a state-funded research center that was established in 1974 to test and certify solar water heaters. By 1980, researchers at the Center had begun to study building techniques that would reduce dependence on air conditioners, and their results attracted FPL (for more on the Florida Solar Energy Center, see *FHB* #30, p. 80).

Using FSEC as a consultant, FPL invited architects from around the state to bid for the job of designing two passive-solar homes for either south, central or north Florida. Three firms were then chosen. One was assigned to each region, and all were issued the following guidelines: none of the homes could use mechanical heat-

ing or cooling; house appearance had to be marketable to the general public and blend into most residential settings; house size was to be 1,400 sq. ft. to 1,600 sq. ft., with three bedrooms and two baths; construction costs, excluding land, were to fall between $70,000 and $80,000 (based on 1983 prices).

By the end of 1983, six designs were made available to the public. The design my wife and I chose to build is known as South Florida #2. It's a three-level, gable-roofed building with about 1,400 sq. ft. of living space, augmented by 620 sq. ft. of screen porches (Craig Sharp, of Osborne Sharp Associates in Sarasota, was responsible for this particular design). The house was completed in the fall of 1986, and has already proven its effectiveness in coping with south Florida's heat. Even when temperatures are consistently above 90°F, the house has remained comfortable. When the air conditioners in most homes pushed monthly electric bills into triple figures, we ended up paying an average of about $35 per month.

The cost of construction stayed within the bounds set out by FPL. As owner-builder I originally estimated the cost at $63,000, but the construction costs for the completed house were closer to $70,000. The increase was due to a low original estimate for the amount of lumber that would be needed and the addition of a solar water-heating system. Also, we changed our minds about using drywall on all the ceilings and switched to T&G cedar.

Cooling strategy—In designing this house, Sharp drew on his own experience with solar designs, in addition to using the research done by the Florida Solar Energy Center. Basically, the design shrugs off high temperatures by forcing air to move, and move in the right direction: warm air up and out of the house, cool air in to replace it.

Passive-cooling technology isn't a recent development. Before the advent of air conditioning, architects and builders had to develop reliable ways to get rid of excess heat. Cajun houses that Sharp spotted during a trip to southern Louisiana provided vernacular examples of proven passive-cooling principles. These old houses have wide verandahs for shade and a crawl space to allow ventilation from beneath. They also have vented cupolas at roof peaks to allow heat to escape. The roofs themselves are corrugated metal, a low-cost material that has good reflective qualities.

Proper siting is also important. Our house is located on a 1¼-acre site dominated by slash pines and palmetto palms. The pines were important for shading, and the house was positioned so that it has pines on all sides. Only one sizable tree had to come down to make room for the house.

The crucial roof—Controlling heat gain through the roof is a critical factor in passive-cooling design. In this house, floors, walls and ceilings are insulated conventionally, but up to 90% of heat gain through the roof is eliminated by using a combination of metal roofing, radiant barriers and double-skin construction, which is also known as vent skin.

The designers chose a metal roof because it's significantly better at reflecting solar heat than shingles. The South Florida #2 plans call for a standing-seam aluminum roof. When the low bid for this type of roof came in at $9,600, I decided that I might go for something a little less expensive. I checked with Sharp and FPL for an economical alternative that would have similar reflective qualities, and they suggested that we use 5-V-crimp galvanized steel, made by Reynolds Aluminum (P.O. Box 310, Eastman, Ga. 31023). This material is manufactured in 26-in. wide sheets that can be ordered to any length. It is best installed over rafters that are spaced

24 in. o. c., since the V-crimps near the edges of each sheet have to overlap.

A circular saw equipped with a metal-cutting blade is all that you need to trim the sheets. Either screws with neoprene washers or lead-headed ring-shank roofing nails can be used to anchor the panels to the purlins. I discovered that there is much debate among roofers as to which is more effective and long-lasting. I chose the nails because I felt that their lead washers (which are part of the head) would hold up longer than neoprene in this climate. Working with a carpenter and his crew, I put the roof on for a total cost of about $3,500—just slightly more than a conventional fiberglass shingle roof would have cost. (For more on metal roofing, see *FHB* #39, pp. 61-65.)

Reflective roofing is just the first line of defense. Hidden below the metal is an airspace that connects soffit vents to a continuous ridge vent. Air that is warmed beneath the metal roof can rise naturally, by convection, and escape through the ridge vent. This draws cooler air under the metal roof through soffit vents near the eaves. Instead of being trapped inside the roof, where it can contribute to high temperatures inside the house, heat can dissipate.

To create this ventilation space beneath the metal roof, I replaced conventional decking with a reflective board, or radiant barrier. The material I used is called Thermo-ply (Simplex Corp., Adrian, Mich. 49221), and it comes in 4x8 ft. sheets and in several thicknesses (I used ¼-in. thick sheets). The board is covered on both sides with foil, which reflects radiant heat.

In order for the radiant barrier to work well, it needs to have an airspace above it. Once the sheets had been stapled to the top edges of the rafters, I nailed 2x2 spacers in place over the rafters, sandwiching the Thermo-ply between rafter and spacer (top drawing, facing page). Then I nailed 1x4 wood purlins across the spacers on 12-in. centers. The 1x4s stiffen the roof structure and act as nailers for the metal roof panels. FPL's plans call for purlin spacing every 24 in., but I chose a closer spacing to ensure against "oilcanning," or excessive flexing. A rainstorm can drum up quite a racket on a metal roof. The 12-in. purlin spacing dampens the sound of rain to a pleasant level and also makes it possible to walk on the roof with no worry of denting the surface.

Both soffit and ridge vents are continuous. The effectiveness of the roof system was evident as soon as the roof was finished. You could feel air being sucked into the soffit vent as the roof heated up. One of the carpenters held a piece of paper against the vent, and the pull was so great that the paper stayed there most of the day.

Hot air out, cool air in—The vent skin conquers heat penetration, but doesn't cool the living space. To do this, you need good indoor ventilation. More specifically, you need a design that naturally exhausts warm air and draws in cool air.

Warm air rises naturally, so its principal exit in this house is through the clerestory windows 16 ft. above the floor of the main level (photo, p. 141). The clerestory, actually a gabled cupola

with seven crank-open windows, is the highest part of the house. Most of the rooms in the house have cathedral ceilings, so warm air can rise comfortably overhead and eventually exit through the clerestory.

As warm air passes out of the house through the upper windows, a slight negative pressure is created inside the house which draws air in through lower openings. Air can also be drawn into the house by what the architect calls a "wind venturi" effect. Adjusting the clerestory windows as shown on the facing page (bottom drawing) effectively harnesses prevailing breezes to increase negative pressure in the clerestory.

To enhance air movement, six ceiling fans were installed throughout the house. The fans, the configuration of the house and the location of the windows ensure good ventilation and comfortable indoor temperatures even on the hottest days.

Complementing the exhaust function of the clerestory are ample openings lower in the house for cool-air intake. Opening onto the porch are three sliding-glass doors. Each pair of doors slides into a pocket on the outside wall, so its doorway can be completely open (bottom photo, next page).

The porch that surrounds the main level is 8 ft. wide in most places, providing a valuable band of shade. Because the porch is screened, it's an integral part of the living space and keeps the home open to the outside environment.

Like the roof, the west side of the house is particularly susceptible to excessive solar-heat gain. In the west wall, there are only four windows (three are bathroom windows; the fourth is in the master bedroom), and they're small. This provides ventilation but minimizes heat gain from the afternoon sun. Exterior shutters, hinged at the top (called "Bahama shutters" in these parts), allow the windows to remain in shade when open or closed.

As another defense against heat gain in the west wall, we used vent-skin construction beneath its siding, like that on the roof. First, the Thermo-ply radiant barrier was stapled to the wall studs, followed by a layer of builder's felt. Before the T-111 plywood siding went on, 1x2 furring strips were nailed vertically into the studs. This created a ¾-in. airspace beneath the siding. The bottom of the wall was left open, save for a screen that keeps pests out. The top of the wall vents into the attic, allowing warm air from behind the siding to exhaust eventually through the vent skin of the roof.

The porch provides some degree of cooling, but the crawl space beneath the house is an even better cool-air source. My crawl space is more like a basement because the local building code requires extra elevation above grade level for houses with septic tanks. Louvers installed in the walls around the basement allow air to enter the shaded space. Floor registers inside the house and spaces between the 2x6 porch decking give basement air a chance to move upstairs.

Orientation is another crucial factor in passive-cooling design. In South Florida, the winds are consistently from the south, southeast or southwest during the hottest months. The porches and clerestory are situated to take advantage of

Drawings: Christopher Clapp

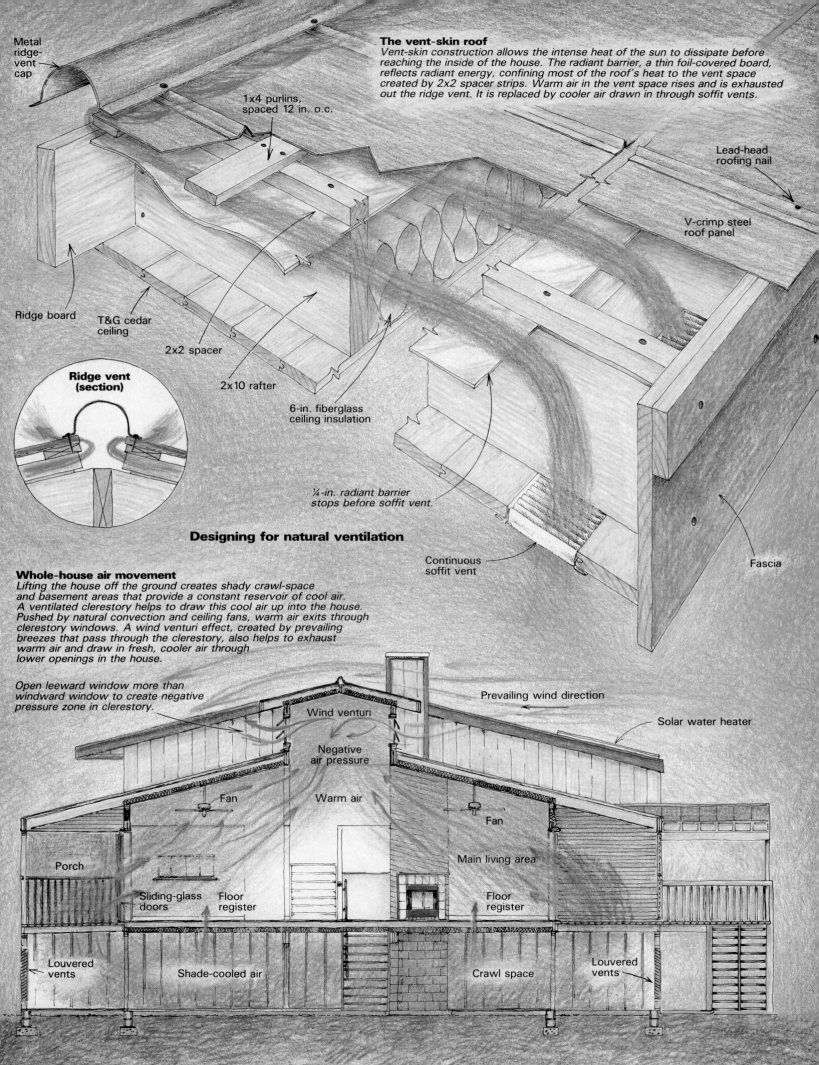

Metal ridge-vent cap

The vent-skin roof
Vent-skin construction allows the intense heat of the sun to dissipate before reaching the inside of the house. The radiant barrier, a thin foil-covered board, reflects radiant energy, confining most of the roof's heat to the vent space created by 2x2 spacer strips. Warm air in the vent space rises and is exhausted out the ridge vent. It is replaced by cooler air drawn in through soffit vents.

1x4 purlins, spaced 12 in. o.c.

Lead-head roofing nail

V-crimp steel roof panel

Ridge board

T&G cedar ceiling

2x2 spacer

Ridge vent (section)

2x10 rafter

6-in. fiberglass ceiling insulation

¼-in. radiant barrier stops before soffit vent.

Designing for natural ventilation

Continuous soffit vent

Fascia

Whole-house air movement
Lifting the house off the ground creates shady crawl-space and basement areas that provide a constant reservoir of cool air. A ventilated clerestory helps to draw this cool air up into the house. Pushed by natural convection and ceiling fans, warm air exits through clerestory windows. A wind venturi effect, created by prevailing breezes that pass through the clerestory, also helps to exhaust warm air and draw in fresh, cooler air through lower openings in the house.

Open leeward window more than windward window to create negative pressure zone in clerestory.

Prevailing wind direction

Solar water heater

Wind venturi

Negative air pressure

Warm air

Fan

Fan

Porch

Main living area

Sliding-glass doors

Floor register

Floor register

Louvered vents

Shade-cooled air

Crawl space

Louvered vents

A shady setting. Yellow pines, treated with care during the construction process, offer some respite from the sun in return. Generous porches and broad eaves combine to create a band of shade around the house. The living space sits above a vented basement that contributes cool air to the ventilation system. Below, sliding-glass pocket doors open onto 620 sq. ft. of screen porch, which substantially increases the living space.

prevailing breezes, so it's important not to deviate more than 7.5° east or west of true north when placing the home on a lot. Because of the location of our driveway, we had to flop the floor plan, keeping the clerestory and porch areas in the same location to retain the effectiveness of the design.

Testing it out—Because all materials and designs have been aimed at the goal of eliminating heat, there are some chilly mornings in the winter. A fireplace in the main living area is the sole source of heat, but in this part of Florida, cold snaps are rare and thankfully short, so we don't mind a few days of electric blankets and space heaters. FPL's designs for the central and north areas of the state have provisions for solar heating and thermal mass to help retain heat.

This was the first South Florida #2 built, and the decision to build it was a difficult one. The living space looked small, and we had no assurance that the concept would work. What I did know was that I had a 1¼-acre lot in the woods and I didn't want to be spend a lot of time inside an air-conditioned box.

FPL's plans came with two manuals prepared by the architect—one for the builder, the other for the owner. The information presented is comprehensive, covering everything from site clearing to landscaping to operating the clerestory and selecting energy-saving appliances. These manuals were invaluable to me in building the house and understanding its passive-cooling features.

Except for the vent-skin roof and west wall, construction details are fairly conventional. The porches are framed and decked with pressure-treated 2x lumber. The foundation is concrete block with a stemwall of pressure-treated 2x4s. The standard plans call for manufactured roof trusses to be used, but I framed the entire roof by hand with 2x10s. This allowed me to have cathedral ceilings in a few more rooms.

The ceilings are all T&G white cedar. Drywall ceilings are specified in the plans, but my lumberyard gave me an excellent price on the cedar because a huge shipment had been rejected. The man who had intended to use it decided he didn't like the smell of the fresh-cut cedar. I do, and in fact I miss the cedar scent now that the wood has aged.

One smell we could do without is the dank odor caused by mildew. Because of the openness of the house, mildew has been our only setback. Stuff stored in the airspace under the main floor is very vulnerable, and so are the insides of closets and kitchen cabinets. Wall-to-wall carpets aren't recommended because of the mildew potential, so our floors are either tile or oak parquet. Louvered doors have helped to control mildew in closets and cupboards, but the architect admits that the problem will be difficult to eliminate. Experiments with desiccants at the Florida Solar Energy Center might provide some non-mechanical solutions. Until then, we're more than happy with the comfort and economy of our new home. □

Ted Hutton works as a journalist for the News and Sun Sentinel Co. in Boca Raton, Fla.

An essential part of the ventilation scheme, a gabled clerestory above the living room takes advantage of convection and prevailing breezes. The floor is oak parquet; ceilings are T&G white cedar.

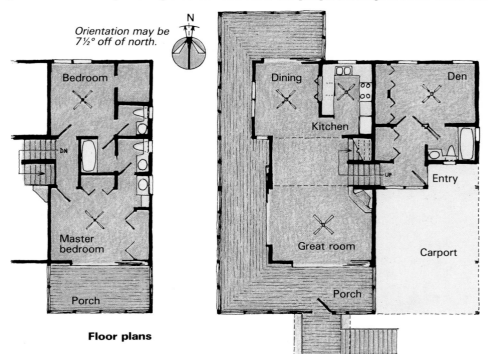

Orientation may be 7½° off of north.

N

Bedroom

Master bedroom

Porch

Dining

Kitchen

Great room

Den

Entry

Carport

Porch

Floor plans

Florida Cracker House

An indigenous form returns in style

by Mark Alvarez

There was no air conditioning for Florida's early residents. They fought stifling summer heat and humidity with shaded overhangs and open windows, and learned to design their houses to take advantage of natural phenomena that would help make them less uncomfortable. The most popular plan featured a belvedere set at the peak of a steeply pitched hip roof that would shed a heavy rain quickly. Rising warm air would be vented out through the windows of the belvedere, thus setting up a natural convection current to give some relief from the muggy heat. The style was the choice of so many native Floridians that it borrowed their nickname and became known with affectionate pride as the "cracker" house.

Architect Dwight Holmes of Rowe Holmes Associates in Tampa had been fascinated by the functional design of these traditional houses for a long time, but the advent of mechanical cooling had all but killed the style. When family friends Rita and Allen Logan asked him to design an energy-efficient, casual house with lots of light and plenty of room for entertaining, they were pleased with his proposal for a traditional Florida house with deck space and a high, central, full-width common space flanked by the family's private rooms. Allen, a lumber dealer, naturally wanted a house that would display his favorite material, and the homegrown style with Holmes' open plan was a perfect vehicle.

Site—The Logan site is suburban, but its location next to a federally protected tidal estuary lends it a rural air. Holmes tucked the house near the rear boundary of the property and left nearby palms and live oaks standing to provide shade and greater privacy.

The proximity of the preserve also imposed certain design constraints. Standing on ground only 2 ft. above sea level, the Logan house would have to be raised at least another 8 ft. to

Dwight Holmes' version of a Florida cracker house is raised above flood level on 10x10 posts of pressure-treated pine.

From *Fine Homebuilding* (June 1981) 3:56-59

meet zoning regulations and sit safely above storm flooding. Pole houses are more common in south Florida than in the Tampa area, but the technique was a natural here, and would also provide a protected space for storage and play beneath the structure. Original plans called for cable-braced utility poles anchored above the ground to concrete footings. Allen, though, located a source of 10-in. by 10-in. pine timbers in Savannah. Study indicated that they would be sturdier and would last longer if they were augered directly into the ground. They were kiln dried, Wolmanized (pressure treated against rot) and set in place. Sunk 6 ft. deep under the house and 4 ft. deep under the decks, these massive timbers connected by beams of triple 2x10s and 2x12s are the house's major structural element, and give it rigidity and resistance to hurricane-force winds.

Building methods—The framing of the house (diagrammed below right) was straightforward, though Holmes and the Logans had a little trouble at first persuading the carpenters that they were deliberately making what Holmes calls "a somewhat crude statement." The triple beams, for example, were connected to the posts with bolts through halves of ⅜-in. steel flanges (drawing and photo, next page). The joints are visible in-

side the completed house, and with the strong horizontal and vertical elements of the rough-sawn posts and beams, give the impression of strgth and solid security in what is otherwise a light and airy space.

Holmes specified standard 2x4 framing between the structural members to hold batts of 3½-in. fiberglass insulation and to serve as nailing surface for sheathing and interior finish. One of Allen's staples as a lumber dealer is T-1-11, tongue-and-groove plywood sheets that are manufactured to look like boards, and can serve as both sheathing and siding. He decided on cedar T-1-11 for the house's exterior. The sheets were fastened with coated nails so that no rust stains would develop in the future, stained with Cabot's Driftwood Creosote stain, and left to weather. Workmen were careful to flash the connection between siding and floor level beams, and caulk all other joints. Fir T-1-11 was used over the exposed rafters and on interior wall surfaces not covered with drywall.

Interior partitions were installed without molding, a trial for both sheetrockers and carpenters, who couldn't conceal inaccuracies. Back when the plans had called for utility poles, Holmes had specified a ½-in. reveal between them and both drywall and interior T-1-11. He felt that the space and the clean edge of the wall

The Logan home is sited near a protected tidal estuary. Trees left standing on the land belie the house's suburban setting.

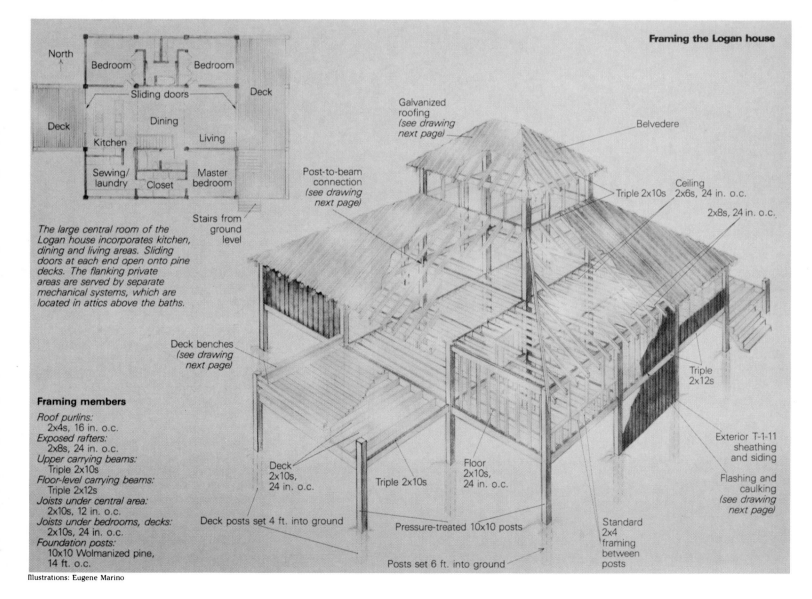

Framing the Logan house

North

Bedroom   Bedroom

Deck

Sliding doors

Deck

Dining

Living

Kitchen

Sewing/laundry   Closet   Master bedroom

Stairs from ground level

The large central room of the Logan house incorporates kitchen, dining and living areas. Sliding doors at each end open onto pine decks. The flanking private areas are served by separate mechanical systems, which are located in attics above the baths.

Galvanized roofing (see drawing next page)

Belvedere

Post-to-beam connection (see drawing next page)

Triple 2x10s

Ceiling 2x6s, 24 in. o.c.

2x8s, 24 in. o.c.

Triple 2x12s

Deck benches (see drawing next page)

Framing members

Roof purlins:
    2x4s, 16 in. o.c.
Exposed rafters:
    2x8s, 24 in. o.c.
Upper carrying beams:
    Triple 2x10s
Floor-level carrying beams:
    Triple 2x12s
Joists under central area:
    2x10s, 12 in. o.c.
Joists under bedrooms, decks:
    2x10s, 24 in. o.c.
Foundation posts:
    10x10 Wolmanized pine,
    14 ft. o.c.

Deck 2x10s, 24 in. o.c.

Triple 2x10s

Floor 2x10s, 24 in. o.c.

Exterior T-1-11 sheathing and siding

Flashing and caulking (see drawing next page)

Deck posts set 4 ft. into ground

Pressure-treated 10x10 posts

Standard 2x4 framing between posts

Posts set 6 ft. into ground

Illustrations: Eugene Marino

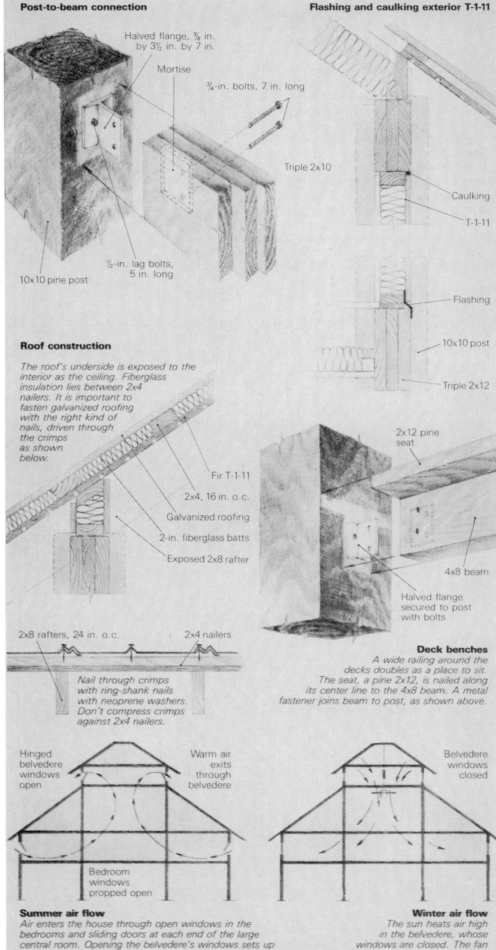

Post-to-beam connection

Halved flange, ⅜ in.
by 3½ in. by 7 in.

Mortise

¾-in. bolts, 7 in. long

Triple 2x10

10x10 pine post

½-in. lag bolts,
5 in. long

Roof construction

*The roof's underside is exposed to the
interior as the ceiling. Fiberglass
insulation lies between 2x4
nailers. It is important to
fasten galvanized roofing
with the right kind of
nails, driven through
the crimps
as shown
below.*

Fir T-1-11

2x4, 16 in. o.c.

Galvanized roofing

2-in. fiberglass batts

Exposed 2x8 rafter

2x8 rafters, 24 in. o.c.   2x4 nailers

*Nail through crimps
with ring-shank nails
with neoprene washers.
Don't compress crimps
against 2x4 nailers.*

Hinged
belvedere
windows
open

Warm air
exits
through
belvedere

Bedroom
windows
propped open

Summer air flow
*Air enters the house through open windows in the
bedrooms and sliding doors at each end of the large
central room. Opening the belvedere's windows sets up
a strong current, venting the warmest air back outside.*

Flashing and caulking exterior T-1-11

Caulking

T-1-11

Flashing

10x10 post

Triple 2x12

2x12 pine
seat

4x8 beam

Halved flange
secured to post
with bolts

Deck benches
*A wide railing around the
decks doubles as a place to sit.
The seat, a pine 2x12, is nailed along
its center line to the 4x8 beam. A metal
fastener joins beam to post, as shown above.*

Belvedere
windows
closed

Winter air flow
*The sun heats air high
in the belvedere, whose
windows are closed. The fan
pulls it down to the large room.*

**Architect Holmes deliberately made what he
calls 'a somewhat crude statement' in the Logan
house. He specified no molding around door casings, top, and wall panels, and left the bolted
joints between posts and beams visible. Outside,
above, cedar T-1-11 plywood sheets are nailed to
standard framing between the posts. The bottoms
of the sheets are flashed with galvanized steel.**

panels would offset the rough and bumpy surface of the posts, and emphasize the thrust of the
members rather than their surface lumpiness.
He stuck with the idea after the switch to
10x10s, and the reveals became a motif, subtly
emphasizing the boundary between structure
and partition.

The roofers were surprised that the plans
called for 5V-crimp, galvanized barn roofing
(what you'd find on an authentic cracker house)
instead of the more elegant and expensive
standing-seam material common in the area.
Horizontal 2x4s were nailed 16 in. on center
over the fir T-1-11, and 2-in. fiberglass batts were
set between them. The 29-ga. galvanized sheets
were fastened to the 2x4s with galvanized ring-
shanked nails whose neoprene washers sealed
the puncture holes (drawing, left).

Floors are standard oak, but they have never
been varnished. Instead, they are oiled once a
month or so with a mixture of equal parts boiled
linseed oil, turpentine and vinegar, well shaken.
The result is a darkly glowing surface.

Interior space—The house's main room soars
up to the peak of the roof, and accepts much of
its light from the belvedere's windows. Wood is
everywhere—fir T-1-11 exposed over the rafters
and used on upper wall surfaces, oak floors, pine
posts and beams, a teak rail around the stairway
to the ground—set off by white drywall on the
lower walls, and the red Westinghouse Micarta
plastic laminate on the kitchen counters. The
room sweeps the full width of the house, and
sliding glass doors at each end lead out to pine
decks. The effect is one of casual but well-
ordered spaciousness.

The children's rooms to the north share a com-

Roof rafters in the Logan house are exposed. The fir T-1-11 over them is also the roof sheathing. In the winter, the fan in the belvedere pulls downward air warmed by the sun; in summer, hot air vents out through the belvedere.

Casual outdoor spaces were an important part of the Logan house design. The decks are surrounded by pine benches that double as railings, and under the house is a combined garage, storage area and play space.

mon bath, and provide plenty of space for kids to play. On the south side, the master suite is connected by a closet/dressing room to Rita's haven, a sewing room that doubles as a laundry. Attics over the private areas carry the house's mechanical systems.

Cooling and heating—Like early cracker homes, the Logan house was designed to promote natural ventilation, though air conditioners were also installed. Allen had the simple windows in the bedrooms and belvedere custom-made of mahogany, which is no longer as scarce or as costly as it once was. Bedroom windows hinged at the top are simply propped open. Those in the belvedere swing inward from the bottom when their latches are unhooked by a telescoping pole of the type used by electric utilities to switch transformers on and off.

Air entering through the lower windows and the sliding doors rises into the belvedere and is vented back outside (drawing, bottom of previous page). The air currents are surprisingly brisk, and increase noticeably as more belvedere sashes are opened. When storm winds blow, the force of the rising air is strong enough to slam the windows shut, saving the Logans the trouble of getting out their pole.

The result of this natural ventilation is that the Logans button up the house and use their air conditioners only intermittently during the summer, rather than 24 hours a day, every day, as many Floridians must. They estimate a savings of one-quarter to one-third on their electric bill.

The design of their house also works for the Logans during Tampa's usually short heating season. Morning sunlight streaming through closed belvedere windows heats air high above the floor, which is then pulled downward by a fan suspended from the ceiling. During a normal winter the Logans turn on the heat pumps of their mechanical system only on one or two dozen evenings, relying on sunlight and a mild climate to keep warm. They have recently installed a freestanding Firedrum II fireplace (made by Fire Drum Corp., 1566 Carroll Ave., San Francisco, Calif. 94124) with firebrick to hold heat instead of sending all of it up the chimney. This past winter, though, with temperatures frequently in the twenties, the heat pumps worked "for 1½ months straight," according to Rita. Nevertheless, their electric bills were at least 25% lower than those of friends living in similar sized houses.

Outdoor living—Holmes and the Logans planned decks at the east and west as integral parts of the house. Parties often flow onto the larger deck off the living area, and members of the family wander in and out of entries they can often leave open, because the breezes at that height keep bugs at bay.

Benches were built as railings along both decks, but their pine seats, fastened along their centers only (drawing, previous page), are warping and cupping badly. The Logans are planning to re-

place them with redwood. They are also thinking of using a bleaching stain to accelerate the weathering of the exterior cedar T-1-11. Rain rebounding from the decks turned the lower portions of the siding gray quickly, while leaving the rest much nearer its original shade.

Underneath the house is a carport, a storage space and a sheltered play area for the Logan children and their friends. Plumbing rises through the two partitions, one of which also encloses stairs to the main floor, and both of which screen heat pumps set on the ground. Plumbing for a house of the same size on slab would run about $2,000, according to Holmes, but running pipes inside partitions and through floor joists doubled the cost. Drywall is mounted on joist bottoms, hiding pipes, wires and 6 in. of fiberglass insulation.

Cracker houses were developed by rural, untrained owner-builders who needed relief from unbearable heat and humidity. Their priorities have begun to make sense all over again in an era of escalating energy costs and dwindling water supplies. Architect Holmes recognized that the style was also a natural for the Logan's casual, outdoor life, and their remote-seeming site. While the original form reflected the idiosyncrasies of materials available to subsistence farmers in a harsh climate, Holmes' use of modern materials and techniques is honest and respectful. His carefully "crude" details and concern for function retain not only the appearance of the vernacular style, but its vigor as well. □

Raised in Florida

A passively cooled house built on stilts to catch the breeze

by Herb Beatty

Passive-solar homes in Fort Myers, Florida, have little in common with those in Minneapolis, Minnesota. Before I moved to Florida in 1981, I built passive-solar houses in the Minneapolis area, where heating bills are steep. But when I decided to build a passive-solar house in Fort Myers, I needed to change my point of view. In an area that averages 4,000 cooling degree days a year, passive solar means passive cooling.

I knew that the state-funded Florida Solar Energy Center (FSEC, 300 State Rd. 401, Cape Canaveral, Fla. 32920) had researched the design of energy-efficient buildings for hot, humid climates. So before I designed my house, I attended several of their seminars to learn the principles of passive-solar cooling. Based on the information I gathered, I designed a three-story "stilt house" with a central cooling core, vented walls and radiant barriers (photo below).

I decided to raise the house 12 ft. up on pilings. This would induce a chimney effect, with warm air exhausting out of the top of the house and cooler air replacing it from the shaded area beneath the main floor. Also, at the higher level the natural wind velocity is greater, which enhances evaporative cooling. And as a bonus I'd get a better view, more privacy and fewer flying insects. Like all passive-solar homes, this one would require an active owner to adjust the ventilation throughout the year.

A three-story core—The central core of the house measures 12 ft. by 12 ft. and rises a full three stories. At ground level, it contains a utility room, an entry, and stairs that lead all the way to the loft on the third floor. On the second level, the main living areas surround the core (drawing, facing page).

The core is the primary conduit for the air flow through the house. It directs warm air up to the loft, where the air is exhausted through awning windows. The resulting negative pressure draws cool air in through two louvered doors in the utility room, where most of it funnels up the stairwell. The rest enters the kitchen through vents at the base of the cabinets.

The vents consist of a ⅜-in. slot routed horizontally down the center of the toeboard. Air enters the base through screened vents in the utility room ceiling (which is uninsulated) and through holes cut in the subfloor beneath the cabinets. Warm air from the main living area exits through vents at the top of the interior walls surrounding the core (photo on p. 149) that correspond to vents in the lower portion of the walls of the loft.

Adjusting to the elements—In Fort Myers, the prevailing summer breezes blow consistently out of the southeast, so I placed a large screened porch at the southeast corner of the

The house is elevated on stilts and arranged around a central core to encourage natural ventilation. Domestic hot water is provided by the flat-plate collector on the loft roof. The photovoltaic cell mounted beneath it powers a water pump in the first-floor utility room.

house to capture them. An adjacent open deck faces south and skirts two 8-ft. Har-Car sliding-glass pocket doors (Har-Car Aluminum Products, 1201 Cornwall Rd., Sanford, Fla. 32773). Each door has top and bottom tracks that extend an extra 4 ft. on one end, allowing the 4-ft. door panels to "stack" out of the way for full ventilation of the living and dining rooms (photo on p. 149). These doors are shielded from the summer sun by the 4-ft. deck overhang. During the rest of the year, sun is admitted for passive heating; a heat-circulating fireplace supplies backup heat. The bedrooms are located on the east and north sides of the house, (away from the late-afternoon sun), and the main entry is reached by exterior stairs on the northwest corner.

The east and west walls get the low-morning or afternoon sun, so here I used a minimum of windows, with none in the main living area. The windows are protected from direct sun by what is generically referred to as "grey film." The translucent film, a flexible lamination of polyesters and aluminum, is applied to the interior side of the windows and reflects 60% to 80% of the radiant heat striking it. I left the tricky job of installing the film to seasoned professionals, who are sometimes referred to as "tinters."

Hurricane-proof foundation—In this hurricane-prone area, wood-piling foundations for stilt houses must be strong enough to withstand the upward thrust created by high winds. The foundation for the house consists of 8x8 pine timbers with a 30-year saltwater intrusion treatment. Wood treated this way is subjected to greater pressure and retains more chemicals than standard pressure-treated lumber.

The pilings were sunk 6 ft. into the ground in hand-dug holes (photo at right). Footings weren't required, but the four pilings in the center were anchored with 4-ft. by 4-ft. by 1-ft. 6 in. thick concrete collars to ensure stability of the core. Pilings were anchored to the collars by drilling two horizontal, perpendicular holes in each piling—one slightly above the other so they wouldn't intersect—about 8 in. up from the bottom. A 3-ft. 8 in. length of ¾-in. rebar was then driven through each hole so that both ends projected about 1½ ft. Once the pilings were set and the collars had been poured, the holes were packed with the excavated soil.

The main floor platform was framed with pressure-treated southern yellow pine. The beams were made by bolting three 2x12s together with a pair of ¾-in. galvanized bolts spaced every 4 ft. The piling tops were then notched and the beams bolted to them. They cantilever out to support the joists beneath the north end of the master bedroom, and the porch and deck on the south side of the house. The floor joists themselves cantilever out 4 ft. beyond the beams to support the entire east wall. Under the deck and porches, 2x10 joists were used, while the main living

areas are supported by 2x12s. All the floor joists were placed 24 in. o. c. and fastened securely with galvanized hurricane straps. The subfloor is ¾-in. T&G waferboard.

Vent skins and radiant barriers—Most of the summer heat comes through the east and west walls on the main level, as well as through the roof, so I specified vent-skin and radiant-barrier designs for those locations. This would reflect solar radiation away from the interior of the house and vent warm air

out of wall and roof cavities through ridge vents in the roof.

The shell of the house features a hard-working collection of details. The 2x4 stud walls were insulated with R-11 fiberglass batts. On the north and south walls, ⅛-in. Thermo-ply "Storm Brace" sheathing (Simplex Manufacturing Co., 3000 W. Beecher Rd., Adrian, Mich. 49221) is sandwiched between 2x4 studs and T-111 plywood siding. Thermo-ply is a laminated structural sheathing with a reflective aluminum surface. On

The pilings were sunk 6 ft. in the ground to resist uplift during hurricanes. For added stability, the four pilings supporting the core of the house were anchored to 4-ft. sq. by 1-ft. 6 in. thick concrete collars. Once the house was framed and sheathed, the bracing was removed.

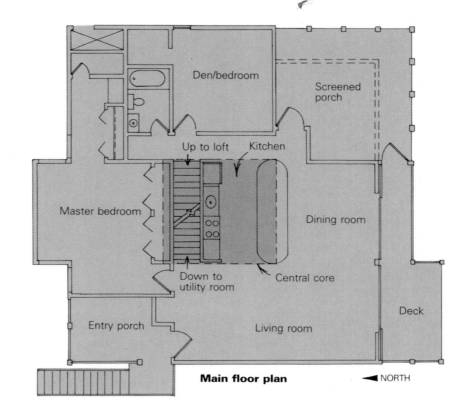

Main floor plan   ◄ NORTH

Den/bedroom

Screened porch

Up to loft   Kitchen

Master bedroom

Dining room

Down to utility room   Central core

Deck

Entry porch   Living room

Section through vent-skin wall and roof

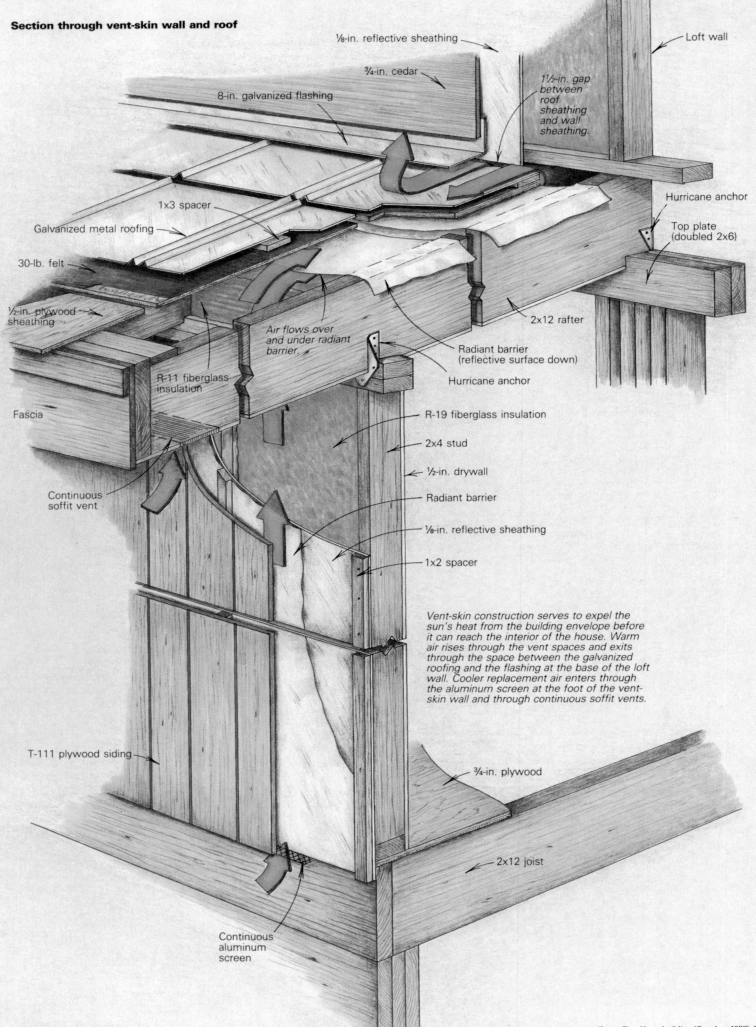

⅛-in. reflective sheathing

¾-in. cedar

8-in. galvanized flashing

1½-in. gap between roof sheathing and wall sheathing.

Loft wall

1x3 spacer

Galvanized metal roofing

Hurricane anchor

Top plate (doubled 2x6)

30-lb. felt

½-in. plywood sheathing

Air flows over and under radiant barrier.

2x12 rafter

Radiant barrier (reflective surface down)

Hurricane anchor

Fascia

R-11 fiberglass insulation

R-19 fiberglass insulation

2x4 stud

½-in. drywall

Radiant barrier

⅛-in. reflective sheathing

1x2 spacer

Continuous soffit vent

Vent-skin construction serves to expel the sun's heat from the building envelope before it can reach the interior of the house. Warm air rises through the vent spaces and exits through the space between the galvanized roofing and the flashing at the base of the loft wall. Cooler replacement air enters through the aluminum screen at the foot of the vent-skin wall and through continuous soffit vents.

T-111 plywood siding

¾-in. plywood

2x12 joist

Continuous aluminum screen

From *Fine Homebuilding* (October 1988) 49:72-75

the radiant-barrier walls east and west, I added a layer of Parsec Thermo-Brite (Parsec Inc., P. O. Box 38527, Dallas, Tex. 75238) over the Thermo-ply for additional radiant-heat control. It's a flexible builder's foil that consists of a thin layer of aluminum laminated to a reinforcing substrate. The foil reflects up to 95% of the heat radiating from a warm exterior surface.

Radiant barriers have to face an open air-space in order to work. Otherwise, they just pass heat by conduction from a hot surface to a cooler one. In this case, the airspace was created by nailing vertical 1x2 furring strips over the Thermo-ply sheathing at each stud location to separate the Thermo-ply and the T-111 siding. Aluminum screening at the bottom of the air space keeps out bugs and birds. The air space also provides a series of "wall chimneys" that let warm air behind the siding escape through the roof ventilation system (drawing, facing page).

Most of the summer heat in a typical Florida home enters through the roof, so the design of the roof was critical. Experiments by the FSEC have shown attic radiant barriers to be cost-effective as far north as Baltimore. Here, a radiant barrier of Parsec Thermo-Brite was stapled over the rafters beneath the plywood sheathing. The foil was installed to droop about 2 in. between the rafters. This created an air space between the foil and the sheathing that channels the warm air up and out through the ridge vents. Though radiant

barriers reflect heat for a time with the reflecting surface facing either up or down, dust may degrade the performance of the foil over a period of time. For that reason, the FSEC recommends installing the foil shiny-side down.

After 30-lb. felt was stapled to the roof sheathing, 1x3s were nailed to the deck horizontally 24 in. o. c., and galvanized metal roofing was installed over them. This created another series of ventilation channels. Galvanized metal roofing is reflective, too. Finally, the roof was insulated with R-19 fiberglass batts. There is a 5½-in. air space between the insulation and the radiant barrier above it. The complete roofing system blocks more heat than a standard roof insulated with R-48 batts, and it's cheaper to install.

Research by the FSEC has shown that radiant barriers work best in concert with soffit and ridge vents. On the main roof, I used continuous soffit vents at the eaves and designed a simple venting system where the roof meets the loft. The vent consists of a 1½-in. gap between the roof sheathing and the loft walls. Eight-inch galvanized flashing was bent to the pitch of the roof and installed behind the finish siding to cover the gap (drawing, facing page). This ventilates not only the main roof but the vent-skin walls below. For the roof over the loft, soffit vents and a ridge vent draw warm air out of the roof cavities.

Mechanicals—My home is equipped with a 4 ft. by 10 ft. flat-plate solar collector, which provides 100% of my hot water requirements. The hot-water storage tank is located in the utility room on the ground floor, where a photovoltaic-powered pump lifts the water up to the solar panel atop the loft roof. The pump operates automatically whenever there is enough sunlight to heat the water.

The house is all-electric, including an oven and range, microwave oven, frost-free refrigerator, dishwasher, clothes washer and dryer, stereo and even a barbeque. There are also five ceiling fans—which aren't essential to the passive cooling—and a 3.5 ton air-conditioning system. An electric-strip heating system was installed in the air-conditioning duct work, but I rarely use it. Occasionally, when high humidity and hot temperatures coincide with breezeless days, I have to turn on the air conditioner, but this is the exception rather than the rule.

The bottom line—The house took just over two months to build, and the passive and active solar features accounted for about 5% of the total cost. I've been rewarded with electric bills averaging about 20% of those for conventional houses of comparable size. □

Herb Beatty is a solar-energy consultant who also distributes and installs radiant barriers in Fort Myers, Fla. Photos by the author, except where noted.

A 4-ft. overhang shades the interior in the summer, but allows for moderate passive heating during the winter. The deck leads to the southeast corner of the house, where a screened porch captures the prevailing summer breezes. Two 8-ft. sliding-glass pocket doors open a full 16 ft. to ventilate the living and dining rooms. The vents in the walls above the kitchen help direct warm air from the main living areas into the loft, where it exits through awning windows. The ceiling fan in the dining room is rarely used. *Photo by staff.*

Passive Cooling

Earth-coupling, shuttered skylights and good venting help keep a North Florida house cool

by Chuck Mitchell and Tom Barr

The problem of keeping cool in a hot, humid climate is an old one here in North Florida. Long before air conditioners became common household appliances, house designs incorporated simple systems for passive cooling. Historically, Florida's vernacular architecture has taken two paths to cooling: the massive masonry building of Spanish origin and the lighter, single-story Florida farmhouse that was raised off the ground and built in the form of a narrow rectangle.

Clearly, there was something to be learned from the proven methods of passive cooling found in these different vernacular forms. Our goal in planning the house shown below was to combine both old and new ideas in an optimum design for a cool, livable house. The Tallahassee house we finished in early 1980 represents what

we feel is a good combination. It also presents several design and construction details that, though not commonly used at the moment, will probably become popular in passive cooling systems in the future.

Before diving into design details, it is important to mention one crucial unknown upon which the effective performance of any energy-efficient house will depend: the inhabitant. In this case, our client was familiar with the passive and active cooling details that made up the entire system. She could, in fact, adjust the system to suit particular variations in temperature, humidity, or sunlight. If it were not for her understanding and willingness to participate in part of the process, the passive cooling systems could not perform as we intended.

Design for cooling—Our strategy for cooling can be divided into four distinct areas of design considerations: heat gain prevention, active and passive ventilation, earth-coupled cooling and active dehumidification. In some instances we used or adapted traditional approaches to enhance warm-weather cooling; in other cases we developed new ideas.

Porches, high ceilings, cupolas and windows placed to maximize cross ventilation are several important traditional elements we used to prevent heat gain. Porches with low roofs that keep direct sunlight out of the house were replaced by overhangs and light-proof skylight shutters, which performed the same function. Roll-down shades on solarium windows and insulated drapes on sliding-glass doors were also used to

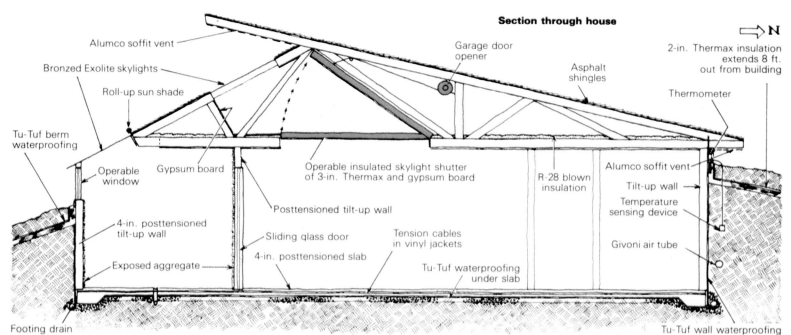

Section through house

⇨ N

- Alumco soffit vent
- Bronzed Exolite skylights
- Roll-up sun shade
- Tu-Tuf berm waterproofing
- Operable window
- Gypsum board
- 4-in. posttensioned tilt-up wall
- Exposed aggregate
- Footing drain
- Operable insulated skylight shutter of 3-in. Thermax and gypsum board
- Posttensioned tilt-up wall
- Sliding glass door
- 4-in. posttensioned slab
- Tension cables in vinyl jackets
- Tu-Tuf waterproofing under slab
- Garage door opener
- Asphalt shingles
- R-28 blown insulation
- 2-in. Thermax insulation extends 8 ft. out from building
- Thermometer
- Alumco soffit vent
- Tilt-up wall
- Temperature sensing device
- Givoni air tube
- Tu-Tuf wall waterproofing

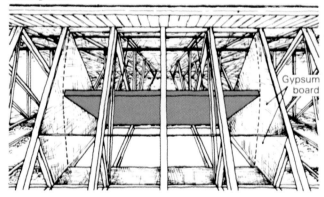

Gypsum board

In the drawing at left, a light well is viewed from outside the building as though the skylight glazing and roof were removed. The ceiling shutter (in color) is drawn up to a ¾-open position in the well. Hot air rises into the light well and is vented over and around the shutter, then outside through the soffit vents. If the shutter is fully opened, the venting is closed off.

- Master bath
- Utilities
- Exhaust fan
- Bath
- Den
- Kitchen
- Master bedroom
- Bedroom
- Great room
- Garage
- Solarium
- Entry
- **Floor plan**

⇧ N

prevent heat gain by direct sunlight. Again borrowing from the farmhouse, we planned to use vegetation as a means of passive cooling around the house. The high ceilings typical of vernacular architecture encourage passive cooling: Hot air to rises and escapes through cupolas and vents in the attic. We used this idea in the new house, providing an exit route for warm air through a series of continuous attic soffit vents. To prevent heat gain through the roof, we isolated this sun-exposed area from the interior with R-26 insulation, specifying oversized roof trusses to hold the extra cellulose.

The ventilation plan we designed began with the traditional narrow, rectangular form of the farmhouse, a shape that maximizes cross-ventilation. We designed two passive systems for venting warm air out of the house interior. The first is the solarium soffit, which siphons warmer air through the attic and out the upper soffit vents mentioned earlier. Adjustable, insulated ceiling shutters (shown above) in the living room and bedrooms form the second system. These multi-purpose shutters can be opened and closed through an infinitely adjustable switch hooked up to an electric garage door opener. When opened three-quarters of the way, ceiling height is increased by about four feet, providing pockets where rising warm air can collect before escaping through the attic soffits.

Passive systems keep this Florida house cool in the summer. The roof overhang (opposite page) shades the skylights. Earth berms surround the house and keep the walls cool; only the roof protrudes above ground level (top). River stones add texture to the exterior wall (above).

Conversely, the shutters are usually closed at night to hold in heat. They can also be opened during sunny winter days to admit direct sunlight through skylights in the roof. An angled roof overhang keeps direct summer sunlight out of the house when the ceiling shutters are open.

We designed the active ventilation system as a backup to the passive. It consists of a 30-in. whole-house exhaust fan located in a common hallway and regulated with a rheostat. The unit controls not only the amount and velocity of breezes through selected rooms, but—more significantly—the exact times when cooler outside air is desired inside. On hot days the owner can raise the four ceiling shutters, thereby providing an effective convection route for warmer interior air. The fan can supplement passive venting action, removing the hot air through the top soffit vents and drawing cooler air into the house from ground level.

Earth-coupled cooling—As in the farmhouse, we relied upon a large surface-to-volume ratio for the walls to dissipate heat. But, recalling the massive, thick-walled Spanish vernacular style, we wanted to take heat dissipation through the wall mass a step further. Our calculations (based on data collected in Tallahassee by D.R. Davis, agricultural meteorologist, and from procedures developed by Dr. K. Labs at Undercurrents En-

The ceiling shutters are fully open (top photo), letting in the maximum amount of solar heat on this winter day. On hot summer days, opening the shutters allows hot air to rise and escape through soffit vents in the attic. The roof overhang prevents direct summer sunlight from entering through the skylight. Sliding windows can be opened in the solarium (above, at right) to catch the breeze, but more often they are closed, and hot air is either vented through the soffit or retained. In hot weather, roll-up shades cover the transparent acrylic glazing on the ceiling.

vironmental Research Station) showed that a large proportion of the house's cooling needs could be met by earth-coupled cooling in a bermed-earth design. Two-thirds of the building's wall area and all of its floor area would be in direct contact with the earth.

With this design decision behind us, the problem then became how to thermally stabilize the berms surrounding the house. Our plan assumed a stable cool temperature just below grade level. However, field data in our area indicated that soil temperatures suitable for cooling could be obtained only at a depth of 5 ft. to 8 ft. Because of this we decided to insulate the berm, reducing the impact of the sun and air on it and creating the desired stable, cool temperatures at a depth of only 4 ft.

When the berm had been filled in around finished exterior walls to a point 12-in. below finished grade, we covered the earth with sheets of 2-in. thick Styrofoam bead board. It extended 8 ft. out from the building wall on both west and north sides. We then covered the Styrofoam with a layer of Tu-Tuf waterproof liner (manufactured by Sto-Cote Products, Inc., Drawer 310, Richmond IL 60071). This was then covered with earth up to the finished grade level. In addition to separating the Styrofoam board from its soil cover, the waterproof liner deflects surface water from the building. (See top right photos.) This is important, since water severely reduces the insulating properties of soil. As far as

---

Typical Seasonal Operations

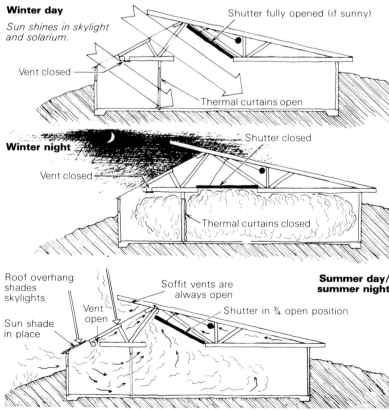

Winter day
Sun shines in skylight and solarium.

Shutter fully opened (if sunny)
Vent closed
Thermal curtains open

Winter night
Vent closed
Shutter closed
Thermal curtains closed

Summer day/ summer night
Roof overhang shades skylights
Soffit vents are always open
Vent open
Sun shade in place
Shutter in ¾ open position

Winter

6:00 A.M.: Open ceiling shutters to allow the sun's rays in. Open drapes in solarium. If you're leaving for work, open doors from solarium; if not, then prepare to enjoy breakfast there.

10:00 A.M.: Air temperature in the solarium should be warm enough so that the doors to the solarium can be opened to allow heat inside.

2:00 P.M.: If it is a sunny day, the temperature inside may be getting too warm. If you're still at home, the doors to the solarium may need to be closed, and perhaps the drapes as well. If it is still too warm, the ceiling shutters may be adjusted to admit less (or no) sun. The dampers for the solarium exhaust vents may also be opened to exhaust excess heat, but if the home can be made comfortable without this operation, it is better to retain as much heat in the solarium and its mass as possible to help heat the house at night.

6:00 P.M.: Since the sun should still be providing good insolation, you may choose to leave all systems open for another few hours. If, however, it is a cold overcast day with little heat gain, it may be time to close the doors to the solarium, close the curtains and close the ceiling shutters. From this point the building's massive heat storage should keep you comfortable through the night. A fire may be started, or the heat pump can be turned on. All systems remain closed until the morning.

Summer

6:00 A.M.: All ventilating systems are still open from the night, and the house is cooled.

10:00 A.M.: As the temperature rises, the doors to the solarium are closed. The curtains are drawn if the vents in the solarium are not removing all excess heat. To vent the inner house you can leave the ceiling shutters three-quarters open for indirect lighting. (The direct sun is blocked by the roof overhang.) You can also close the ceiling shutter to seal the building and retain the coolness.

2:00 P.M.: The temperature inside may have risen to the point where the heat pump goes on to provide backup cooling for extra comfort.

6:00 P.M.: As ambient temperatures begin to drop, the house may still be closed up and remain cool without the necessity of the heat pump. When ambient temperatures drop into the comfort zone of 78° (usually around sunset), the house may be opened up and the whole-house exhaust fan turned on to augment cooling. The home may remain open through the night, and should cool to the low to mid-70s (typical August low temperature). Of course, should you choose to keep the house closed through the night, cool temperatures can be maintained through storage in the bermed-earth mass.

—Chuck Mitchell and Tom Barr

the physical aspect of this insulating job is concerned, we found that we could drive our Uniloader over the Styrofoam without damaging it once a foot of soil had been distributed over the insulation and its waterproof cover.

We are also experimenting with another element in berm conditioning: blowing cool night air through tubes in the berm to remove heat that has built up in it during the day. This system is being developed in Israel by Dr. Baruch Givoni, author of *Man, Climate and Architecture*. (It can be purchased for £16 from Applied Science Publications Ltd., 22 Rippleside, Ripple Road, Barking, Essex England.) At this point we have installed only one Givoni air tube under our berm insulation. We are monitoring this system with temperature sensors in the berm, and preliminary data show that we are able to reduce the berm temperature enough to justify the cost of running the fan.

Because of the stability of the berm temperature, this cushion of earth could also be relied upon for passive heating during the occasional cold spells that come to North Florida. During December 1980, a five-day period of overcast days and below-freezing nights failed to drop the solarium's temperature below 62°F; this area is a totally passive-conditioned zone.

Augmenting the berm as a cold-weather heat source are several backup systems. Direct solar gain through the solarium's sliding doors and ceiling shutters is an additional source of passive heating. For active heating we installed a Lennox 1½-ton heat pump which also serves as a dehumidifier. The heat pump has been called on more as an air handler and heat distributor than as a heat generator. It comes on rarely in the winter. The house also has an energy-efficient Heatilator fireplace, but this is more of an aesthetic feature than a necessary part of the heating system. The owner hasn't used this unit very much because of the efficiency of the other parts of the system.

Active dehumidification was the final part of our strategy for warm-weather cooling. It was also a necessary accessory to the bermed wall design, since underground dwellings have an inherently high humidity index when compared to above-ground structures. The Lennox heat pump is designed to remove excess humidity without affecting the temperature.

Posttensioning the foundation—Standard foundation construction was not feasible due to potentially shifting soils with low permeability. While a standard 2,500 psi (lbs. per sq. in.) concrete slab can carry a considerable weight, it cannot withstand significant pressure from lateral shifting or torquing due to unstable soils. Consequently, we chose a method of construction that is relatively new to the home-building industry: posttensioned concrete. This is a system based on 3,500 psi concrete slab containing steel cables under tension. Each slab has

Above, prior to berming the wall, waterproof sheeting is installed (left). Cables attach the wall to deadman anchors set in the ground; they will be tensioned before backfilling begins. At right, the berm has been compacted to within 12 in. of its final height. An 8-ft. band of 2-in. insulation board is laid on the berm, followed by a layer of waterproof sheeting. Then the final 12 in. of earth is spread over the berm. This way, an 8-ft. band of earth around the house is insulated from the sun and ambient air temperature, helping to maintain stable house temperatures during hot or cold weather.

Wall slabs are cast on the floor slab and tilted up into place by a small crane. Here a wall slab is being placed in a keyed slot at the perimeter of the posttensioned floor slab.

Once the walls are tilted into place, they are temporarily braced as shown above, until the whole system can be locked together with interlocking top-plate hardware. The openings in the wall will enclose sliding glass doors.

The two men below are torquing and welding a corner bracket. The corners are pulled together and joined to stabilize the form. Slab corners are drawn together with a torquing device (bottom).

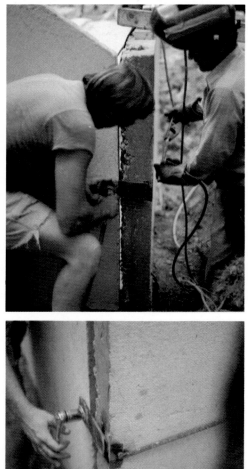

the wall sections. Our engineer advised casting the sections horizontally, on top of the finished surface. After they had been posttensioned, they were tilted up onto the foundation with a small crane. Next, we held the walls in place with temporary braces until special connecting hardware had been secured. The hardware consisted of interlocking top plates and steel cables running diagonally down to concrete deadmen, which we located in the ground about 8 ft. from the building, as shown in the top photo at left.

Although posttensioning is not a construction technique commonly used in single-family houses, we found it to be an important part of our final design. All phases of the concrete work were done on the site, with little need for special equipment. We, as designers and builders, can share the owner's confidence that the house will stand up to the expected soil shifting that can buckle or crack standard concrete foundations.

The interior side of the wall was coated with adhesive and finished with plaster. For the interior sides of the solarium walls (and the exposed exterior wall near the entry) we cast a 1-in. layer of river rock into the reinforced wall when the concrete was poured into the wall forms. When these walls were tilted up, the bottom face revealed a mat of rock embedded in the wall as a textured finish surface.

We used Tu-Tuf for water protection, running one continuous piece from the top wall plate to below the crushed stone beneath the foundation. This was the logical choice, since this waterproofing material provides a seamless seal over the entire foundation, and allows the concrete walls to expand or contract without breaking the waterproofing surface.

greater compressive strength than a standard poured slab and, additionally, substantial tensile strength, which enables it to withstand severe earth movement in any direction.

The floor slab (shown in the photo above) was formed and prepared much like a standard monolithic slab, except that ⅜-in. steel cables jacketed in plastic were used for reinforcement instead of steel rebar and wire mesh. These cables were interwoven 3 ft. on center throughout the slab. Their ends were left protruding through the forms at points along the perimeter. Each intersection of the cable within the slab was supported by a chair 1½-in. high, to keep the cable in the middle of the 4-in. thick slab during the concrete pour.

After the rough plumbing and termite treatment, we put in 6 in. of crushed stone before the concrete was poured into the forms and finished as usual. Three to five days after the pour we installed specially made steel slip washers around the dozen or so exposed ends of cable. Through the use of a special posttensioning machine, the cable was stretched to a tension of 30,000 lbs. per inch, and pulled taut through the washers, which prevented the cable from slipping back. Stretching and locking off each cable end causes the slab to be uniformly strengthened through tension. A slab of this type can support a three-story building anywhere on its surface, and can also withstand shifting earth (a problem on our site) and sinkholes without cracking.

Because we were also concerned with lateral pressures the earth would exert on the walls of the building—especially during periods of heavy rains—posttensioning was also planned for exterior walls. With this in mind, we cast the foundation slab with a perimeter slot to receive

Costs and conclusions—The Tallahassee house totalled 1,768 sq. ft. and cost about $35/sq. ft. to build. The garage and driveway brought construction expenses to $67,800. This falls within the medium price range in our market. We think the house works successfully. This is due largely to the research and planning that took place as a part of the design process. We were fortunate to have a client whose desire for a thermally efficient house enabled us to utilize several ideas we had been developing for passive cooling and warm-weather house design.

On a more specific level, our design strategy for warm-weather cooling turned out to be an integrated program dependent on not one but several systems: heat gain prevention, passive and active ventilation, earth-coupled cooling, and dehumidification. The multi-faceted nature of the program ensures its effectiveness, since different systems can be used in combination or as backups to achieve the most comfortable interior climate possible. □

Chuck Mitchell and Tom Barr are principals of Mad Dog Design and Construction Inc., in Tallahassee, Fla.

A Modern Mississippi House

Traditional forms find new expression in this design for a hot, humid climate

by Robert M. Ford

Northeastern Mississippi has mild winters, hot summers and high humidity throughout most of the year. The well-ventilated houses built by early settlers in this region responded well to these conditions, and established an architectural tradition that I wanted to incorporate in my design for a modern house. Passive cooling was a major goal, since many home owners in this part of the country pay monthly electric bills in excess of $130 when air-conditioning demand is high. My house has an average electric bill of $30 per month because I used the same design principles that were developed by early Mississippi builders. Beyond energy-efficient design, I was also looking for traditional forms that would link a contemporary house to the rich heritage of the region. So I named it Deja-vu.

The formality of antebellum homes is closely linked with the graciousness of Southern hospitality, and I wanted my house to restate this tradition. Many old mansions have long drive-

Resting on concrete piers, above, the house perches on its sloping site, overlooking a pond. Windows, porches and a belvedere maximize views and ventilation. The symmetrical plan of the house is most noticeable from the street (top photo), where twin carports are linked to the house by a 66-ft. long walkway.

ways with detached stables or carriage houses. My building site could also accommodate such a plan. The lot is wedge-shaped, with a dead-end street at its narrow south side. Growing wider, it slopes down to the edge of a pond.

In order to shelter two cars and to provide much-needed storage space, I located the carports near the road, flanking a 66-ft. long bridge leading to the house (photo above). This long entryway, with its detached carriage-house appearance, helped to create the formal feeling I had in mind. It would also work well with my plan to put the house as close to the pond as local zoning regulations would allow. The carports needed to be at grade, but the slope of the lot suggested a raised house. Lifting the structure off the ground would provide a beautiful view of the pond.

Passive cooling—The traditional strategy for cooling in large houses was simple: Ventilate from at least three sides of every room and al-

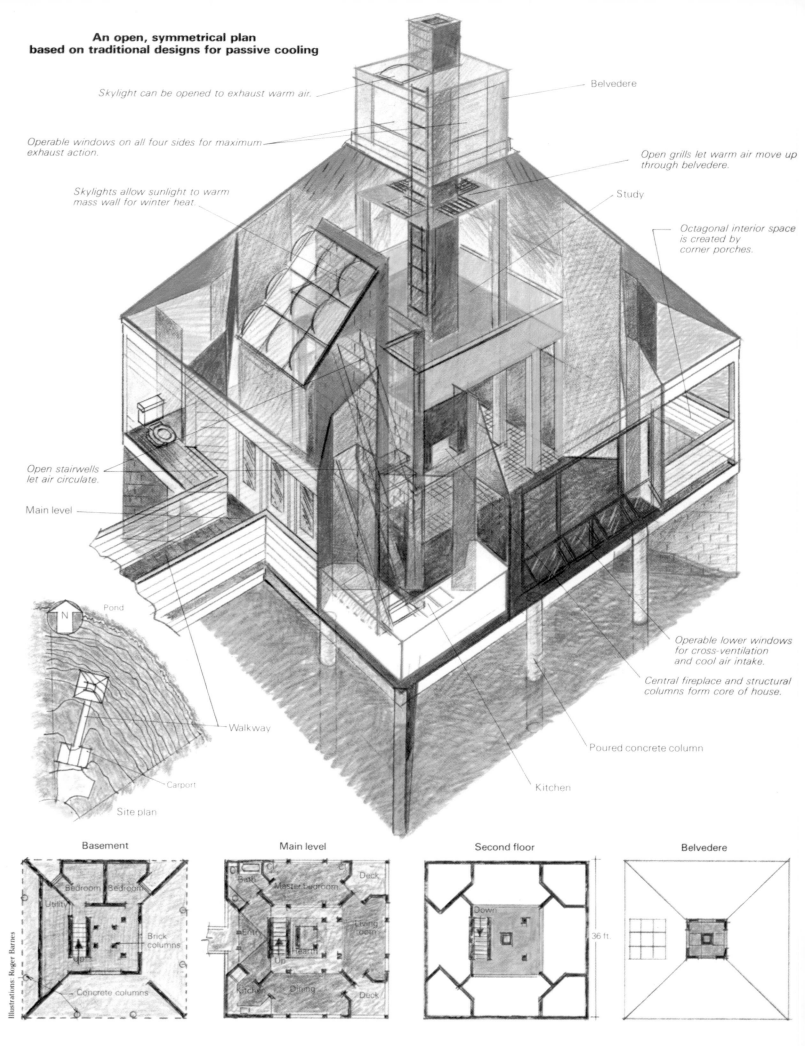

An open, symmetrical plan based on traditional designs for passive cooling

Skylight can be opened to exhaust warm air.

Operable windows on all four sides for maximum exhaust action.

Skylights allow sunlight to warm mass wall for winter heat.

Open stairwells let air circulate.

Main level

Belvedere

Open grills let warm air move up through belvedere.

Study

Octagonal interior space is created by corner porches.

Operable lower windows for cross-ventilation and cool air intake.

Central fireplace and structural columns form core of house.

Poured concrete column

Kitchen

Pond

N

Walkway

Carport

Site plan

Illustrations: Roger Barnes

Basement

Bedroom Bedroom

Utility

Brick columns

Up

Concrete columns

Main level

Bath

Cl

Master bedroom

Deck

Entry

Hearth

Up

Living room

Kitchen Dining

Deck

Second floor

Down

36 ft.

Belvedere

low warm air to rise and escape through a belvedere (see *FHB* #3, p.58). In my house, drawing cool air from the lake and surrounding foliage into the house could keep temperatures down, so this exhaust action through the belvedere was important. I planned to install ceiling fans on the main level to boost the natural circulation pattern. Since stairwells would be a major pathway for rising warm air inside the house, I decided to eliminate the risers in my stair design. In addition to preventing warm air from being trapped inside the house, it also helped to keep the construction details simple and inexpensive.

The belvedere at the top of the roof in the center of the house offers a pleasant view of the countryside. A steel ladder, set into the chimney that the belvedere surrounds, provides access to this high space. Windows on all four sides can be opened selectively to control the airflow, and in the winter the floor gratings can be replaced by solid panels, which reduce heat loss through the belvedere.

Early Mississippians learned that raising living areas off the ground reduces in-house humidity and allows heat to dissipate through the floor. It also discourages fungi and termites—two major enemies of wood structures in the South. Deja-vu's main living areas, framed in wood, are supported on brick walls and 14-in. dia. concrete columns (photo, above right).

Floor to ceiling Thermopane windows in the north, east and west walls of the main level look out on the pond. They include 12 large awning sash sections so that the windows can remain open even during summer rains.

A symmetrical plan—Antebellum houses in Mississippi are often square, though a number of octagonal homes were also built in the South. Combining the two approaches, my house is an octagon inscribed in a 36-ft. square. On the main level, I formed the octagon by placing triangular spaces—the bathroom, kitchen, and two decks—at each corner (drawing, facing page). A porch is accessible from each major room, and there is ventilation throughout from three sides. The open plan recalls rooms connected with sliding pocket doors in early plantation houses.

The house has one central fireplace, open on three sides to heat the dining room, the living room and the master bedroom. This fireplace, with its raised hearth and surrounding columns, has become the social center of the house, as well as a source of heat in the winter. The masonry mass radiates warmth to the entire main floor. The brick Trombe wall facing the entryway absorbs some solar gain through the skylights in the south-facing roof; it helps to heat the house on sunny winter days. An electric, forced-air heating and air-conditioning unit in the basement acts as a back-up.

Keeping it simple—The symmetry of the plan had yet another purpose: ease of construction. The square shape with its pyramid roof allowed for simple, repetitive framing, and posed no thorny problems for carpenters and masons.

Because the construction was uncomplicated,

I decided to act, along with my son, as my own general contractor. We hired subcontractors for most of the work but reserved cabinets, flooring, finish carpentry and painting for ourselves.

The house is four stories high, with the second and third floors enclosed under a pyramid roof. The four floors are actually squares of different dimensions centered about the square fireplace and its chimney. Using structural columns around the hearth made more sense than creating walls, doors and hallways in the small floor space. It also is a definite Southern touch. Even modest "dog-trot" cabins are often enhanced with roughsawn columns in this part of the country.

Local concrete men regularly pour reinforced concrete slab floors, but not concrete walls. So we decided on block walls, concrete block up to grade level, topped off with locally produced 8x8x4 bricks. We had trouble getting an estimate for pouring the six concrete columns that would help support the main floor. Their 12-ft. height, combined with the slope of the site, would make it difficult to position the round forms and place the concrete.

My solution was to build temporary supports alongside standard cardboard Sonotube column forms. We then framed up the main floor on these supports, making it possible to wheelbarrow concrete from the road, over the bridge, onto the platform and into the cardboard column forms. By forming and pouring the concrete columns ourselves, my son and I saved the $600 in labor cost the subcontractor would have charged us. We finished pouring the six columns in 1½ hours. The completed and fully supported main floor then became the stage from which we built the progressively smaller balcony and belvedere floors.

The roof was framed with 2x10 rafters and sheathed with ½-in. plywood. Then we rolled on a layer of asphalt felt and installed a corrugated galvanized steel roof. Similar roofs have covered Mississippi houses and barns for generations. Galvanized roofs are inexpensive and

Diagonal corner walls and columns support the house. The lowest floor is a poured slab.

maintenance-free over their 30 to 40-year lifespan, weathering to a rich reddish brown. They also do a good job of reflecting the sun, preventing heat build-up under the roof. And I like the sound of the rain on the metal. The sheathing beneath the metal was a concession to modern materials, though. Traditionally, metal roofs were nailed to oak purlins set across the rafters. The plywood serves as backing and protection for the fiberglass insulation batts I installed between the rafters.

Interiors—I was able to complete the detailing and cabinetwork using only basic tools. Since doors are the most costly and difficult part of kitchen cabinet construction, I eliminated the problem by purchasing pine interior shutter panels from Sears. Their wide range of panel sizes enabled me to design my cabinets to standard dimensions. These louvered doors are moderately priced and ensure good ventilation in humid climates. To make the cabinets, I built simple boxes of ⅝-in. particleboard (drawing, p. 159), covering all exposed edges with 1x2 edging (glued and nailed in place).

Shelving inside the cabinets is also particleboard, edged with ¾-in. screen molding. I prime-coated the particleboard, then painted

The central hearth and its surrounding columns, seen from the living room, form the structural core of the house. The front door is at right, the dining room and kitchen to the left.

it with semi-gloss white enamel. The white shelving contrasts nicely with the grain of the wood doors and edging, and gives a surprisingly elegant appearance to these low-cost cabinets. All shelves are adjustable using simple drilled holes and pin-type shelf brackets.

The stairways were kept simple, too. I nailed 2x12 treads to 2x10 standard cutout stringers, notching the back corners of each tread as shown in the drawing on the facing page. Then the exposed edges of the stringer and the top end of each tread were trimmed with 1x2 fir, mitering the joints for a more finished appearance. Since I had already decided to eliminate the risers in order to promote air circulation between floors, I encircled each tread with carpet, stapling it in place from underneath. Not having tried this type of stair design before, I was pleased with the clean lines that resulted.

Interior walls are ½-in. gypsum board. With so many edges and corners in a relatively small space, I dispensed with wood casing. The drywall crew used plenty of metal corner beads, and the look is crisp and more in keeping with the open plan of the house. When the interior work was done, I stained all the wood in the house with semi-transparent stain. A coat of satin varnish finished the job.

The house is too young for a true evaluation of energy efficiency, but during the summer of 1981 the air-conditioning back-up system was used only seven days.

Mixing traditional architectural forms with new designs has its risks, but Deja-vu seems to do more than just work well. Native Mississippians who come to visit can still sense the traditional hospitality, formality and simplicity of design that their ancestors must have known in houses built generations ago. □

Architect Robert Ford teaches at Mississippi State University in Starkville.

Crisp, clean and simple
Ford's decision to leave corners, doors and windows uncased created clean lines where drywall panels intersect. Above, the dining room as seen from the third-level study. One of the house's two small, triangular decks can be seen through the door at the top of the photo. At right, the dining room and kitchen. Apart from reducing construction cost, the white-painted, uncased drywall contrasts nicely with the carpeting, cabinetwork, and oak and tile floors.

Easy, elegant detailing using standard materials

Upper-cabinet design

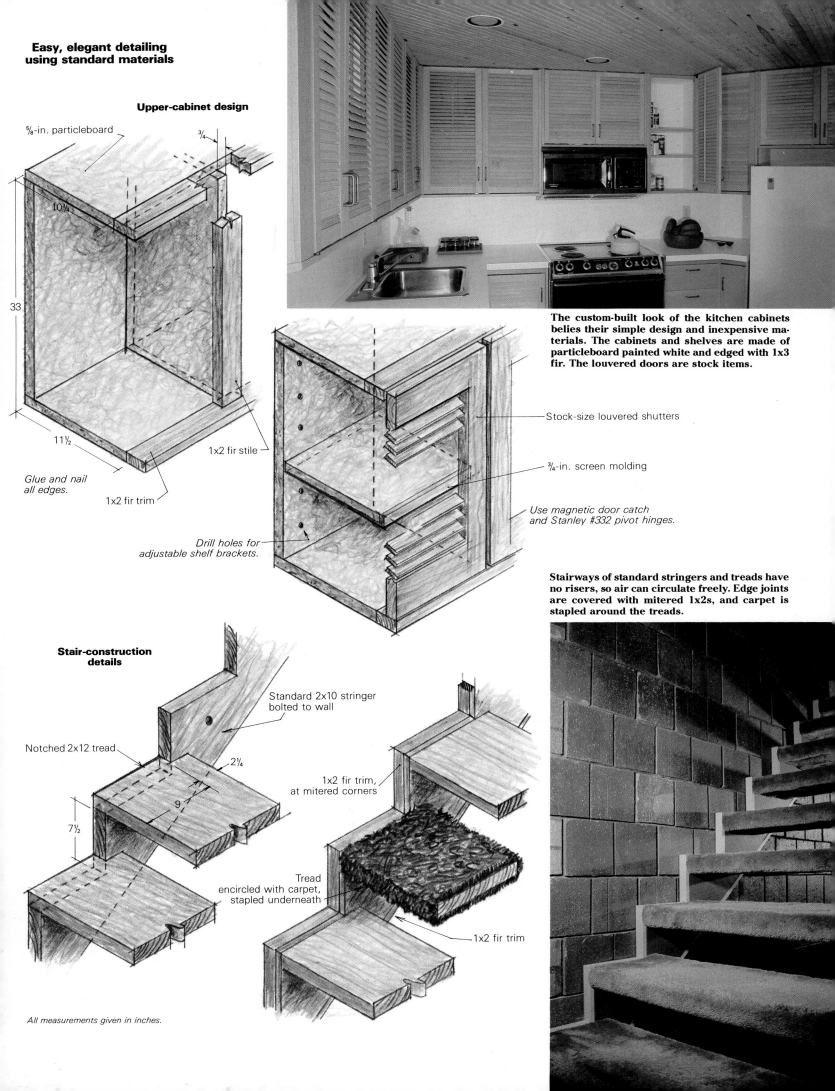

5/8-in. particleboard

3/4

10¾

33

11½

Glue and nail all edges.

1x2 fir stile

1x2 fir trim

Drill holes for adjustable shelf brackets.

The custom-built look of the kitchen cabinets belies their simple design and inexpensive materials. The cabinets and shelves are made of particleboard painted white and edged with 1x3 fir. The louvered doors are stock items.

Stock-size louvered shutters

¾-in. screen molding

Use magnetic door catch and Stanley #332 pivot hinges.

Stairways of standard stringers and treads have no risers, so air can circulate freely. Edge joints are covered with mitered 1x2s, and carpet is stapled around the treads.

Stair-construction details

Standard 2x10 stringer bolted to wall

Notched 2x12 tread

2¼

9

7½

1x2 fir trim, at mitered corners

Tread encircled with carpet, stapled underneath

1x2 fir trim

All measurements given in inches.